MICROSOFT® WINDOWS® SECURITY

ESSENTIALS

MICROSOFT® WINDOWS® SECURITY
ESSENTIALS

Darril Gibson

WILEY

Wiley Publishing, Inc.

Senior Acquisitions Editor: Jeff Kellum
Development Editor: Candace English
Technical Editors: Naomi Alpern; Tom Carpenter
Production Editor: Dassi Zeidel
Copy Editor: Tiffany Taylor
Editorial Manager: Pete Gaughan
Production Manager: Tim Tate
Vice President and Executive Group Publisher: Richard Swadley
Vice President and Publisher: Neil Edde
Book Designer: Happenstance Type-O-Rama
Compositor: James D. Kramer, Happenstance Type-O-Rama
Proofreader: Rebecca Rider
Indexer: Ted Laux
Project Coordinator, Cover: Katie Crocker
Cover Designer: Ryan Sneed
Cover Image: © Linda Bucklin / iStockPhoto

Copyright © 2011 by Wiley Publishing, Inc., Indianapolis, Indiana
Published simultaneously in Canada
ISBN: 978-1-118-01684-8
ISBN: 978-1-118-11454-4 (ebk.)
ISBN: 978-1-118-11457-5 (ebk.)
ISBN: 978-1-118-11456-8 (ebk.)

For general information on our other products and services or to obtain technical support, please contact our Customer Care Department within the U.S. at (877) 762-2974, outside the U.S. at (317) 572-3993 or fax (317) 572-4002.

Wiley also publishes its books in a variety of electronic formats and by print-on-demand. Not all content that is available in standard print versions of this book may appear or be packaged in all book formats. If you have purchased a version of this book that did not include media that is referenced by or accompanies a standard print version, you may request this media by visiting http://booksupport.wiley.com. For more information about Wiley products, visit us at www.wiley.com.

Library of Congress Cataloging-in-Publication Data is available from the publisher.

10 9 8 7 6 5 4 3 2 1

Dear Reader,

Thank you for choosing *Microsoft Windows Security Essentials*. This book is part of a family of premium-quality Sybex books, all of which are written by outstanding authors who combine practical experience with a gift for teaching.

Sybex was founded in 1976. More than 30 years later, we're still committed to producing consistently exceptional books. With each of our titles, we're working hard to set a new standard for the industry. From the paper we print on, to the authors we work with, our goal is to bring you the best books available.

I hope you see all that reflected in these pages. I'd be very interested to hear your comments and get your feedback on how we're doing. Feel free to let me know what you think about this or any other Sybex book by sending me an email at nedde@wiley.com. If you think you've found a technical error in this book, please visit http://sybex.custhelp.com. Customer feedback is critical to our efforts at Sybex.

Best regards,

NEIL EDDE
Vice President and Publisher
Sybex, an Imprint of Wiley

To my wife, who brings so much joy
and happiness into my life.

ACKNOWLEDGMENTS

I love the process of writing a book. From the first idea to the last written word, it's an enjoyable process where I'm able to work with many talented people. I'm grateful to the many people at Wiley who have helped me with this project. First, thanks to Jeff Kellum for inviting me to write this book. I appreciate the work put into this project by Candace English, the development editor, and Tom Carpenter, the technical proofer. Thanks also to Dassi Zeidel, a dedicated production editor who helped guide the book to completion in the final stages of production.

ABOUT THE AUTHOR

Darril Gibson is the CEO of Security Consulting and Training, LLC. He has written, coauthored, and contributed to more than a dozen books, and he regularly consults and teaches on a wide variety of IT topics. Most of the books he's been involved with are available on Amazon by searching for *Darril Gibson*. He has been a Microsoft Certified Trainer (MCT) since 1999 and holds a multitude of certifications including Security+, CISSP, MCSE (NT 4.0, Windows 2000, and Windows 2003), MCITP (Windows 7, Windows Server 2008, and SQL Server), and ITIL Foundations. Darril lives in Virginia Beach with his wife of more than 18 years and two dogs. Whenever possible, they escape to their cabin in the country with more than 20 acres of land, where his dogs wear themselves out chasing rabbits and deer. You can reach the author by writing to darril@mcitpsuccess.com.

CONTENTS AT A GLANCE

CONTENTS

CHAPTER 7   **Protecting a Network**   **147**

CHAPTER 8   **Understanding Wireless Security**   **171**

INTRODUCTION

Attacks on computers have become as common as computers themselves. Criminals have discovered that they can separate money from uninformed users with very little work and, often, with very large paydays. IT professionals must include sound security practices when maintaining any network today.

The first step is to understand the risks. Once you understand the risks, the security controls implemented to protect the computers and networks from these risks make a lot more sense. This book covers the basics of security in a Microsoft IT environment and is geared toward preparing you for one of the three certification exams in the Microsoft Technology Associate (MTA) Information Technology (IT) Professional track.

The MTA certification is a new certification level. It includes three separate tracks: IT Professional, Developer, and Database. The IT Professional track is for individuals pursuing work as administrators. The Developer track is for individuals pursuing work as programmers and software engineers. The Database track is for individuals pursuing work as database administrators and database developers.

The MTA IT Professional series includes three certifications:

Networking Fundamentals   This is the first certification in the MTA IT Professional track. It lays a solid foundation of basic networking knowledge needed for the other MTA certifications and also for the more advanced Microsoft Certified Technology Specialist (MCTS) and Microsoft Certified IT Professional (MCITP) tracks. You earn this certification by taking and passing exam 98-366.

Security Fundamentals   Security Fundamentals is the second certification in the MTA IT Professional track. It builds on the knowledge learned in the Networking Fundamentals certification and adds fundamental security knowledge needed by administrators. IT administrators in any environment need to be aware of the risks associated with IT systems. You earn this certification by taking and passing exam 98-367, covered by this book.

Windows Server Administration Fundamentals   This certification builds on the knowledge gained in the Networking Fundamentals and Security Fundamentals certifications. It digs deeper into knowledge and skills needed by Windows Server administrators. You earn this certification by taking and passing exam 98-365.

Each of these certifications can serve as a stepping-stone to Microsoft's next levels of certification: Microsoft Certified Technology Specialist (MCTS) and Microsoft Certified IT Professional (MCITP).

Who Should Read This Book

This book is for current or aspiring professionals seeking a quick grounding in the fundamentals of security in a Microsoft environment. The goal is to provide quick, focused coverage of fundamental security skills. If you have a basic understanding and want to expand your knowledge into security, this book is for you. It will help you grasp many fundamental security concepts and how they apply to Microsoft systems. Also, you can use the knowledge gained from this book as a foundation for more advanced studies.

This book is focused on the objectives of the Microsoft Technology Associate (MTA) Security Fundamentals certification. This is one of the certifications in the MTA IT Professional series. It's best if you start with the Networking Fundamentals topics, covered in *Microsoft Windows Networking Essentials* (Wiley, 2011). You can then move into the Windows Server Administration Fundamentals MTA certification.

You can read more about the MTA certifications and MTA exam certification paths at **www.microsoft.com/learning/en/us/certification/mta.aspx**.

What You Will Learn

You will learn the essentials of security in a Microsoft environment. This book covers all the objectives of the Microsoft Technology Associate Security Fundamentals exam (exam 98-367).

Details on this exam, including the objectives, are available at **www.microsoft.com/learning/en/us/exam.aspx?ID=98-367**.

Prerequisites

This book is focused on the 98-367 exam, which is the second Microsoft exam in the MTA IT Professional series. The first exam is Networking Fundamentals (98-366), and it's expected that you have the knowledge tested in that exam, although you don't need to have taken and passed that exam.

The Networking Fundamentals exam (and the associated knowledge) does provide a solid foundation, and there simply isn't enough room in this book to include basic networking knowledge. However, when a networking topic is important, this book does provide some key information to remind you about the underlying networking concepts. For a more detailed look at networking essentials, consult *Microsoft Windows Networking Essentials* (Wiley, 2011).

What You Need

Because this book is focused on providing you with only the essentials, the biggest requirement is a desire to learn. You aren't expected to have a lot of knowledge about or experience in security before starting the book. It starts with the basics in Chapter 1 and steadily builds on the knowledge through the end of the book.

Ideally, you'll have some hardware that you can use. Because this is a Microsoft book focused on Microsoft technologies, it would be good to have a system running Microsoft Window Server 2008 or Windows Server 2008 R2.

If you're running another operating system, such as Windows 7, you can create a virtual server running Windows Server 2008. I have included an optional lab for this book, which you can download at **www.sybex.com/go/securityessentials**. It will lead you through the following steps:

- ▶ Configuring Windows 7 with virtualization

- ▶ Locating and downloading an evaluation copy of Windows Server 2008

- ▶ Creating a Virtual PC machine for Windows Server 2008

- ▶ Installing Windows Server 2008 on a virtual machine

- ▶ Promoting Windows Server 2008 to a domain controller

What Is Covered in This Book

Microsoft Windows Security Essentials is organized to provide you with the knowledge needed to master the basics of security in a Microsoft environment.

The objectives for this book are primarily focused on Microsoft Windows Server 2008. Although Microsoft Windows Server 2008 R2 does include a lot of under-the-hood enhancements, there aren't many differences covered in this book. Unless specific differences are mentioned, the topics apply equally to both Windows Server 2008 and Windows Server 2008 R2. Occasionally, I mention both to remind you; but to avoid repetition, I often just refer to Windows Server 2008, implying both Microsoft Windows Server 2008 and Microsoft Windows Server 2008 R2.

Chapter 1, "Understanding Core Security Principles"   Most security principles can be traced back to the security triad of confidentiality, integrity, and availability. This chapter introduces these concepts along with basics of risk and the importance of implementing a defense-in-depth strategy.

Chapter 2, "Understanding Malware and Social Engineering" One of the most common threats to computers today is malicious software, or malware. Malware comes in many forms, such as viruses, worms, and Trojan horses. It's important to understand how serious the threat is and what you can do to protect computers and networks. Additionally, attackers often use social-engineering tactics to trick users into giving up valuable data. This chapter covers how to thwart those attacks, plus how to safeguard email.

Chapter 3, "Understanding User Authentication" One of the primary methods of ensuring security is to restrict access to known users. This requires users to authenticate themselves, or prove their identity by providing credentials. Authentication is commonly classified using three types or three factors of authentication: something you know, something you have, and something you are. This chapter helps you understand these factors, including their strengths and weaknesses.

Chapter 4, "Securing Access with Permissions" Permissions are the primary method used to restrict access to resources in a Microsoft domain. You can assign permissions to NTFS drives, shares, Active Directory objects, and the Registry. This chapter covers the many types of permissions and how some of these permissions interact with each other.

Chapter 5, "Using Audit Policies and Network Auditing" Auditing provides administrators with an easy method of tracking activity on systems. You can track when users access files, shut down systems, create or modify accounts, and much more. Windows Server 2008 includes multiple categories of auditing that you can manipulate, and you'll learn about them in this chapter.

Chapter 6, "Protecting Clients and Servers" In this chapter, you'll learn common techniques used to protect clients and servers, including User Account Control. Additionally, this chapter covers the importance of keeping every system in an organization up to date. You'll also learn about many of the server roles, including some specific security steps used to protect them.

Chapter 7, "Protecting a Network" Attackers are out there, constantly trying to attack networks. In this chapter, you'll learn some of the common well-known attack methods and techniques to protect a network. You'll learn about network-based firewalls and how they provide network isolation for an internal network. This chapter also covers Network Access Protection (NAP), a new technology in Windows Server 2008 used to inspect clients for health and isolate unhealthy clients.

Chapter 8, "Understanding Wireless Security"   Wireless networks have become quite popular in recent years. They're relatively inexpensive and don't require you to run cables for connectivity. However, security for wireless networks had a rough start. If you don't use up-to-date technologies, your wireless networks will be highly vulnerable to attacks. This chapter covers many current wireless security standards and protocols.

Chapter 9, "Understanding Physical Security"   One of the basic security steps you can take is to restrict physical access to systems. Most organizations use a variety of methods to enforce physical security, such as locked doors, cipher locks, guards, and more. You can also use Group Policy to enhance physical security by restricting access to systems. The Deny Log On Locally Group Policy setting prevents users from logging onto a computer, and a Removable Storage Access policy can restrict what users can do with different types of removable devices including USB flash drives. In addition to specific Group Policy settings, this chapter provides a big picture view of how Group Policy works. You'll also learn about mobile-device security.

Chapter 10, "Enforcing Confidentiality with Encryption"   A key part of the security triad (confidentiality, integrity, and availability) is confidentiality. The two primary ways of encrypting data are via symmetric or asymmetric encryption. You can also provide one-way encryption with hashing functions. This chapter covers many of the generic encryption methods along with some specific Microsoft methods such as Encrypting File System (EFS) and BitLocker Drive Encryption.

Chapter 11, "Understanding Certificates and a PKI"   A Public Key Infrastructure (PKI) includes all the pieces required to issue, use, and manage certificates. Certificates (also called public-key certificates) are used for a wide variety of purposes to provide different types of security. This chapter explains the details of certificates and explores the components of a PKI.

Chapter 12, "Understanding Internet Explorer Security"   Internet Explorer (IE) is the primary web browser used on Windows Server 2008 and Windows 7. Because it's so common to use the Internet to research and do regular work, it's important to understand some of the security risks and some of the security mechanisms that help protect users. This chapter covers many of the browser settings, the different security zones, and some of the IE tools used to identify malicious websites.

Appendix A, "Answers to Review Questions"   This appendix includes all of the answers to the review questions found in "The Essentials and Beyond" section at the end of every chapter.

Appendix B, "Microsoft's Certification Program"   This appendix maps the objectives in the MTA Security Fundamentals exam (exam 98-367) to the specific chapters where each objective is covered.

I have created an online glossary as well as provided the suggested or recommended answers to the additional exercises included at the end of each chapter. You can download these at **www.sybex.com/go/securityessentials**.

Sybex strives to keep you supplied with the latest tools and information you need for your work. Please check its website at **www.sybex.com/go/securityessentials**, where we'll post additional content and updates that supplement this book if the need arises. Enter security essentials in the Search box (or type the book's ISBN—978-1-118-01684-8), and click Go to get to the book's update page.

CHAPTER 1

Understanding Core Security Principles

Every computer presents a certain level of risk. You can't eliminate risk unless you simply never turn on the computer. However, you can manage risk. You start by understanding what risk is and understanding that risk mitigation is accomplished by reducing vulnerabilities.

Several core security principles guide the protection of information technology (IT) systems and data. When you understand these core security principles, it's easier to grasp the reasoning behind many of the security practices.

Most security principles can be traced back to the *security triad* (also called the AIC or CIA triad). The security triad mandates protection against the loss of confidentiality, the loss of integrity, and the loss of availability of IT systems and data. Other principles include defense-in-depth and the principle of least privilege. Administrators *harden*, or secure, IT systems by attempting to configure them more securely than the default configuration and reduce vulnerabilities. This chapter covers all of these topics in the following sections:

▶ **Understanding risk**

▶ **Exploring the security triad**

▶ **Implementing a defense-in-depth security strategy**

▶ **Enforcing the principle of least privilege**

▶ **Hardening a server**

Understanding Risk

▶

Minimizing risk is also known as *risk mitigation*.

Risk is unavoidable. You can't eliminate it. However, it's possible to minimize risk by first understanding it and then taking steps to mitigate it.

For example, every time you step into a street, you run the risk of being hit by a car. The real threat of a car colliding with your body, and your body's vulnerability to this collision, convinces you to take steps to reduce the risk. Unless you're Superman, you can't stop the threat. If the car is coming, it's coming. But you can minimize the risk by using crosswalks and looking for approaching cars before stepping into the street.

Similarly, risks are reduced in IT networks by taking steps to reduce the vulnerabilities. Consider Figure 1.1. Risk occurs when *threats* exploit *vulnerabilities*. In an IT environment, threats are any events that can result in the loss of *confidentiality*, *integrity*, or *availability* of IT systems or data. Threats can be man-made or natural.

The next section explains the concepts of confidentiality, integrity, and availability in more depth.

FIGURE 1.1 Threats exploit vulnerabilities, creating risk.

NIST's DEFINITION OF RISK

The National Institute of Standards and Technology (NIST) is a U.S. agency that includes the Information Technology Laboratory (ITL). The ITL regularly conducts research and publishes papers on behalf of NIST.

Much of NIST's research focuses on what the U.S. government can do to improve security for its IT systems and data. However, these papers are publically available, and many non-government organizations adopt the techniques and methodologies.

NIST's Special Publication 800-30 (SP 800-30) is titled "Risk Management Guide for Information Technology Systems." The definition of *risk* in SP 800-30 is as follows: "Risk is a function of the likelihood of a given threat-source's exercising a particular potential vulnerability, and the resulting impact of that adverse event on the organization." Although you don't need to memorize this quote, it's worth noting that it does add more depth than just *Risk occurs when a threat exploits a vulnerability.*

Risk management is a complex topic that includes multiple facets. At this stage of your study, you don't need to master all the different topics of risk management, but you should be aware that much more detail is available.

(Continues)

NIST'S DEFINITION OF RISK *(Continued)*

If the topic appeals to you, you can use the Microsoft Technology Associate Security Fundamentals certification as a springboard to more advanced security certifications such as ISC(2)s Certified Information Systems Security Professional (CISSP) certification.

Man-made threats are any threats from people. These can be intentional threats such as attacks or malware distribution. Intentional threats can also include the access, modification, or deletion of data. Other threats include theft, fire, and vandalism. Man-made threats can also be unintentional, such as the accidental deletion of data. Natural threats include weather events such as hurricanes, floods, tornadoes, and lightning. Environmental threats include long-term power failures or the inadvertent release of hazardous chemicals.

An important point to keep in mind is that you can't stop threats. If someone wants to write malicious software, you can't prevent it. If Mother Nature wants to create a tornado, it's coming. However, you can reduce risks by reducing vulnerabilities.

Vulnerabilities are weaknesses. These can be inherent weaknesses in your software or hardware, such as bugs in the code or faulty power supplies. They can be weaknesses in procedures that allow users to give up valuable data to social engineers. They can be weaknesses in security configurations, such as when unneeded services or protocols are left running on a system. They can be weaknesses in physical security that allow unauthorized personnel access to servers or network devices.

Reducing vulnerabilities is the core of risk management in an IT environment. Every step you take to reduce weaknesses reduces your risks. The following list identifies some common techniques you can use to reduce weaknesses. Don't worry if you don't understand them all right now—they're covered in more depth throughout this book:

- ► Enforce the principle of least privilege.
- ► Implement strong authentication mechanisms.
- ► Train employees on risks of social engineering.
- ► Regularly remind employees about their security responsibilities.
- ► Implement multiple layers of security (defense-in-depth).
- ► Remove or disable unneeded services and protocols.

► Implement host-based and network-based firewalls.

► Keep all systems up to date with patches.

► Install and update antivirus software.

► Add redundancies for critical systems.

► Secure access to data with permissions.

► Back up data and store a backup copy off-site.

► Track access to data and systems with audit trails.

► Encrypt critical data at rest and when transmitted on the wire.

► Protect systems, data, and facilities with strong physical security.

Although this book isn't a comprehensive source for mitigating all risks, it does include basic information you can use as a foundation.

Exploring the Security Triad

The security triad includes three key security principles that are at the core of all security practices. These are sometimes called the AIC triad or the CIA triad, using the first initials of each (*availability, integrity,* and *confidentiality*).

Any study of IT security requires an understanding of these basic principles. Figure 1.2 shows the three elements in the security triad. These three elements combine to provide a solid layer of protection for assets within an organization:

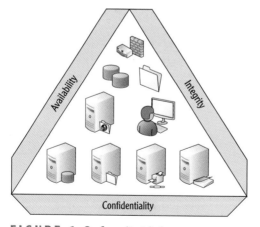

FIGURE 1.2 Security triad

Confidentiality   This element ensures that only authorized people are able to access data.

Availability   Availability ensures that systems and data are up and available when needed.

Integrity   Data integrity prevents the unauthorized modification of data and ensures that unauthorized modification is detected.

Protecting Against Loss of Confidentiality

The loss of confidentiality occurs when unauthorized individuals access data. A company needs to keep its secrets secret. If unauthorized people can access the secrets, they just aren't secret any more.

You can take several steps to ensure confidentiality. You start by ensuring that everyone who accesses data is authenticated. In other words, users log onto a system with a username and password or another authentication method.

You then use access-control methods to control who can access the data. For example, you can assign permissions to specific files and folders. If a user doesn't need access, they aren't granted permissions.

Encryption is another layer of security to protect against the loss of confidentiality. You can encrypt individual files, entire hard drives, and data transmissions traveling across the network. If an individual does obtain an encrypted file, it's scrambled in such a way that it's unreadable until it's decrypted. Strong encryption standards ensure that unauthorized individuals aren't able to decrypt any encrypted data.

Protecting Against Loss of Availability

Loss of availability simply means that systems or data aren't available when the user needs them. Some systems need to be up and operational 24 hours a day, 7 days a week, such as web servers available on the Internet. Other systems only need to be available from 9 a.m. to 5 p.m. Monday through Friday, such as computers used by employees during the day.

You ensure that systems stay operational by protecting against different threats and building in redundancies. One of the most common threats to systems today comes from malicious software (malware). *Malware* includes viruses, worms, Trojan horses, and more.

Backups are important to consider. If you've never lost any data, you're luckier than most. However, it's just a matter of time. You'll lose data. And when you do, the difference between a major catastrophe and a minor inconvenience is the existence of a backup. If you have a copy of your data, you can simply restore it, and you're back in business. If you don't have a copy, you'll have to rebuild the data from scratch.

Chapter 3 covers authentication in more depth, including the three factors of authentication: something you know, something you have, and something you are.

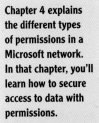

Chapter 4 explains the different types of permissions in a Microsoft network. In that chapter, you'll learn how to secure access to data with permissions.

Chapter 10 explains the different types of encryption that are available to enforce confidentiality in Microsoft networks.

Chapter 2 presents the different types of malware and methods to protect against it. You'll also learn about threats from social engineering.

Organizations implement sophisticated backup plans to ensure that they have copies of all their important data. Additionally, organizations with mature backup plans maintain a copy of data off-site.

Fault-tolerant or redundant technologies can be built into systems at multiple levels. A fault-tolerant system ensures continued operation even if a failure, or fault, occurs. Redundant Arrays of Independent Disks (RAIDs) provide fault tolerance for hard drives. Failover clusters provide fault tolerance for servers. Hot, warm, or cold sites provide fault tolerance for entire locations.

Of course, not every business has an alternate location. Similarly, not every system and every drive includes fault tolerance. The organization determines what to implement based on the value of the systems and data and the cost to protect them.

Protecting Against Loss of Integrity

The loss of integrity occurs when data is modified without authorization. This can occur if unauthorized individuals modify data.

Access controls work to ensure that only authorized people have access. However, malicious users may bypass the controls, or the controls may fail. Audit logging can show if anyone accessed data and may include details such as who they are, what they did, and when they did it.

In addition to auditing, hashing detects when data has lost integrity. In its simplest form, a *hash* is simply a number. A *hashing algorithm* is a mathematical calculation that you can execute against a file or a message to create the hash, or the number. As long as the data stays the same, a hashing algorithm will always produce the same hash (or the same number). If the data changes, the hashing algorithm will produce a different hash indicating the data has changed.

Hashes are created at a given time to identify the original state of the data. They're then re-created at a later time to see if the hash has changed. If the two hashes are different, the data has lost data integrity. However, if the two hashes are the same, the data has maintained integrity.

As a simple example, a message may have a hash of 12345 when a user creates and sends it. The sending computer sends both the message and the calculated hash. Another computer receives the message and calculates the hash again. If the recalculated hash is 12345, the receiving computer knows the message hasn't been modified. It hasn't lost data integrity. However, if the recalculated hash is 98765, the receiving computer will recognize that this is different from the original hash of 12345. Because the hashes are different, the data is different. The data has lost its integrity.

▶ Organizations keep a copy of backups in a separate geographical location, such as a separate building. This ensures that the organization can recover from a major catastrophe such as a fire.

▶ Chapter 5 covers audit policies and network auditing. You'll learn about what can be audited in a Microsoft network.

▶ Chapter 10 includes information on how email can be digitally signed to provide both authentication and integrity.

Many organizations implement a Public Key Infrastructure (PKI) so that they can issue their own certificates. For example, a PKI can issue certificates to users to digitally sign email and ensure integrity.

Implementing a Defense-in-Depth Security Strategy

Defense-in-depth is a strategy employed by security professionals that includes multiple layers of security. Instead of implementing one security technique and then celebrating success, you must treat security as an ongoing process. You can't simply password protect your systems and files and say you're done.

Think about an attacker. Attackers often get money when they successfully attack a network. Sure, some attackers are just thrill seekers hacking into a system for the fun of it. But most attackers today are dedicated criminals trying to break into systems for monetary gain.

Imagine that an attacker can make $5,000 a week from attacks. He is likely highly motivated to learn everything he can about security procedures and methods. Moreover, he knows how to break into networks and systems to get the information he needs. If you employ just a single security procedure that he's already cracked, his job is easy. However, if instead you employ multiple layers of security, he must know how to break each one. It takes time and effort to break down each layer.

Defense-in-depth strategies defend against threats at multiple points and at multiple layers. They use a combination of policies, operations procedures, people, and security technologies. Figure 1.3 outlines many of the elements of a defense-in-depth strategy and identifies the chapters where these topics are covered.

Notice that policies and procedures represent a first line of defense. Behind that is physical security, which provides a second line of defense. Then, within each of the technical topics (such as data, auditing, and so on), multiple security methods are employed to provide additional layers of protection. The lines of defense and security methods outlined here aren't all-inclusive, but they do cover many of the typical security measures used to protect IT infrastructures:

Administrative Policies and Procedures These are written rules that outline security requirements. They let administrators know what security to implement, and they let users in the organization know what is expected of them. These often include steps to maintain a high level of security awareness by all users. For example, users may be reminded of the dangers of malicious software (malware) and about current social

Chapter 11 presents information on a Public Key Infrastructure and digital certificates.

Defense-in-depth strategies often slow down or deter an attacker. This delay can provide extra time to detect the attack and respond to it.

Chapter 2 presents information on malware and social engineering. Chapter 3 covers the different methods of authentication.

engineering tactics employed by attackers. Acceptable methods of authentication are also outlined as part of a basic access policy.

▶

Defense-in-depth also provides protection if one layer of security fails. Even if one fails, other layers remain in place.

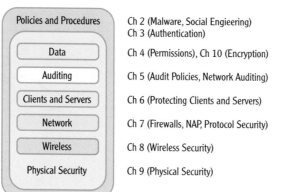

Policies and Procedures	Ch 2 (Malware, Social Engieering)
	Ch 3 (Authentication)
Data	Ch 4 (Permissions), Ch 10 (Encryption)
Auditing	Ch 5 (Audit Policies, Network Auditing)
Clients and Servers	Ch 6 (Protecting Clients and Servers)
Network	Ch 7 (Firewalls, NAP, Protocol Security)
Wireless	Ch 8 (Wireless Security)
Physical Security	Ch 9 (Physical Security)

FIGURE 1.3 Defense-in-depth strategies, and the corresponding chapters in this book

▶

Chapter 4 covers NTFS, share, registry, and Active Directory permissions in more depth.

▶

Chapter 5 covers audit policies and methods for auditing a network for security compliance.

▶

Chapter 6 goes into more depth on protecting clients and servers.

▶

Chapter 7 covers firewalls, NAP, and protocol security.

Data   You can protect data with permissions and encryption. Files, folders, and shares are secured with New Technology File System (NTFS) permissions and share permissions. Other permissions include registry permissions and Active Directory permissions.

Auditing   Auditing is the process of tracking access. It identifies what was done, when it was done, where it was done, and who did it. For example, you may have proprietary data and want to track all access to it. You can enable auditing to create an ongoing audit trail that will show which users have accessed the content, when they accessed it, and what actions they performed.

Clients and Servers   Clients and servers within a network must be secured. At the most basic level, antivirus software protects these systems from malware. Additionally, systems must be kept updated with current security patches and hotfixes.

Network   Almost all data used in organizations today travels through the network at one time or other. Attackers can use tools such as sniffers to capture and analyze data traveling through a network if it isn't secure. Securing a network includes using tools such as firewalls to control the traffic, or Network Access Protection (NAP) to control the clients accessing the network. You can also encrypt critical data using Internet Protocol Security (IPSec).

Wireless   Wireless networks are very valuable, allowing you to quickly set up a network without running cables to every system. However, wireless traffic can easily be intercepted, so wireless networks require additional steps to secure. Whereas early wireless networks were highly insecure, today there are protocols and methods you can use to provide a higher level of security.

◄

Chapter 8 covers wireless security, including WEP, WPA and WPA2.

Physical Security   This uses locked doors and other physical security measures to protect assets. For example, servers and network devices are often locked in server rooms or wiring closets, and only a limited number of people have access.

◄

Chapter 9 covers physical security, including the use of technical policies to restrict the use of removable devices and drives.

Enforcing the Principle of Least Privilege

Another core security principle is the principle of least privilege. Users, resources, and applications should be given the rights and permissions to perform necessary tasks, and nothing else.

For example, if users need access to project data on a computer, they should be given minimal access to that data. A gross violation of the principle is to give these users full administrator access. Yes, they will be able to access the project data with administrator access, but they can also do anything else on the computer. Some administrators may be tempted to give everyone administrator access instead of managing the permissions. Admittedly, this is easier in the short term. However, people can accidentally cause problems. They can access data they shouldn't see (like other employees' pay data), and some may even maliciously delete or modify the data. When the incidents start, it'll take a lot of time and energy to get things back in order, and some of the damage may be irreversible.

MALWARE AND LEAST PRIVILEGE

When malware infects a computer, it attempts to escalate its privileges to the highest level possible. If a user has administrative privileges on a system, the malware can usually escalate its privileges to the same level. However, if a principle of least privilege is used, few users will have administrative permissions. Therefore, the possibility of malware escalating its privileges is reduced.

Many organizations issue administrators two accounts: one account is used for regular work, and the second account is used for administrative work. Administrators only use the administrator account when doing administrative work. The administrator will typically be logged on with their regular account the majority of the time.

This reduces the risk of malware escalating its privileges to the administrator level. Note that by itself, this doesn't prevent a system from becoming infected; that's done with a strong anti-malware program. But if an administrator uses the administrator account only 10 percent of the work time, this reduces the likelihood of a system becoming infected and subsequently the malware from obtaining administrator access.

Additionally, any accounts that are created for service accounts should also use the principle of least privilege. These service accounts should be granted the minimal necessary rights and permissions for the service or application to run as needed.

As an example, Figure 1.4 shows the Log On tab of the DNS Server service properties page. Each time the DNS server starts, it uses the Local System account to access any resources. Notice that you have the capability to change this setting to This Account and add an account name and password to start the service (including the administrator account), but this isn't necessary for the DNS Server service. The minimal access that the DNS Server service requires is local access from the Local System account.

> **A *service account*
> is an account used
> to start a service or
> application. Service
> accounts can be
> built-in accounts,
> local accounts,
> or domain-level
> accounts.**

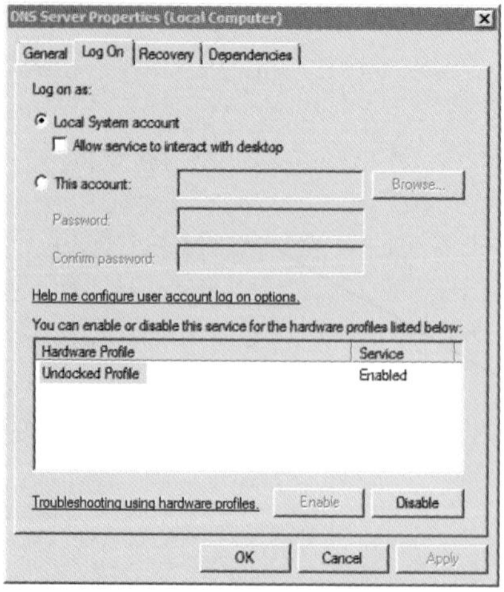

FIGURE 1.4 DNS Server service Log On settings

Hardening a Server

Hardening a server indicates that you're making changes to the default configuration in order to enhance the system's security. You can take multiple steps to harden a server. These include the following:

▶ Reduce the attack surface.

▶ Keep the operating system up to date.

▶ Enable firewalls.

▶ Install and update antivirus software.

The following sections explore these steps in more depth.

Reducing the Attack Surface

You *reduce the attack surface* of a computer by ensuring that only necessary services and protocols are running or installed on the system. If a protocol isn't installed on a system, it can't be attacked.

As an example, consider a web server. It's primary purpose is to host web pages that users access over the Internet or intranet. A web server uses Hypertext Transfer Protocol (HTTP) and HTTP with Secure Socket Layers (HTTPS) as the protocols to serve these web pages. On the server, HTTP and HTTPS are required and must be running in order to present users with both plain text and secure web pages. However, other protocols such as Telnet and the Simple Mail Transport Protocol (SMTP) aren't needed.

If the Telnet Server service is running, it may be possible for an attacker to connect into the server using Telnet and launch an attack. However, if the Telnet Server service is disabled, a Telnet attack isn't possible. Similarly, if SMTP is installed and running, the system is susceptible to possible attacks that exploit vulnerabilities in SMTP. Remove SMTP, and all SMTP attacks are blocked.

Figure 1.5 shows two web servers. The server on the left is running several additional unneeded protocols. These additional protocols are all subject to attack. The server on the right is much more secure simply by having the unnecessary services and protocols removed or disabled.

Some web servers use SMTP. Of course, if SMTP is required by the website, it's a necessary protocol. In our example, SMTP isn't needed.

A server with a reduced attack surface is still subject to attack. However, there are fewer attack possibilities.

Server Running
Unnecessary Protocols

Server with
Minimized Attack Surface

FIGURE 1.5 Minimizing the attack surface of a server

There's an added benefit to reducing the attack surface. If there are fewer protocols running on a system, there is less to manage. The administrator only needs to focus on the installed protocols. Unfortunately, when all the extra protocols are running, administrators sometimes still focus only on the required protocols. In other words, the administrator may simply forget about these extra protocols and not manage or monitor them. Attacks may go unnoticed until the damage is catastrophic.

Although it's simple to say that unnecessary services and protocols should be disabled and removed, it's not as easy to identify which are necessary and which aren't. However, there are tools that can help. For example, the Security Configuration Wizard (SCW) is built into Microsoft Windows Server 2008 and Microsoft Windows Server 2008 R2. It can analyze a system and recommend more secure settings for services, firewall rules, the registry, audit policies, and more. Figure 1.6 shows one screen of the SCW where the wizard is recommending changes to the startup mode of different services.

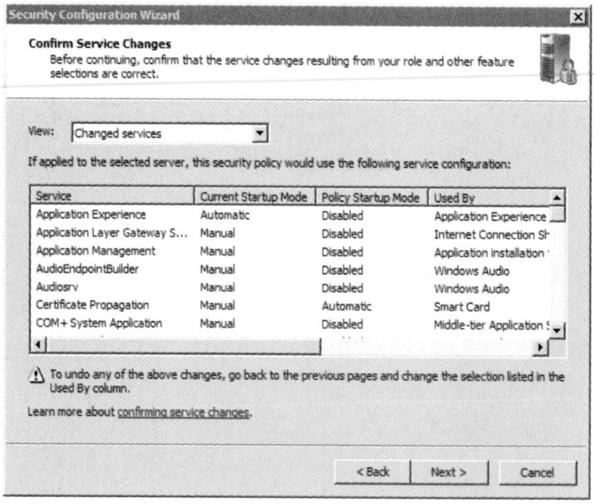

FIGURE 1.6 Security Configuration Wizard service startup mode recommendations

You can launch the SCW on a Windows Server 2008 system by choosing Start ➤ Administrative Tools, and selecting Security Configuration Wizard. The wizard leads you through several screens, allowing you to create, edit, apply, and roll back settings for security policies.

The following steps show how to create a security policy on a Windows Server 2008 server using the SCW:

1. Choose Start ➤ Administrative Tools, and select Security Configuration Wizard.

2. Review the information on each of the screens. Click Next to accept the defaults on each of the screens until you reach the Security Policy File Name page.

3. On the Security Policy File Name page, enter a name of Test at the end of the line. It will have this full path:

   ```
   C:\Windows\security\msscw\Policies\Test
   ```

   Click Next.

4. Ensure that Apply Later is selected on the Apply Security Policy page, and click Next.

5. Click Finish.

6. Launch Windows Explorer by clicking Start and selecting Computer.

7. Browse to `C:\Windows\security\msscw\Policies\Test`, and open the `test.xml` file you just created by double-clicking it. Your display will look similar to Figure 1.7.

SCW saves this as an Extensible Markup Language (XML) file. You can open XML files in many applications, including Internet Explorer and Notepad.

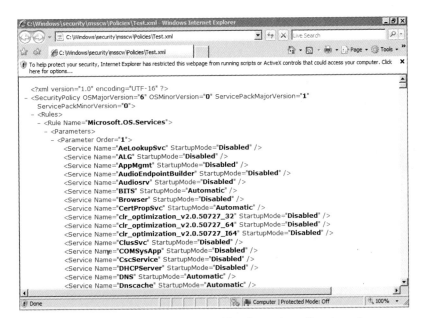

FIGURE 1.7 Security Configuration Wizard security policy shown in Internet Explorer

8. Scroll through the security policy file to view the settings. As you can see, the policy is extensive. It includes several primary nodes, including the following:

   ▶ Microsoft.OS.Services (to secure the services)

   ▶ Microsoft.OS.Networking.Firewall (to implement firewall rules)

▶ Microsoft.OS.Registry.Values (to secure the registry)

▶ Microsoft.OS.Audit (to enable auditing)

You can copy this .xml file to another computer and apply it. For example, if you have five identical web servers in a web farm, you can create one security policy, test it, and then apply it equally to all the servers.

It's often useful to create a policy using the SCW, but sometimes you may want to focus on a specific server role to determine what the most secure settings are. The SCW includes an extensive database that you can browse for different security settings. Figure 1.8 shows the entry page of this database. It includes security settings for just about all the possible server roles, client features, administration options, service settings, and Windows Firewall settings. You can view this page by clicking the View Configuration Database button on the fourth page in the SCW.

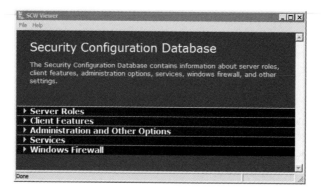

FIGURE 1.8 Security Configuration Database viewed from the SCW

Some high-profile security patches are released out-of-band. If a security threat is high and immediate, Microsoft sometimes releases the patch earlier than the second Tuesday of the month.

▶

Keeping a System Updated

Operating system software is often insecure. That may sound like a strong statement, but it's true. As long as you're using a computer, there are operating system vulnerabilities that can be exploited. The trick is to discover the known vulnerabilities and fix them as quickly as possible.

Microsoft routinely investigates bugs and flaws in released operating systems. The company regularly writes and releases patches and hotfixes to correct the problems. A *patch*, or *hotfix*, is a small amount of code that corrects a problem.

Microsoft releases security updates on the second Tuesday of every month, known as *Patch Tuesday*. Because administrators know when patches will be released, they can plan for them and manage their deployment.

Many organizations use Automatic Update to automatically install the updates when they're released. Unfortunately, sometimes a patch that is intended to fix one problem may create another. For example, a security update may address a known security issue, but an unwanted side effect of the update may be to prevent an application from running. If one computer stops working, it's inconvenient. However, if all 500 computers in an organization suddenly stop working, it can be catastrophic.

Organizations often use a tool such as Windows Server Update Services (WSUS) or Microsoft System Center Configuration Manager (SCCM) to manage the deployment of updates.

Both WSUS and SCCM allow administrators to test updates before deploying them. Updates that create conflict with existing computer configurations aren't deployed. Other updates can be easily deployed to all systems in the organization. It doesn't matter if the organization has 50 computers, 5,000, or more; a few clicks send the update to all of the targeted computers.

WSUS is a free product available on Microsoft's download site. SCCM is an add-on server product. SCCM has more capabilities than WSUS.

◄

◄

One benefit of SCCM over WSUS is that SCCM supports scheduling. In other words, an administrator can schedule updates to deploy at certain times.

ALL OPERATING SYSTEM SOFTWARE HAS VULNERABILITIES

Because you hear about Microsoft systems being attacked and exploited, you may think they're the only operating systems that have security issues. Some people believe it so much that they repeat it. For example, some people say that Macs are so secure that antivirus software and updating aren't needed. Not true.

For example, in November 2010, *Computerworld* published an article titled "Apple Smashes Patch Record with Gigantic Update" (www.computer world.com/s/article/9196118/Apple_smashes_patch_record_ with_gigantic_update). It mentions that Apple fixed 134 flaws with Mac OS X. Mac OS X is based on a version of Unix known as Snow Leopard.

More than 90 percent of the systems in use are Microsoft based, so Microsoft systems get more press. This includes positive press demonstrating the power of these systems and negative press when vulnerabilities appear. If the most popular operating systems were produced by another company, you can bet these would have the most attacks and known security vulnerabilities.

Operating systems are very sophisticated and include billions of lines of code. Despite excellent programmers and extensive testing, bugs and flaws appear during the life cycle of any operating system. Many of these flaws are security related. Attackers can exploit them, and they do. The only way to ensure that an operating system stays as secure as possible is to keep it current with system updates.

Chapter 7 explores firewalls in more depth, including the Windows Firewall.

▶

▶

A host firewall is installed on the client or server. A network firewall is installed at a network boundary, such as between the Internet and an internal network.

▶

Drive-by attacks download malware without the user's knowledge when the user visits a website. Chapter 12 covers Internet Explorer security that can protect users.

Enabling the Firewall

The Windows Firewall has been a part of Windows systems since Windows XP and Windows Server 2003. Since Windows XP Service Pack 2 (SP2) was first released, the Windows Firewall has been enabled by default. If you're using Windows Server 2008 or Windows Server 2008 R2, the Windows Firewall is enabled by default.

When you're hardening a server, it's important to ensure that a host firewall is enabled. Some companies purchase various third-party firewalls for use on their systems. However, the built-in Windows Firewall is natively installed and doesn't have any additional costs.

Installing Antivirus Software

Every system that is on and accessible to people is susceptible to malware. Antivirus (AV) software can detect and block known malware, and it can often detect suspicious activities by unknown malware. Although malware is most often distributed through email, it can also be distributed through many other methods.

For example, if a user visits an infected website, the user's system can be infected. If a user inserts an infected USB into a system's USB port, the malware can install itself on the system. If a system is running on a network infected with a worm, the system can become infected.

Every system should have AV software installed, although different systems need different protections. For example, the AV software installed on an email server is different from AV software you'd install on a database server or an end user's computer.

THE ESSENTIALS AND BEYOND

This chapter introduced many of the basics related to IT security. Risk occurs when a threat has the potential to exploit a vulnerability, and risk mitigation reduces risks by reducing vulnerabilities. The security triad mandates the protection against loss of confidentiality, loss of integrity, and loss of availability of systems and data. A primary principle to protect against these losses is a defense-in-depth strategy, which includes multiple layers of security. Defense-in-depth increases the difficulty of exploiting systems and ensures that security remains in place even if one layer fails. The principle of least privilege states that users, resources, and applications are granted rights and permissions needed to perform their jobs, but no more. Last, hardening a server means making it more secure than the

(Continues)

THE ESSENTIALS AND BEYOND *(Continued)*

default installation and includes performing actions that reduce the attack surface, keep it up to date, enable host firewalls, and use up-to-date antivirus software.

ADDITIONAL EXERCISES

▶ Draw a diagram that shows the security triad.

▶ Run the Security Configuration Wizard on a Windows Server 2008 server. Identify the recommended state of the SMTP service (SMTPSVC) for the server's current configuration.

▶ Run the Security Configuration Wizard on a Windows Server 2008 server. Identify the recommended state of auditing for Logon events for the server's current configuration.

▶ Identify whether Windows Firewall is enabled on your system.

To compare your answers to the author's, please visit **www.sybex.com/go/ securityessentials**.

REVIEW QUESTIONS

1. What is a simple definition of risk?

2. True or false: You can reduce risk by reducing vulnerabilities.

3. An implementation of which security principle ensures that secrets stay secret?

   A. Authentication   C. Integrity
   B. Availability   D. Confidentiality

4. The implementation of techniques that map to which security principle help to ensure that an unauthorized change to data is detected?

   A. Accessibility   C. Integrity
   B. Availability   D. Confidentiality

5. A basic security principle states that users, resources, and applications should be granted only the rights and permissions needed to perform a task. What is this principle?

6. What is meant by *reducing the attack surface* of a system? (Choose all that apply.)

   A. Disabling needed services   C. Keeping a system up to date
   B. Removing unneeded protocols   D. Disabling the firewall

(Continues)

THE ESSENTIALS AND BEYOND *(Continued)*

7. What tool can you use to create a comprehensive security policy as an XML file on a Windows Server 2008 system?

   A. Microsoft Baseline Security Analyzer (MBSA)

   B. System Center Configuration Manager (SCCM)

   C. Security Configuration Wizard (SCW)

   D. Windows Server Update Services (WSUS)

8. Of the following choices, what is the best method to protect against malware?

   A. Installing antivirus software and keeping it up to date

   B. Disabling unneeded services

   C. Removing unnecessary protocols

   D. Enabling a firewall

CHAPTER 2

Understanding Malware and Social Engineering

One of the most common threats to computers today is malicious software, or malware. Malware comes in many forms, such as viruses, worms, and Trojan horses. It's important to understand how serious the threat is and what you can do to protect computers and networks. The primary protection is antivirus (AV) software. Most AV software will protect against all types of malware, not just viruses.

Social engineering is another common threat. An overwhelming number of attackers out there want to steal people's identities, steal their financial data, steal their money, or simply trick them into adding their computer to a massive robot network ready to attack others. Social engineers are tricky, conniving, and dishonest. However, a little bit of education goes a long way toward stopping them. This chapter covers all of these topics in the following sections:

▶ **Comparing malware**

▶ **Protecting against malware**

▶ **Thwarting social-engineering attacks**

▶ **Protecting email**

Comparing Malware

Malicious software (*malware*) is software that is installed on a system without the user's knowledge or consent. It includes viruses, worms, Trojan horses, spyware, and more.

If a computer is turned on, it's susceptible to infection from malware. The majority of malware is delivered through the Internet (such as via email), but there are many other delivery mechanisms. For example, an infected USB flash drive may install malware on a system as soon as the flash drive is plugged in.

The primary purpose of malware today is making money. Malware attempts to gather as much data as possible, and then attackers use that data for monetary gain. This is sometimes done by stealing identities, stealing financial data, and clearing out bank accounts. Sometimes attackers are willing to collect small amounts at a time from millions of users. Another purpose of malware is espionage—both corporate espionage and government espionage.

Table 2.1 introduces some of the common malware types, and the following sections explore these in more depth.

TABLE 2.1   Common Malware Types

Type	Protection	Comments
Virus	Up-to-date AV software, educated users	Requires interaction by a user
Worm	Up-to-date AV software, firewalls	Doesn't require user interaction
Trojan horse	Up-to-date AV software, educated users	Looks like something helpful but has a hidden component
Buffer overflow	Up-to-date operating systems and applications	Exposes memory by sending unexpected code to a system
Spyware	Up-to-date AV software or antispyware software	Collects information about the user without the user's knowledge

BOTNETS AND MALWARE

Much of today's malicious software has the primary purpose of taking over a computer and having it join a *botnet* (or robot network). The computers act as clones or zombies and do the work for the attacker. Many botnets include tens of thousands of clones, and some have more than a million.

(Continues)

BOTNETS AND MALWARE *(Continued)*

A server known as a *command-and-control server* controls the clones within a botnet, and an attacker controls the server. It's not unusual for the attackers to have almost as much control of a user's computer as the user does.

Clones check in periodically with the command-and-control server for instructions on what to do. They can be instructed to launch denial of service (DoS) attacks against targets on the Internet or send massive amounts of infected spam to unsuspecting users. This is all completely unknown to the user.

Any computer with access to the Internet (even computers within private networks) can become a zombie. The best protections are up-to-date and active AV software and educated users.

Viruses

A computer *virus* is an executable program that spreads from one computer to another. One of the key functions of a virus is to replicate itself. It's through this self-replication that it's propagated. Virus authors write them to interfere with the normal operation of a computer. Some of the damage that a virus can cause includes the following:

- ▶ Join your computer to a botnet
- ▶ Corrupt or delete data on your system
- ▶ Erase everything on your hard disk
- ▶ Email itself to other computers using your address list

Viruses come in many forms. The most common method of delivering a virus is as an attachment in an email message or through instant messaging. For example, *spam* often includes malware. Spam can include harmless advertisements, but today it's much more common for spam to be malicious.

Some of the common ways that viruses are delivered are as follows:

Attachment in Unwanted Email   Spam often includes malware and is the most popular way to transmit viruses. Such messages may look like greeting cards, audio files, video files, or images. When the user double-clicks the attachment to open it, the virus installs itself on the computer.

◀

Spam **is unwanted or unsolicited email. It often includes malware as an attachment, embedded scripts that can cause damage, or links to malicious websites.**

Script in Unwanted Email   Some email messages have scripts embedded within them. When the user opens the email, the script runs and installs the virus. Some email programs (such as Microsoft Outlook) block the scripts by default, but other email programs may allow the scripts to run.

Installed on USB Drives   Viruses sometimes look for a USB drive and automatically infect the drive when it's plugged into a system. When the user inserts the drive into another system, the virus infects this system too.

Embedded in Downloaded Files   Files available as free downloads are sometimes infected. This can include both freeware and shareware.

Worms

Freeware is software available at no cost. *Shareware* is software available at no cost for a trial period; the user is obligated to pay if they continue to use it after the trial ends.

A *worm* is a software program that copies itself from computer to computer over a network. After a worm installs itself on a computer, it can do many of the same types of damage as a virus.

The biggest difference between a worm and a virus is that a virus must be executed through some type of human interaction but a worm doesn't require any human interaction at all. Worms can spread themselves over the network through one of several methods. For example, a worm can identify IP addresses of other computers on the network and then look for open ports. When it finds an exploitable port, it infects the other computer. Worms can also read email addresses stored in a user's address book and then send themselves via email.

Because the worm spreads over the network, it has the potential to slow down network performance. Some worms flood the network with so much traffic that the entire network slows to a crawl.

Some of the famous worms that have attacked and infected networks and systems include the following:

Morris   Morris was one of the first worms and was named after its creator, Robert Morris. It exploited vulnerabilities in Unix programs, such as Sendmail and Finger, and cracked weak passwords. It infected systems multiple times, and each infection consumed system resources until eventually the infected system became inoperable or simply crashed.

Conficker   Conficker (also known as Kido, Downadup, and Downup) is the largest known worm. It attacks unpatched Windows systems. It's estimated to have infected more than 7 million computers, each of which is controlled in a massive botnet spread over 200 countries.

Sasser Sasser exploits a buffer-overflow vulnerability in certain Windows systems. The worm component searches for other systems on the network that have port 445 open and then starts the buffer-overflow attack on this port. Infected systems randomly crash and reboot. This worm has caused massive problems for multiple companies. For instance, X-ray machines in a hospital were shut down, which prevented emergency X-ray services. It also caused another company to close all 130 of its offices due to the destructive nature of the worm.

Blaster Blaster also exploits a buffer-overflow vulnerability in some Windows systems. It spreads by sending itself to other users on the network without requiring users to open an attachment. Infected systems quickly become unstable and reboot.

Trojan Horses

Trojan horse malware is software that looks like one thing but is actually something else. For example, a user may be enticed into downloading a game or utility. However, in addition to the game or utility, the download includes malicious software embedded within it. When the user installs the application, the Trojan horse is also installed.

The name comes from the mythological Trojan horse. In Greek mythology, the Greeks tried to take the city of Troy for several years but were unsuccessful. Then they built a giant wooden horse and convinced the people of Troy that it was a gift from the gods. Greek soldiers hid in the horse, and the rest of the Greek army packed up their camp and left as though they had given up. The people of Troy rolled the horse into the city and celebrated their good fortune with plenty of grog. The soldiers emerged later as the partiers slept and opened the gates to let the Greek army (who had returned) into the city. The Trojan horse looked like one thing (a gift from the gods) but was something else (a vehicle for soldiers, which led to the destruction of the city of Troy). Similarly, Trojan horse software looks like one thing but is something else.

A popular type of Trojan horse today is *rogueware*. Rogueware is a fake program that advertises a specific function, such as AV. The program will alert the user that their computer is infected and will then ask for payment in order to remove the threat. The program's intention is to solicit the payment, and whether or not a threat exists on the machine is never actually checked. For example, a user may visit a website and see a pop-up dialog box similar to Figure 2.1. The warnings can be scary for uninformed users.

◄ Buffer overflows are covered later in this section. The best defense against buffer-overflow attacks is to keep a system up to date with current patches.

◄ PandaLabs reported almost a million variants of rogueware in 2009. Attackers are making more than $400 million per year from rogueware.

I created the dialog box in Figure 2.1, but warnings created by rogueware authors look similar.

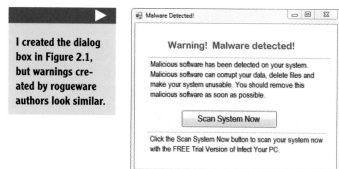

FIGURE 2.1 Rogueware warning

If the user clicks the Scan System Now button shown in Figure 2.1, it starts the download and installation of the malicious software. Some rogueware installs other viruses. More often, it reports that the user's system is infected with specific viruses but, unfortunately, the free trial version won't remove them. The user is prompted to purchase the full version. Many users gladly purchase the software to "fix" their computer. Some attackers then sell the purchaser's credit-card data.

Microsoft Security Essentials is covered later in this chapter, including how to download and install it on your system. Microsoft Security Essentials is *not* rogueware.

In Figure 2.1, the rogueware version is named Infect Your PC. Although this is a giveaway that something is wrong, actual rogueware isn't so obvious. For example, one version of rogueware is named Security Essentials 2010. This isn't the valid Microsoft Security Essentials program created and published by Microsoft, but the name is close enough that it fools many users.

Rogueware continues to pop up with different names and different interfaces, but they all attempt the same thing—to fool the user into installing them on the user's system and ultimately to solicit payment from the user. The attackers are sophisticated and create very realistic-looking programs. The best defenses are up-to-date AV software from a reliable source and educated users.

STUXNET

Stuxnet is the first known malware that has shown it is capable of having an impact on industrial control system hardware. Stuxnet has successfully penetrated networks and reached this internal hardware, even when networks are isolated from the Internet.

It starts as malware that infects Windows systems. Stuxnet is primarily transferred via USB flash drives. When a user plugs an infected USB flash drive into a computer running Windows, the virus infects the system. Stuxnet doesn't damage the Windows systems but instead uses a worm component to seek out a specific type of hardware.

(Continues)

Buffer-Overflow Attacks

Applications use areas of memory (buffers) to store temporary data. For example, when you fill out a form on a web page, your information is stored temporarily in a program buffer. Buffer-overflow attacks take advantage of known vulnerabilities within operating systems and applications. A buffer overflow occurs when an application receives unexpected data that it can't handle, resulting in an error. The error then causes the application to write more data to a buffer than the buffer can handle and the unexpected data then overflows to other memory.

Consider Figure 2.2. Applications often have memory available to them in a program buffer. The application can use this buffer but won't have access to other memory. On the right of Figure 2.2, the application is getting unexpected input that is causing an internal error. This error is exposing other system memory to the application, essentially resulting in a buffer overflow.

Not all application errors cause buffer overflows. However, when a buffer overflow occurs, it may be exploited.

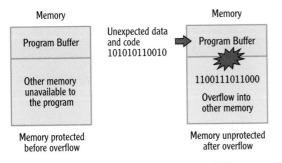

FIGURE 2.2 Buffer-overflow vulnerability

When attackers discover data that causes a buffer overflow, they then add code to the end of the data. This data causes the buffer overflow, and their code is inserted into the exposed memory. In other words, they write malicious code and insert it into the system.

You may be wondering *unexpected data* is. It's anything that the application developer didn't predict and plan for. For instance, you probably know that you can't divide anything by the number zero. If you were to try, you would receive an error. If an application developer didn't anticipate a user inputting the number zero and therefore program for the possibility, the number zero would be considered unexpected by the application and might cause the system to enter an unknown state.

> **Most programs will gracefully handle divide-by-zero errors. The program displays an error to the user but continues to run.**

Most application developers know to check for valid input. They use error checking to gracefully let the user know what is allowed and ignore the user's invalid input. However, there's an almost infinite number of possible data entries, and if one is discovered that wasn't planned for, a buffer overflow may occur.

There are three primary methods to avoid problems related to buffer-overflow attacks:

Input Validation   The application developer should validate all data before using it. For example, if a number between 1 and 100 is expected, the program should verify that the inputted data is a valid number between 1 and 100. When the user enters invalid data, the application doesn't use it but instead gives a user-friendly error letting the user know what data is considered valid.

Application Testing   Application testing puts an application through its paces before it's released. The goal of testing is to identify and correct any problems. Functionality testing is one type of test used for application testing. For example, if a number between 1 and 100 is expected, the numbers 0, 1, 2, 99, 100, and 101 are entered to see how the program handles data at the edge of accepted input. Discovered problems are sent back to the developer to correct.

Up-to-Date Patching   When buffer-overflow vulnerabilities are discovered, the vendor or application developer typically releases a patch to correct the problem. Of course, this patch is only useful if it's applied. Many worms exploit buffer-overflow vulnerabilities, but they're only successful on unpatched systems. If the patch is applied to a system, the worm can't exploit the vulnerability.

Spyware

Spyware is software that installs itself on a system without the user's consent, or without giving the user any notice or control. Spyware may not display any symptoms because it's largely passive. It sits in the background collecting information and doesn't want to be discovered.

Years ago, spyware was satisfied with tracking a user to identify buying habits so that they could target the user with specific advertisements. However, spyware has become much more malicious.

Spyware is often looking to gather personal information about a user and a user's online habits. More malicious spyware tries to discover personally identifiable information (PII) about the user. This PII can be used for identify theft or to hack into a user's online financial accounts.

One method popular with spyware is the use of a *keylogger*. A keylogger is a program that records all keystrokes on a system. The keystrokes are recorded into a log, which the attacker later views. The log includes everything that a user types, including URLs, usernames, and passwords. For example, when a user logs onto their bank's website, a keylogger can record the username, password, or PIN typed in by the user. The attacker can later impersonate the user by using the same credentials.

Understanding the Threat

Many people underestimate the actual threat posed by malware. It's worthwhile knowing how extensive the threat actually is. The MessageLabs Intelligence 2010 Annual Security Report shows some interesting statistics, presented in the following list. The report is sponsored by Symantec and available here:

```
http://www.messagelabs.com/mlireport/MessageLabsIntelligence_2010_
Annual_Report_FINAL.pdf
```

▶ Spam continues to increase, with 89 percent of all global email being spam.

▶ Approximately 5 million active botnets regularly send spam.

▶ Over 88 percent of spam is sent by botnets.

▶ The Rustock botnet includes between 1.1 million and 1.7 million clones and sends about 44 billion spam emails a day.

▶ Over 339,600 strains of malware were detected in email.

▶ Approximately 95.1 billion phishing emails were estimated to be in circulation in 2010.

▶ Tracked phishing attacks impersonated more than 1,500 different organizations.

No, these aren't typos. The Rustock botnet had more than 1 million clones and sent out billions of spam emails a day. At least until Microsoft helped take it down in March 2011.

> ► Almost 43,000 websites were identified with malicious web threats.

> ► Almost 90 percent of blocked websites were legitimate websites that were compromised with malware.

Clearly, the threat of malware is real. You can't just stick your head in the sand and pretend the danger doesn't exist. Organizations must understand this and take proactive steps to protect against malware.

Protecting Against Malware

Chapter 1, "Understanding Core Security Principles" introduced the concept of defense-in-depth. At the top of the list of defense-in-depth concepts are policies and procedures, as shown in Chapter 1 (Figure 1.3). These policies and procedures can include requirements to protect against both malware and social-engineering attacks.

The primary protection against most malware is the use of *antivirus (AV)* software. AV software is discussed in depth in the following section. However, there are additional security steps that can be taken to protect systems from malware. Many organizations establish policies and procedures to ensure that these additional steps are in place. These additional steps include the following:

Use Firewalls   Both network-based and host-based firewalls provide an added layer of protection against worms. If a worm does get into a network (such as from a USB flash drive), the host-based firewalls provide protection for internal clients.

Keep Systems Up to Date   As software vulnerabilities are discovered, vendors release updates to address the vulnerabilities. These are only effective if the systems have the updates installed.

Reduce the Attack Surface   Remove all unneeded protocols, and disable unused services. If a protocol or service isn't running, malware can't compromise it. Fewer protocols and services running on a targeted machine results in fewer successful attacks.

Educate Users   The single best method of addressing social-engineering attacks is to educate users. When users understand the threats, they're better able to counter them. This includes letting users know what the threats are and providing simple guidelines in order to help them thwart attacks.

Minimize Use of Administrator Accounts   Users should use accounts that have the least privilege for their job. Administrators should have two accounts: one

The "Thwarting Social-Engineering Attacks" section (later in this chapter) covers social engineering.

Chapter 7 covers firewalls in more depth.

Read about how important it is to keep a system updated and ways to do so in Chapter 1.

Chapter 1 discussed the concept of reducing the attack surface on systems.

for regular work and one for administrative work. Administrators should only use the administrator account when performing administrative activities.

Using Antivirus Software

AV software protects systems against different types of malware. Although the name implies that it only protects against viruses, most AV software also protects against most, if not all, types of malware.

Many organizations use a three-pronged approach to protecting systems in their network, as shown in Figure 2.3. In the figure you can see 1) a content-filtering firewall used to scan all incoming Internet traffic, 2) a mail server with AV software, and 3) AV software on internal systems. Content-filtering firewalls can scan for risky attachments and strip them off email messages; some also include spam scanners to remove spam messages.

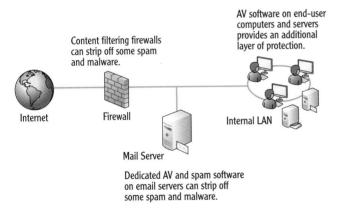

FIGURE 2.3 Three-pronged protection against malware

Email servers use databases that require specialized AV software. This software can scan email within the databases and also strip off malicious attachments or embedded scripts from valid email messages. Email servers can also delete or quarantine spam before it reaches a user's mailbox.

Microsoft's Exchange Server includes built-in spam fighting capabilities with its Content Filter agent. Additional software (such as Microsoft Forefront products) can be installed for more comprehensive protection.

Fighting spam is a balancing act. Most organizations try to set spam filters so that valid emails are never deleted or quarantined. This often results in more false negatives, equating to spam getting through to users' mailboxes.

◀ Chapter 1 discussed the principle of least privilege and the use of dual accounts for administrators.

◀ Chapter 7 covers firewalls in more depth.

AV software on end-user computers and servers provides real-time protection and can perform scheduled scans of servers and users' computers. Microsoft Security Essentials (discussed in the next section) supports each of the following three methods:

Figure 2.4 also shows that scheduled scans are enabled.

Real-Time Protection This monitors your system all the time and can alert you to threats. For example, if you visit a website that attempts to install malware, real-time protection can detect the malicious activity, block the threat, and alert you. Similarly, real-time protection can detect malware when you attempt to open an infected file. In Figure 2.4, you can see that real-time protection is enabled.

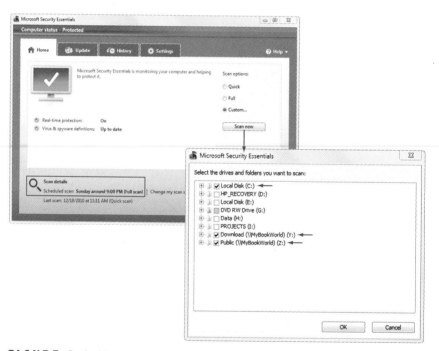

FIGURE 2.4 Microsoft Security Essentials scan options

Scheduled Scans Most AV software supports scheduled scans. You pick a time when you want the scan to occur, such as every Sunday night at 9 p.m., and the scan will automatically start (as long as your computer is on).

On-Demand Scans When you notice suspicious activity on your computer, you can perform an on-demand scan. Most AV software allows you to pick the type of scan you want to have executed (such as quick, full, or custom) and start a scan immediately. For example, Figure 2.4 shows the screen to start a custom on-demand scan. In the figure, only the local C: drive and two mapped drives are selected for scanning.

AV software primarily detects malware using predefined definitions. Viruses have known identifiers similar to a fingerprint for a person. These identifiers include sizes of files, names, embedded code, behaviors, and so on. AV software examines files and their behavior and compares them against a database of known malware. If a match is found, the AV software alerts on the find.

With this in mind, one of the most important actions is to keep the AV definitions up to date. Malware authors are constantly updating and modifying malware to try to get around the definitions. If definitions are old, a slightly modified virus can infect a system without being detected.

Some advanced AV software also includes a heuristics component. If the AV software includes heuristics, it has a better chance of detecting new malware, or recently modified malware, even if the AV software doesn't have a definition for it. Heuristic-based AV software detects malware-like behavior. In other words, it detects the malware based on what it does instead of what it is. For example, malware often attempts to modify system files that regular software would never modify. Because this behavior is suspicious, if a program attempts this type of a modification, the heuristic-based AV software would alert that the software may be malware. Some AV software takes this a step further. Instead of letting a new application make a change and then detecting it, the software temporarily blocks the execution of new programs. Then, it starts the application in a quarantined space on the machine (commonly called a *sandbox* or a *virtual machine*) and observes the behavior. If it appears to be safe, the software allows the actual application to run. If it looks suspicious, the software alerts the user.

Using Microsoft Security Essentials on Desktops

Microsoft Security Essentials is a free AV tool for end users and small businesses. It includes real-time protection against viruses, worms, Trojan horses, and other malware. You can download it free here: `www.microsoft.com/security_essentials`.

Figure 2.5 shows the settings screen of the Microsoft Security Essentials tool. It provides real-time protection to detect malware activity and supports both scheduled and on-demand scans. When it detects malicious activity, it will send an alert and then take an action based on the setting.

Microsoft Security Essentials Software includes several alert levels, as shown in Table 2.2.

Small businesses can use the free Microsoft Security Essentials on up to 10 devices, assuming the devices don't fall within the documented restrictions.

◀

◀

A quarantined threat is moved to an area where it can't cause any harm. However, it remains available for examination.

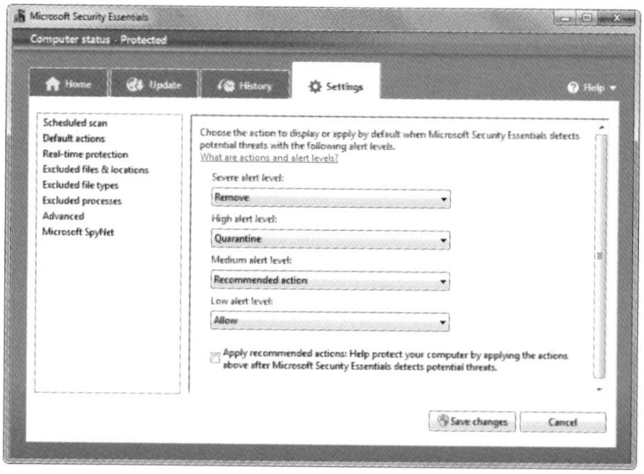

FIGURE 2.5 Microsoft Security Essentials Settings page

TABLE 2.2 Microsoft Security Essentials Alert Levels

Alert Level	Recommended Action	Comments
Severe	Remove the software immediately.	Indicates a widespread or exceptionally malicious program. Can affect the privacy and security of the computer or damage the computer.
High	Remove the software immediately.	Program may collect personal information, negatively affect privacy, or damage the computer.
Medium	Review the alert and consider blocking or allowing the software.	Program may affect privacy or may make unauthorized changes to the computer.
Low	Review the alert and consider blocking or allowing the software.	Relatively harmless. Includes potentially unwanted software that might collect information about the user or the computer or change some settings on the computer.

Businesses with more than 10 devices can use one or more of the Microsoft Forefront family of products for malware protection. Microsoft Forefront includes software for desktop computers, laptops, and servers. Management software is available that can automate the deployment and administration of Microsoft

Forefront on these systems. For example, you can configure the settings remotely, configure schedules for downloading updated definitions, and schedule scans, all from a central console.

MICROSOFT WINDOWS MALICIOUS SOFTWARE REMOVAL TOOL

Microsoft has developed the Microsoft Windows Malicious Software Removal Tool, which can check Windows systems for a wide variety of infections. Microsoft releases a new version of the software on the second Tuesday of every month (Patch Tuesday). This is the same day that Microsoft releases security updates.

This free download is available from Microsoft's download site (**www .microsoft.com/downloads**) when you search for Microsoft Windows Malicious Software Removal Tool, or from the following site: **www.microsoft .com/security/malwareremove**. There are separate versions for 32-bit systems and 64-bit systems.

You can double-click the download to install and run the tool. You'll be prompted to choose a type of scan, as shown in the following graphic.

Although this tool isn't a replacement for AV software on your system, it can help you to discover and remove recently released malware. Also, unlike Microsoft Security Essentials, the Malicious Software Removal Tool will run on Windows Server 2008.

Thwarting Social-Engineering Attacks

No matter how secure a computer or network is, a single person can undo the steps that have been taken by the administrator. Instead of taking endless hours and expensive resources to crack passwords, attackers have found they can sometimes get what they want just by asking. Or, instead of hacking into networks to install malicious software, they can simply ask a user to install it.

This sounds a little outrageous. Would users actually give up their passwords or willingly install software that turns out to be malicious? The answer is yes, and it happens all the time.

Social engineering is a broad term indicating that an attacker is using techniques to trick people into giving up sensitive information or perform actions on behalf of the attacker. Social engineers use deceit and trickery to get users to do what they want, and they succeed without using extensive technical skills. Social engineering can take many forms, including the following approaches:

- ▶ In person
- ▶ Via a phone call
- ▶ Phishing with email

Social Engineering in Person

Attackers can impersonate others to get information or access that they wouldn't normally have. Impersonation is a common method used in social engineering.

For example, an attacker can impersonate a repairman and show up at an organization's doorsteps to "fix" a problem. The attacker may have actually caused the problem by disconnecting a phone line and then he shows up to fix it. He may be welcomed with open arms and led straight to a locked wiring closet, which workers happily unlock to give him access.

The attacker can connect a wireless access point to capture all the traffic going through network devices in the wiring closet. He can then sit in a parking lot next door with a wireless sniffer and capture data sent through the network. Of course, he also repairs the phone line that he disconnected, providing "proof" that he was the repairman.

A *wireless sniffer* is a protocol analyzer that can capture traffic transmitted wirelessly. The attacker can then read any data transmitted in clear text.

Social Engineering with a Phone Call

A social-engineering attack can come as a simple phone call. An attacker can call the help desk, identify herself as an executive in the company by name, and then say that she's forgotten her password. A simple request like this may give the attacker access to the account: "Can you unlock my account so that I can get back to work?"

If procedures aren't in place, the help-desk employee may simply say "Sure," reset the password, and tell the attacker the new password. There are two important procedures to consider in this situation.

Verifying Identity Prior to Resetting Passwords   Instead of help-desk personnel simply believing that people are who they say they are, a verification process can be used, requiring some type of identity proofing before the password is reset. For example, users may be required to provide specific information that isn't publically available, such as a PIN used for their account.

Limiting Password-Reset Rights   The passwords that help-desk personnel can reset should be limited. At the very least, only high-level IT administrators should be able to reset accounts for high-level executives.

LIMITING RIGHTS AND LEAST PRIVILEGE

Limiting rights is also required to implement the principle of least privilege. If a help-desk technician can reset any account, he can change the password for any manager and then access the manager's documents using the manager's account. For example, a help-desk tech may want to know how much other people are making. By logging onto the HR manager's account, he may be able to access payroll information. By limiting rights, you can avoid this type of situation.

Recognizing Phishing Attempts

Attackers often use *phishing* (pronounced *fishing*) attempts to steal a person's identity or access personal information such as usernames and passwords. Phishing is the practice of sending out an email and trying to trick users into giving up their information.

Phishing attempts often have several specific elements:

▶ The email message looks like it originates from your bank or another company or website that you use.

▶ The email message indicates that there is some type of problem with your account and requests you to revalidate your information.

▶ The email message includes a sense of urgency, indicating that if you don't validate your information, you'll lose access.

◀

Phishing attacks throw out bait hoping to hook a victim, similar to how a fisherman throws out bait hoping to catch a fish.

For example, consider the following text from an email phishing message regarding a bank account:

```
We have noticed suspicious activity on your account. To protect
your financial data you are required to validate your account's
information. Please log on immediately and verify your account.
http://yourbankurl.xxx
Failure to validate your account will result in disabling all account
access to protect you.
Thank you for your business.
Bank logo
```

Although the bank URL may look exactly like your bank's URL, the actual embedded link will be different. In most email applications, you're able to hover over the link to determine the actual embedded destination of the link. Figure 2.6 shows a mockup of an email with a masked web address embedded into it.

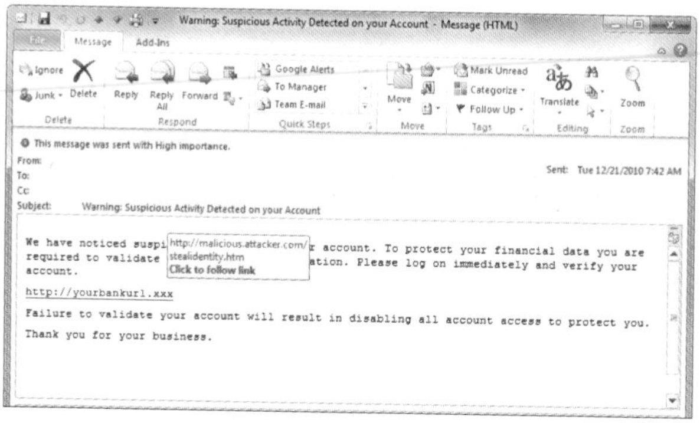

> A *masked* web address is a web link that looks like one address in plain text, but hovering over it shows that the actual link goes somewhere else on the Internet.

FIGURE 2.6 Masked web address in an email

In the figure, the displayed URL is **http://yourbankurl.xxx**, but the actual link is **http://malicious.attacker.com/stealidentity.htm**. One simple rule can help users avoid these traps:

Never follow links embedded in email messages.

If you receive a message like this and think it's valid, open a web browser and type in the URL yourself. You'll be sure that you're going to the correct website.

Another common phishing email may appear to come from your ISP and asks you to validate your email account. It could look something like this:

> Be wary if the embedded link is different from the displayed link. Reputable companies don't mask their web addresses.

```
Your mailbox has exceeded the quota set by your administrator. This
quota can be increased, but to ensure that your account has not been
taken over by spammers, you will need to validate your account.
```

```
To validate your account, reply to this email with the following
information:
Email address:
Password:
Date of birth:
If you fail to validate your account, your account will be deactivated
permanently.
Thank you for your prompt attention in this matter.
```

In this email, the message looks like it's coming from your ISP. For example, the From address could be something like admin@your_isp.com. However, it's easy to spoof an email address in an email message, so you shouldn't automatically trust the From address.

If you click Reply on a spoofed email address, you'll see that the Reply To address is different. Sometimes the Reply To address is clearly different and has completely different names. However, attackers sometimes use typo-squatting techniques to make the address look similar, but not quite the same.

For example, you may receive an email that looks like it came from Microsoft .com. When you click Reply, it shows email addresses that are subtly different, such as these:

▶ microsft.com (without the second *o*)

▶ mircosoft.com (with the *r* and *c* transposed)

▶ validate-microsoft.com (which isn't a Microsoft.com address but is instead a validate-microsoft.com address).

Spear phishing is another variant of phishing. The sender's address is forged so that it appears to come from someone within the employee's organization.

There are many variations on phishing attempts. Here are two additional examples:

You've Won   "Congratulations. Your email has been selected in our lottery, and you've won $100,000. All you have to do is send us all of your personal and banking information."

Here's the implied fine print: "We'll use this information to withdraw all of your money, and you'll never hear from us again."

Help Me Get Money Out of the Bank   "Dear friend. My uncle died leaving over $18 million but it must be transferred to an overseas account in order for me to access it. If you assist me, I'll give you 30 percent of the funds."

Here's the implied fine print: "There is no uncle and there is no $18 million. However, we'd still like access to your bank account."

◀

Email spoofing changes the email message so that the To address makes it appear as if the email is coming from someone other than the actual sender.

◀

The request for information won't be so transparent. However, every piece of personal information you give away puts you at risk, and no one will send you any winnings.

Here are some simple steps any users can take to protect themselves from phishing attacks:

Never Send a Password to a Company Through Email   Be suspicious of any email with an urgent request for any of your personal information. Legitimate companies will never request your credentials through email.

Don't Click Links in an Email   Phishers use masked web addresses. If you open the web browser and manually type in a URL directly, you'll avoid these malicious links. If you're very concerned about a message you received, call the company to verify its legitimacy.

Never Send Other Personal Information via Email   Some phishing attempts ask for your credit-card data, banking information, Social Security number, birth date, or other personal information. Don't submit your personal information to any company in an email message. If an organization really needs this data, it will provide a web page (using HTTPS for security) where you can enter it. Remember, though, don't go to this page from a link provided in an email.

If you want to read more about phishing and current Internet scams, checkout the Anti-Phishing Working Group (APWG) at **www.antiphishing.org**.

Recognizing Pharming

Pharming (pronounced *farming*) redirects victims to unwanted websites even if the user types the correct URL into their web browser. Pharming hijacks name-resolution methods in order to redirect users to these unrequested websites.

Name resolution is the process of resolving a hostname to an IP address. The primary method of name resolution on the Internet is the Domain Name System (DNS). The user's system queries a DNS server, requesting resolution of a hostname, and DNS performs a lookup and then returns an IP address. The TCP/IP suite on the machine uses this IP address to connect with the target system. Other methods for name resolution include utilizing data contained within the host cache on a machine, and using a hosts file on a machine (located at `c:\windows\system32\drivers\etc` on most Windows computers).

The order of processing for name resolution for host names on the Internet is as follows:

> Name resolu-
> tion is covered in
> depth in *Microsoft
> Windows Networking
> Essentials* (Wiley,
> 2011), which covers
> exam 98-366.

1. If a name mapping exists in the hosts file, it's automatically placed in the host cache and is always used first.

2. When a name is resolved by DNS, it's placed in the host cache. The system checks the host cache second to see if the name is there before querying DNS again.

3. If the name isn't resolved with either of these methods, the system sends a query to a DNS server to resolve the name.

A pharming attack will manipulate one of the following three methods to redirect a user to a bogus website:

Hosts File   Malware sometimes modifies the hosts file to map a website to a different IP address. For example, imagine that the IP address of the Windows Update site is 207.46.18.94. An attacker can modify the hosts file to map the Windows Update site to a different IP address. The client computer accesses address content in the hosts file before attempting a DNS lookup, and because the IP address it's attempting is incorrect, the machine can no longer reach the Windows Update site.

DNS Server   In the past, attackers have used social-engineering techniques to convince DNS administrators to modify DNS records for valid websites to IP addresses of the attacker's website. After the DNS record is modified, users can no longer access the intended website.

DNS Cache Poisoning   In a *DNS cache poisoning* attack, cached data on the DNS server is modified, or *poisoned*, resulting in users being redirected to different sites.

◄

You can view the contents of the host cache with the following command at the command prompt: `ipconfig /displaydns`.

Protecting Email

Because the majority of malware is delivered via email, it's important to understand the attacks on email and some of the different steps to take for protection.

This section summarizes the important elements that many organizations implement to protect email:

Antivirus Software   This is a primary protection. Some AV software can strip off or quarantine malicious attachments. Other AV software uses real-time protection to detect malware as soon as a user tries to open it. In addition to installing AV software on the client systems, organizations install AV software on the email server to filter out malicious email.

Antispam Techniques   Spam is a major source of malware, so by filtering out spam, the computer has an added layer of protection. Most email programs have

◄

As mentioned previously, email delivers the majority of malware, often in the form of spam.

> **Microsoft Exchange Servers (used to route email) also include antispam technologies.**

some type of spam or junk filter. For example, Outlook includes a Junk E-mail filter. Email identified by the filter as spam is moved to a Junk E-mail folder in the user's mailbox. The Junk E-mail filter can be configured as shown in Figure 2.7. Links to graphics are blocked, HTML links are blocked, attachments are blocked, and the Reply and Reply All functionality is disabled. Users can move legitimate email from the Junk E-mail folder into the Inbox.

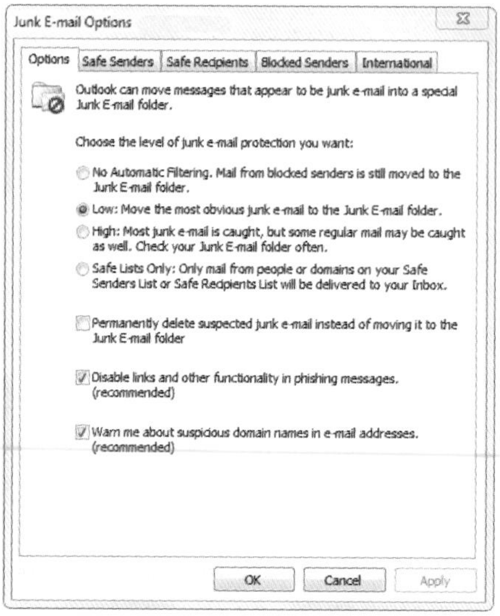

FIGURE 2.7 Junk E-mail options in Microsoft Outlook

Disable Automatic Display of Pictures   This blocks images used as web beacons. An image used as a web beacon isn't sent in the email but is instead retrieved from a web server using a link within the email. Embedded in the link is a code that identifies the recipient's email address. When the server receives a request for the image, the web beacon identifies the recipient's email address as a valid email address. Attackers sell valid email addresses to other spammers, so the result of displaying images automatically is more spam for the recipient. Users should only display images from known senders.

Protection from Phishing   The best protection from phishing attacks are educated users. When users understand the scams, they're better able to detect them. A couple of simple rules can help:

▶ Never send a password to a company through email—legitimate companies will never request it.

▶ Don't click any suspicious links such as masked web addresses. If you want to visit the site, open the browser and type in the URL manually, especially if the email requires you to enter credentials.

THE ESSENTIALS AND BEYOND

In this chapter, you learned about malware. Viruses require user interaction to execute, whereas worms can spread to other computers across the network without user intervention. Trojan horses appear to be one thing but have a hidden malicious element. Buffer-overflow attacks take advantage of vulnerabilities in unpatched operating systems. The primary protection against malware is AV software that is kept up to date.

You also learned about social engineering—a technique used by attackers to trick users into giving up sensitive data or taking actions such as installing malware on their computers. Social engineers commonly try to trick people in person, on the phone, and via email. Phishing is a popular social-engineering tactic. The best prevention against social engineering is education.

ADDITIONAL EXERCISES

▶ Download and run the Malicious Software Removal Tool.

▶ Identify what some of the common computer threats were last month as identified by MessageLabs.

▶ Review the Microsoft Security Intelligence Report (SIR), and identify what threats it's currently focusing on.

▶ Read the Microsoft SIR data on rogueware.

To compare your answers to the author's, please visit **www.sybex.com/go/ securityessentials**.

REVIEW QUESTIONS

1. What is the primary difference between a virus and a worm?

   A. There is none. They're both the same.

   B. A worm requires user intervention to spread, but a virus doesn't.

   C. A virus requires user intervention to spread, but a worm doesn't.

   D. A virus is malware, but a worm is antivirus software.

2. True or false: A buffer-overflow attack can gain access to a system's memory.

3. Which of the following is a type of malware that appears to be something else?

   A. Buffer overflow   **C.** Virus

   B. Trojan horse   **D.** Worm

4. True or false: Botnets don't represent a real threat today.

5. The majority of spam is sent out by _____.

(Continues)

THE ESSENTIALS AND BEYOND (Continued)

6. Microsoft has created an antivirus tool for desktop operating systems. It's available for free for home and small-business users and provides real-time protection. What is this tool?

7. True or false: Security Essentials 2010 is a type of Trojan horse known as rogueware.

8. What tool can you use for free on Windows Server 2008 to check for and remove many types of malware threats? (Choose all that apply.)

   A. Security Essentials 2010

   B. Microsoft Security Essentials

   C. Microsoft Windows Malicious Software Removal Tool

   D. Microsoft Forefront

9. One method of conducting pharming is through DNS _____.

10. Which of the following can protect email from potential threats? (Choose all that apply.)

   A. Antivirus software

   B. Disabling automatic display of graphics

   C. Enabling pharming

   D. Educating users

CHAPTER 3

Understanding User Authentication

One of the primary methods of ensuring security is to restrict access to known users. This requires users to authenticate themselves, or prove their identity by providing some type of credentials. Authentication is commonly classified using three types, or three factors of authentication: *something you know, something you have*, and *something you are*. It's important to understand these factors, including their strengths and weaknesses and how they can be used together to enhance security.

Passwords are the most common method used to authenticate. It's important to know what a strong password is and how to create one. Windows Server 2008 includes many tools you can use to ensure that users follow best practices when using passwords. This includes the option to lock out accounts if users try to guess passwords. Smart cards and biometrics are stronger methods used for authentication and may be used alone or in combination with a username and password.

Kerberos is the primary authentication protocol used in a Microsoft domain, but it has a stringent time requirement you need to understand. These topics and more are presented in the following sections.

▶ **Comparing the three factors of authentication**

▶ **Using passwords for authentication**

▶ **Using smart cards and token devices for authentication**

▶ **Using biometrics for authentication**

▶ **Starting applications with Run As Administrator**

▶ **Preventing time skew with Kerberos**

▶ **Identifying RADIUS capabilities**

▶ **Identifying unsecure authentication protocols**

Comparing the Three Factors of Authentication

Authentication occurs when an entity presents credentials and the credentials are verified as valid. For example, when a user logs on with a username and password, the system checks to ensure that the username and password are valid and, if so, authenticates the user.

You've probably accessed systems using a username and password before, but there are other methods of authentication that may be configured in higher-security environments. The three primary types, or factors, of authentication are as follows:

Something You Know   This includes information such as passwords or personal identification numbers (PINs).

Something You Have   This includes items you can hold, such as a smart card.

Something You Are   This includes distinguishable characteristics about you, such as a fingerprint, and can be verified using biometrics.

Any one of these methods can be used for authentication. However, you can also increase security by using two or three of the factors simultaneously. *Multifactor authentication* uses two or more factors. For example, when a user uses both a smart card and a PIN, they're using the two factors of *something you have* and *something you know*.

There is a difference between authentication and authorization. Just because a user can prove their identify by logging on doesn't necessarily mean they have the authority to access resources on a system. However, authentication is the first step in the process. Chapter 4, "Securing Access with Permissions," covers steps you can take to authorize a user to access resources with permissions.

IDENTIFICATION VS. AUTHENTICATION

There is a difference between identification and authentication. For example, when a user logs on with a username and password, the username provides the identification, and the password provides the authentication.

Identification is when a user professes to be someone or claims a specific identity. *Authentication* verifies the claim with additional information such as a password. In a Windows system, individual computers have local Security Account Manager (SAM) databases that hold account information for local

(Continues)

IDENTIFICATION VS. AUTHENTICATION *(Continued)*

accounts on the system. In a Microsoft domain, a domain controller hosts Active Directory and centrally holds account information for all accounts in the domain.

Using Passwords for Authentication

Passwords are the most common form of authentication. However, they're also the weakest form and the most susceptible to compromise. It's important to understand what a strong password is and how to create one. Additionally, it's valuable to know how strong passwords can be enforced within a Microsoft environment. This section identifies many of the weaknesses of passwords and how they can be strengthened.

Comparing Password Attack Methods

Attackers recognize that passwords are among the weakest form of authentication and use a variety of methods to discover them. If they can discover the password for a user, they can access the user's account and impersonate the user.

Within a Microsoft domain, an attacker will be able to access any resources the user can access. The attacker can read, modify, and delete data that the compromised account can normally access. If the organization is using audit trails, the audit trail will document that the compromised user account took these actions but won't indicate the presence of an attacker.

If an attacker can access a user's password for an online account, they can do anything the user can do. For example, if an attacker has discovered a user's password for a bank account, the attacker can log on and transfer funds out of the account.

Most users are cautious about giving out their bank password. However, they often use the same password for other accounts, and they aren't as cautious about protecting these accounts. For example, a user may use the same password for their Hotmail account that they do for an eBay or PayPal account, or even for their bank account.

The following list identifies some of the common methods used by attackers to discover passwords:

Social Engineering   Social engineers have discovered that if they ask a question in just the right way, users freely give up their passwords. This includes phishing

Chapter 2 covers social-engineering attacks, including phishing.

attacks and other methods to get users to reveal their passwords. User education is the best defense against social engineering.

Dictionary Attacks   A dictionary attack tries using every word in a word list (similar to a dictionary) as a password, until a successful match is found. Most dictionary attacks use word lists from multiple languages, so using a foreign word as a password doesn't help. In addition, most dictionary attacks try commonly used passwords such as *123456, 12345678, qwerty, abc123, 111111, letmein* (let me in), and others. Using strong passwords is the best protection against a dictionary attack.

Brute Force   In a brute-force attack, an attacker simply tries to guess every possible combination for a password. Automated cracking tools are available that can speed up this process. Using strong passwords and account-lockout policies provides the best protection against brute-force attacks.

You may notice a theme in the protection methods: Using strong passwords is one of the best methods for protecting passwords. The next section defines strong passwords and presents methods you can use to create strong passwords that can be easily remembered.

PASSWORD-CRACKING TOOLS

Many automated tools are available that attackers use to crack passwords. Some are advertised as password-recovery tools used by administrators to recover passwords but are also used by attackers.

As an example, imagine that you're a network administrator and someone has changed the local administrator password for a Windows 7 system. You can either rebuild this system from scratch or use a password-recovery tool to recover the administrator password. Obviously, it's easier if you can recover the password.

Ophcrack is a free tool used to recover passwords. You can download an .iso image of the program, burn the image to a CD, and boot to the CD. The tool can quickly recover all the passwords on Windows 7 and other Windows systems. Even a 10-character password can be recovered in less than a minute. Longer passwords take longer to recover.

Although administrators can use Ophcrack to recover a password, attackers can also use Ophcrack to crack a password. The process is the same, but the intent is different.

(Continues)

PASSWORD-CRACKING TOOLS *(Continued)*

Similarly, Nessus is a popular vulnerability-assessment tool. It can capture traffic going across the network and analyze the data to discover passwords. Passwords sent across the network in clear text are easy to discover. However, even when cryptographic methods are used to protect passwords, Nessus can discover them when the passwords are weak.

Security professionals use Nessus to assess a network for weaknesses, but attackers can also use it to discover and exploit weaknesses if they have access to the network.

Creating Strong Passwords

One of the best things you can do to increase security with a password is use a *strong password*. Strong passwords are harder for attackers to crack. However, password-cracking tools have consistently improved, further arming attackers and requiring passwords to become stronger to resist attacks.

A password-cracking tool can discover a weak password without any prior knowledge of the password.

The two primary elements that make a strong password are the length and complexity. Microsoft recommends using a password at least 14 characters long that contains a variety of character types, in order to obtain sufficient complexity. Table 3.1 shows the characteristics of a strong password.

TABLE 3.1 Characteristics of a Strong Password

Characteristic	Description
Sufficient length	Microsoft recommends at least 14 characters.
Mixture of cases	Use both upper- and lowercase letters.
Use of numbers	Include numbers from 0–9.
Use of special characters	Include special characters such as !@#$%^&*()_+.
Isn't in the dictionary	Passwords shouldn't be found in the dictionary of any language.
Doesn't include personal information	Passwords shouldn't include the user's name, the names of family members or pets, or other public information.

Many organizations require administrators to use passwords with at least 14 characters.

If you use a 5-character password, you may think that no one uses a 14-character password because it's impossible to remember. Although some organizations are still using shorter passwords of six or eight characters for most users, the industry trend is to require longer passwords.

The challenge is ensuring that users create strong, complex passwords but don't write the passwords down to remember them. There are techniques you can use to create long, complex passwords that become memorable. The following exercises show two possible methods:

1. Start with a phrase that includes at least 14 characters. As an example, you could use one of these:

   I will be certified

   I love technology

2. Remove the spaces, and change the first letter in each word to uppercase:

   IWillBeCertified

   ILoveTechnology

3. Convert each letter *e* to the number 3:

   IWillB3C3rtifi3d

   ILov3T3chnology

4. Convert each letter *i* to an exclamation mark (!):

   !W!llB3C3rtifi3d

   !Lov3T3chnology

You can replace any letters with symbols or numbers that make sense to you. For example, you could change each letter *a* to @, or change each letter *o* to 0 (zero).

At this point, you have a strong password that is 14 characters (or more) and that you can remember. You can use other techniques such as starting and/or ending the password with a number or symbol. You can also change other letters to symbols, such as changing each letter *s* to $.

Here's another example.

1. Start with a phrase that includes at least 10 words. For example, you could use the following:

   I am learning and will become MTA Security Fundamentals certified

2. Identify the first letter of each word:

   ialawbmsfc

3. Change every other letter to uppercase:

   IaLaWbMsFc

4. Add a number and a symbol at the beginning, such as 1*:

   1*IaLaWbMsFc

5. Add the same number and symbol to the end, but in reverse order (such as *1):

   1*IaLaWbMsFc*1

If someone asked you to memorize *1*IaLaWbMsFc*1*, you might find it difficult to do without writing it down. However, if you took a couple of minutes to create the password using this technique, you would be more likely to remember it. Also, a password with this length and level of complexity would take a significant amount of time and processing power for an attacker to crack.

Enforcing Strong Passwords

You have the ability to enforce strong passwords in Windows Server 2008. The primary method is to use *Group Policy* to configure a *Password Policy*. You can use the local Group Policy or Local Security Policy for an individual computer, or Group Policy in a domain. The Local Security Policy settings apply to all the accounts on the local computer, and the domain-based Group Policy settings apply to all the user accounts in the entire domain.

The local Group Policy applies only to the local computer. It includes thousands of settings. Within the local Group Policy is a single node called Security Settings. If you only want to manipulate the Security Settings node, you can access it by launching the Local Security Policy console, as shown later in this section.

For example, Figure 3.1 shows the Default Domain Policy for a domain named `security.mta` expanded to show the Password Policy section. Table 3.2 explains each of these elements.

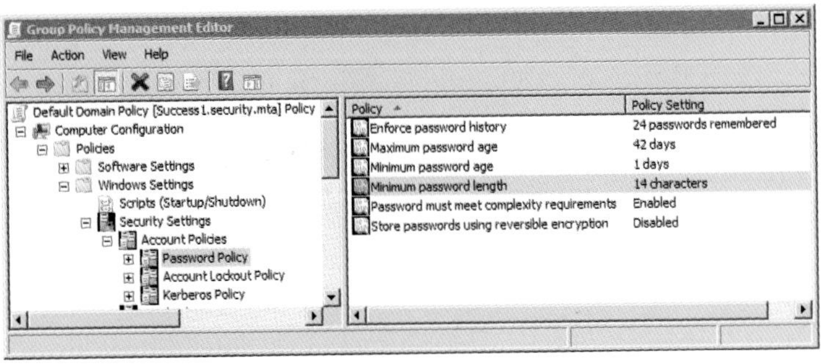

> **Group Policy is a built-in toolset that allows you to configure settings once and then apply the settings across accounts within the scope of the Group Policy.**

FIGURE 3.1 Domain Password Policy

It's worth noting that all the settings in the Account Policies node apply only when set at the domain level in a domain. If you try to configure any of these settings with a Group Policy linked to an organizational unit, they aren't applied. However, you can set all these settings at the local computer using the local Group Policy or Local Security Policy.

TABLE 3.2   Domain Password Policy Elements

Item	Description
Enforce Password History	A password history remembers passwords previously used. Users can't reuse any password in the history. Figure 3.1 shows that the Password Policy is set to remember the last 24 passwords. In other words, when users reset their passwords, they can't reuse any of the last 24 passwords they've used on the system.
Maximum Password Age	This identifies the longest period users can wait before changing their password. If a user hasn't changed their password before the time expires, they won't be able to log on until they change it. Many organizations set this to a time between 30 and 60 days.
Minimum Password Age	This identifies the minimum amount of time a user must wait before changing their password again. Figure 3.1 shows that users must wait at least one day before changing their password again.
Minimum Password Length	This indicates the minimum number of characters in the password. Most organizations have this set to 6 or 8, and Microsoft currently recommends setting it to at least 14.
Password Must Meet Complexity Requirements	When enabled, this requires users to use passwords of at least six characters, using three of the four character types (uppercase, lowercase, numbers, and symbols). Additionally, the password can't contain any part of the user's account name or full name exceeding two characters. For example, Mary Smith's password couldn't contain *Mar*, *ary*, *Smi*, and so on. If you configure a minimum password length greater than six characters with this setting, the minimum password length setting will take precedence for the password length.
Store Passwords Using Reversible Encryption	Some non-Microsoft systems require that the password be stored using reversible encryption. Because it's possible for an attack to use reversible encryption to discover the original password, this isn't recommended.

Some of these policy elements prevent users from circumventing a written password policy. For example, some users may want to switch back and forth between two passwords. However, using the Enforce Password History setting within the Password Policy section of the Group Policy prevents this.

Additionally, some users may want to use the same password successively so they don't have to memorize a new one. They may attempt to change their password repeatedly to get to their original password. If the password history is set to 24, they have to change it 25 times before getting to the original password. Although this may take 15 to 20 minutes, a determined user may be willing to take the time to do it. A Minimum Password Age setting prevents even the most determined users from changing their password until at least one day has passed. Combined with a password history of 24, it would take a user 25 days to get back to the original password. This is enough to discourage most users from trying to circumvent the password policy.

The example showed the Password Policy for a domain, but the Password Policy looks identical for a single computer. You can view the local Group Policy for a server with the following steps:

1. Click Start, type **MMC**, and press Enter.

2. Choose File ➢ Add/Remove Snap-in.

3. Select Group Policy Object Editor, and click Add.

4. Click Finish, and then click OK.

5. Expand Local Computer Policy ➢ Windows Settings ➢ Security Settings ➢ Account Policies, and select Password Policy. Your display will look very similar to Figure 3.1. The only difference is that the top node is Local Computer Policy instead of Default Domain Policy.

You can also view the local Password Policy for a computer by using the Local Security Policy tool. Take the following steps:

1. Click Start, type **Local Security**, and select Local Security Policy.

2. Expand Security Settings ➢ Account Policies, and select Password Policy.

Exploring Account Lockout Policies

In addition to configuring a password policy, most organizations also configure an *Account Lockout Policy*. The Account Lockout Policy will lock out accounts

> A written security policy identifies security requirements such as using strong passwords. Technologies such as Group Policy may be used to enforce the written security policy.

> The Local Security Policy tool includes many of the same security settings in Group Policy for a domain. However, it only applies to the local computer.

Account Lockout Policies help prevent attackers from hacking into an account by repeatedly attempting to guess the password.

if the incorrect password is entered too many times. Users can't use a locked-out account to authenticate successfully.

For example, you can configure a lockout policy to lock out an account for 30 minutes after three incorrect passwords have been entered. If an attacker is trying to guess the password, they can only attempt a few passwords consecutively before the account is locked out.

Figure 3.2 shows the Account Lockout Policy for a local Windows Server 2008 server. Table 3.3 explains each of these elements.

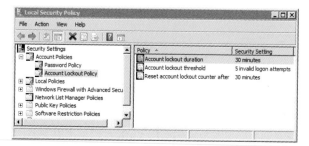

FIGURE 3.2 Account Lockout Policy

TABLE 3.3 Account Lockout Policy Elements

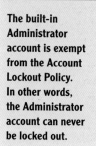

The built-in Administrator account is exempt from the Account Lockout Policy. In other words, the Administrator account can never be locked out.

Item	Description
Account Lockout Duration	The duration identifies how long an account will remain locked out. A value of 0 indicates that the account remains locked out until an administrator unlocks it. Figure 3.2 shows that the account will remain locked out for 30 minutes, after which time the user can try again.
Account Lockout Threshold	The threshold identifies how many incorrect passwords are allowed before the account is locked out. If the threshold is reached, the account will be locked out for the time identified in Account Lockout Duration.
Reset Account Lockout Counter After	The counter counts incorrect passwords, but not forever. This setting indicates how long failed password attempts are counted before the counter resets to 0. For example, Figure 3.2 shows this value set to 30 and Account Lockout Threshold set to 5. You can enter 4 incorrect passwords, wait 30 minutes for the counter to reset to 0, and then enter 4 incorrect passwords again without locking out the account.

Locked-out accounts can be unlocked by administrators or other administrative personnel with the appropriate permissions. The following section shows how to unlock an account.

Unlocking an Account

When an account is locked out, the user sees something like the following message: "The referenced account is currently locked out and may not be logged onto." The user can wait until the Account Lockout Duration time passes, as long as it isn't set to 0. Alternatively, they may ask an administrator to unlock the account.

You can use the following steps to unlock a local account on a Windows machine:

1. Start Computer Management by clicking Start, typing **Computer**, and selecting Computer Management.

2. Expand System Tools ➤ Local Users And Groups, and select Users.

3. Identify the locked user account. Right-click the user account, and select Properties. Your display will look similar to Figure 3.3.

◀ If Account Lockout Duration is set to 0, the account is locked out until it's unlocked by an administrator.

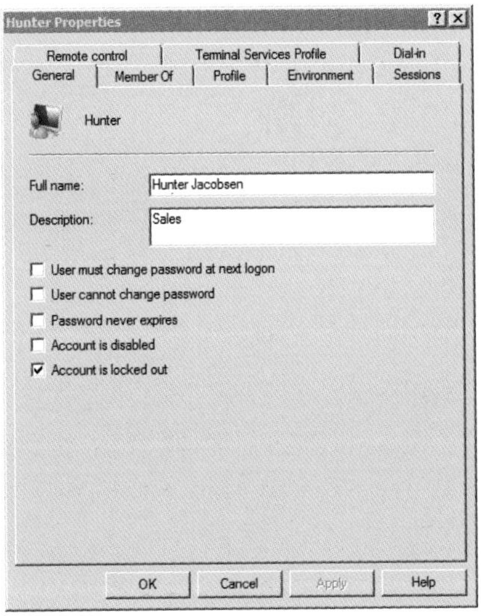

FIGURE 3.3 Viewing the properties for a local user account

◀ The only way an account can be locked out is by entering too many incorrect passwords. An administrator can disable an account from the screen displayed in Figure 3.3 but can't manually lock it out.

4. Deselect the Account Is Locked Out check box. Click OK.

At this point, the account is unlocked, and the user will be able to log on (as long as the user knows the correct password).

If the locked-out account is a domain account, you need to reset the account using the Active Directory Users and Computers (ADUC) tool. The following steps show this procedure:

ADUC is installed by default on servers that have been promoted to domain controllers.

1. Start Active Directory Users And Computers by choosing Start ➢ Administrative Tools ➢ Active Directory Users And Computers.

2. Expand the domain, and select the organizational unit that holds the user account.

3. Right-click the user account, and select Properties.

4. Select the Account tab. Select Unlock Account check box. You'll see a display similar to Figure 3.4.

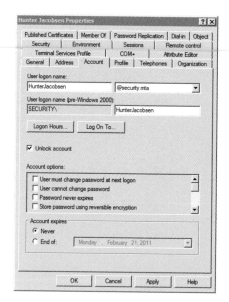

FIGURE 3.4 Unlocking a domain account

5. Click OK.

At this point, the account is unlocked, and the user will be able to log on (as long as they know their password). Of course, there may be times when the user can't remember their password. If that's the case, they may need their password administratively reset. The following section shows how to reset a password.

Resetting a Password

Occasionally, users may forget their password. If this happens, an IT worker such as a help-desk professional may need to reset the password. You can do this in two ways, both detailed here: within a domain using ADUC with the first set of steps, and on a local server using the second set of steps.

You'll need to have administrative permissions to reset passwords. Regular user accounts won't have these permissions.

Here are the steps to use within a domain:

1. Start Active Directory Users And Computers by choosing Start ≻ Administrative Tools ≻ Active Directory Users And Computers.

2. Expand the domain, and select the organizational unit that holds the user account.

3. Right-click the user account, and locate Reset Password. You'll see a display similar to Figure 3.5.

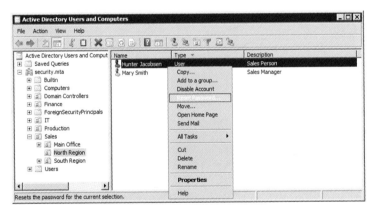

FIGURE 3.5 Resetting a password

4. Select Reset Password. Enter the new password in the New Password text box, and press the Tab key.

5. Enter the new password in the Confirm Password text box.

6. Ensure that the User Must Change Password At Next Logon check box is selected, as shown in Figure 3.6.

7. If the account is locked out, you can also select the Unlock The User's Account check box. Click OK. As long as the passwords match and meet the complexity requirements, you'll see a confirmation that the password has been changed.

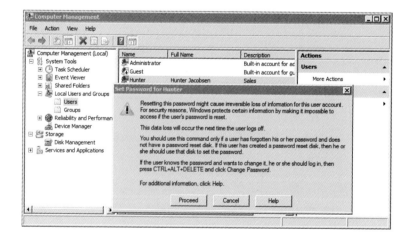

FIGURE 3.6 Modifying the password

> **Attackers are unable to change the password of a local account to gain access to encrypted data.**

Servers can host local accounts that only provide access to the server instead of access within a domain. You can reset local account passwords just as you can reset passwords for accounts within a domain. However, if the user has encrypted data with a local account using Encrypting File System (EFS) within New Technology File System (NTFS), they will lose access to this data. This doesn't apply when you're resetting passwords for a domain account.

The following steps show how to reset the password for a local account on a server:

1. Start Computer Management by clicking Start, typing **Computer**, and selecting Computer Management.

2. Expand System Tools ➢ Local Users And Groups, and select Users.

3. Identify the user account that needs the password reset. Right-click the user account, and select Set Password. Your display will look similar to Figure 3.7.

> **This warning occurs only when a local user account password is reset. You won't see it when resetting a domain password account.**

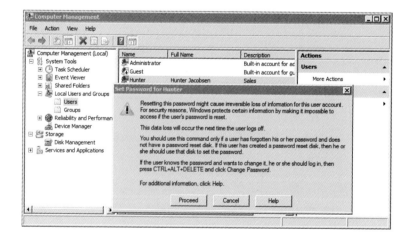

FIGURE 3.7 The warning that appears when resetting the password on a local account

4. Review the information on the page. If the user has forgotten the password and doesn't have a password reset disk, click Proceed.

5. Enter the new password in the New Password text box, and press the Tab key.

6. Enter the new password in the Confirm Password text box, and click OK. As long as the passwords match and meet the complexity requirements, you'll see a confirmation that the password has been changed. Click OK.

PASSWORD RESETS AND SOCIAL ENGINEERING

Most organizations implement procedures for password resets to prevent social-engineering attacks. The goal is to ensure that only users within the organization can request a password reset for their own account.

Consider this type of attack. Disgruntled Joe knows that the company uses the first letter and last name of individuals to create user accounts. For example, Mark Smith's account is msmith. If Disgruntled Joe knows the name of an employee (who is currently on a short business trip), he also knows their username. Next, he calls the help desk, claiming to be the employee, and requests a password reset for the account.

If there aren't procedures in place to validate the identity of the caller, Disgruntled Joe can successfully get a new password for the user's account, allowing him to log on and impersonate the user. He can then access any resources the vacationing employee can access, and, depending on how disgruntled he is, he can cause quite a bit of damage. If he's able to impersonate a manager, he can access any of the manager's files and even their email.

Organizations often require the individual to provide some proof of their identity prior to changing a password to prevent this type of attack.

Changing a Password

When a password policy is set for a system, users are reminded to change their password before the maximum password age passes. Users can use the following steps to voluntarily change their passwords:

1. Press Ctrl+Alt+Delete (all three keys simultaneously).

2. Click Change A Password. You'll see a display similar to Figure 3.8.

◄

These steps work on Windows Server 2008, Windows Server 2008 R2, and Windows 7 systems.

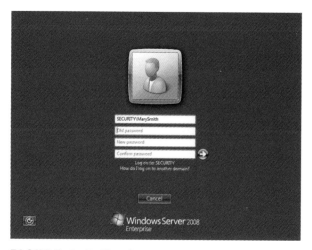

FIGURE 3.8 Changing a password

3. Enter the old password in the Old Password text box, and press the Tab key.

4. Enter the new password in the New Password text box, and press the Tab key.

5. Enter the new password again in the Confirm Password text box, and press Enter.

As long as the old password is correct, the new and confirm passwords are entered identically, and the new password adheres to the requirements enforced by the password policy, the password will be changed.

Creating a Password-Reset Disk

A *password-reset disk* allows you to reset a password even if you've forgotten the original password. However, you must create the password-reset disk before you've forgotten the password. The password-reset disk information can be stored on a USB flash drive or a floppy disk, depending on what is available.

You can use the following steps to create a password-reset disk for a local account:

1. Insert a USB flash drive into the system. This flash drive will be the password-reset disk.

2. Press Ctrl+Alt+Delete (all three keys simultaneously).

3. Click Change A Password.

4. Click the Create A Password Reset Disk link.

5. Review the information on the Welcome To The Forgotten Password Wizard screen, and click Next.

6. On the Create A Password Reset Disk page, select the USB drive from the drop-down list. This display will only show removable disks. Click Next.

7. Enter the current password of the logged-in user, and click Next.

8. A file is written to this disk. When the progress bar shows 100% complete, click Next. Click Finish. This disk can now be used as a password-reset disk if the user forgets the password.

Using Smart Cards and Token Devices for Authentication

Up to this point, we have been focusing on passwords, which are considered part of the first authentication method: *something you know*. The second factor of authentication is *something you have*. For this method, the user must have something in their possession to successfully authenticate. Two common examples are smart cards and token devices.

A *smart card* is a credit-card sized card that has a certificate embedded in it. It also has electrical contacts that allow data from the card to be read when the card is inserted into a smart-card reader. Figure 3.9 shows a smart card and a smart-card reader.

It's common for smart cards to also include information about the user, such as a picture and their name.

Smart Card

Smart Card Reader

FIGURE 3.9 Smart card and smart-card reader

The smart-card reader can be a separate hardware device, or you may purchase system components, such as keyboards, that have smart-card readers built into them.

An organization needs to have a PKI in place to effectively utilize smart cards. The PKI system includes certificate authorities that can issue and manage certificates. Each smart card has at least one certificate embedded in it and may be used by the user to log on or to access resources while they're logged on.

A smart card is rarely used by itself. Instead, after the user inserts the card into the reader, a prompt appears, requiring them to enter additional information such as PIN or a username and password.

Token devices are similar in that they require the user to have something, but they work a little differently. A token is also called a *key fob* and can be hooked onto a key chain so that it can easily be carried. Consider Figure 3.10. It shows a token-based authentication server on the left and a token held by the user. The number displayed in the screen on the token changes regularly, such as every 60 seconds. The server and the token are synchronized with each other so that whenever the number in the token changes, the server knows the new number.

> When a user is required to have something (the smart card) and know something (a PIN), the authentication is using multifactor authentication.

FIGURE 3.10 Token used for authentication

When users want to log on, they enter the number shown in their token and additional information such as their username and password, or a PIN. As long as all the information is accurate (and entered before the number in the token changes), users are able to authenticate.

> The token provides multifactor authentication because it proves that users have something (the token) and know something (their username and password, or PIN).

Using Biometrics for Authentication

Biometrics (*something you are*) is a much more secure method of authentication compared to the *something you know* and *something you have* methods mentioned previously. Biometrics measures specific physical information about a user. For example, everyone has unique fingerprints. Because they're unique, fingerprints can be used to accurately validate a user's identity.

Biometric authentication is configured by capturing a sample of the biometric information ahead of time. This data is stored in an authentication database, and when the user tries to authenticate, the database information is compared to the authentication attempt. If the data matches, the user is successfully authenticated.

Biometric methods used for authentication include the following:

Fingerprints and Handprints Many laptops include fingerprint readers that can be used to authenticate. Some USB flash drives have built-in fingerprint readers that only allow individuals with a registered fingerprint to access data on the drive. Some facilities use full handprints to authenticate individuals.

Retinas and Irises Retina scans are the most accurate biometric method. They map the blood vessels in the back of the eye. However, retina scans take about 10 seconds and require the user to place an eye very close to the scanner as it shines a light into the eye. An iris scan maps the details around the pupil, such as the various color bands. A user can be about 20 inches away from the iris scanner, making it much less intrusive than a retina scan.

Weight Some facility access points measure weight along with another authentication method. For example, a user may be granted access to a small foyer and then use their fingerprint to access the next room. However, the total weight in the room is tracked to prevent more than one person from entering at a time.

Although biometric authentication methods can be more accurate than other methods, they're also more expensive. In general, when an organization wants to increase authentication, it typically uses multifactor authentication by combining the use of smart cards or tokens with the use of passwords or PINs.

Starting Applications with Run As Administrator

Many organizations require administrators to use two different accounts. One account is for regular day-to-day work and doesn't have administrative rights or permissions. The second account has elevated (administrative) permissions. Administrators only use the elevated-permissions account when performing administrative work.

The majority of the time, an IT worker will be logged on as a regular user. If they need to perform administrative work, they can launch an application with administrative permissions or by using their administrative credentials. For example, users can run many commands as an administrator by right-clicking an item and selecting Run As Administrator, as shown in Figure 3.11.

◀

In previous versions of Windows (before Windows Server 2008), the Run As Administrator command was known as Run As.

Windows Server 2008 includes User Account Control (UAC). UAC uses two logical tokens: a regular user token and an elevated administrator token. Even if a user is logged on as an administrator, the operating system only grants the user access with the regular user token by default. If the user attempts to perform a task requiring elevated permissions, UAC may prompt the user to approve the request for administrative access.

FIGURE 3.11 Using Run As Administrator

If an administrator is logged on with a regular user account and attempts to perform an action requiring elevated permissions, UAC still goes into action. However, instead of requiring the user to approve the action, UAC prompts the user to provide the credentials of an account that has the required permissions.

Chapter 6 explains UAC in more depth. The logical tokens aren't the same as the hardware tokens described earlier.

THE NEED FOR DUAL ACCOUNTS

There are several reasons why organizations may require administrators to use two accounts, one for regular day-to-day work and the other for administrative work:

Access by Non-administrators If an administrator logs onto a computer as an administrator and is called away for an emergency, the administrator may forget to log out or lock the computer. A passerby can then access the computer and enjoy full administrative permissions.

(Continues)

THE NEED FOR DUAL ACCOUNTS *(Continued)*

Accidental Damage   An administrator has full control over resources as an administrator. If the administrator always logs on as an administrator, there is increased potential for accidental damage. For example, a regular user can view many configuration settings but not change them. An administrator can accidentally modify a setting with an errant mouse click.

Malware Elevation   Certain malicious software is able to use the permissions of the logged-in user. If a threat successfully infiltrates the network while a user is logged on with administrative credentials, the malware may gain the elevated permission of the administrator. However, if administrators normally log on with a regular account, there is less possibility that the malware will gain access to the elevated permissions.

Preventing Time Skew with Kerberos

Kerberos is the primary network authentication protocol used in Microsoft domains. It has been the preferred authentication protocol for Active Directory domains since Windows 2000.

After a user has authenticated to the domain with Kerberos, Kerberos is also used behind the scenes to ensure that only authenticated entities can access resources. Kerberos uses a system where users and computers are issued tickets to access resources. A Key Distribution Center (KDC) manages these tickets.

An important requirement with Kerberos is that every system within a domain must be using the same time. If any system is more than five minutes off from the domain controllers in the environment, the result is a time-skew error. Systems that have the incorrect time are refused access to network resources, and users may fail to authenticate.

All computers within a domain are synchronized to prevent time-skew errors. The following elements provide the time synchronization:

▶ A single domain controller within a domain holds the operations master role of primary domain controller (PDC) emulator. This computer should be configured to regularly synchronize with an external time source.

Kerberos uses port 88. Routers within a network infrastructure that is using Kerberos for domain-based user authentication must allow traffic to pass through on port 88.

◀

◀

The Kerberos five-minute time requirement prevents attackers from intercepting data, modifying it, and replaying it to impersonate a user at a later time. It isn't feasible to accomplish this within five minutes.

> ► Each domain controller within a domain receives its time from the PDC emulator.

> ► Each computer within a domain receives its time from one of the domain controllers.

Problems may occur if users are able to change the time on their system. Because the ability to change the time requires elevated permissions on Windows Server 2008 and Windows 7 systems, this is less likely to occur today.

If a domain computer's time is off, rebooting it will often resolve the problem. When the computer reboots, it updates its time from a domain controller.

Identifying RADIUS Capabilities

Remote Authentication Dial-in User Service (RADIUS) is an authentication service used to authenticate a wide range of clients. Although it was originally designed to authenticate clients that dialed in using modems, its usage has expanded.

If an organization provides access to the network for remote users with a virtual private network (VPN), RADIUS can provide authentication for these clients. RADIUS is useful as a central authentication point. For example, if an organization includes 10 VPN servers, it can use a single RADIUS server to provide authentication services for clients accessing any of the 10 VPN servers.

Chapter 7 presents some concepts related to VPNs. The *Microsoft Windows Networking Essentials* book in this series presents more in-depth information on VPNs.

Similarly, if an organization is supporting wireless clients, a RADIUS server can provide authentication services before clients are granted access. For example, WPA2 Enterprise includes a RADIUS server configured to provide 802.1x support. Requiring authentication with WPA2 Enterprise for wireless clients provides much more security than just using WPA2 Personal.

RADIUS servers support several different protocols. Figure 3.12 shows protocol configuration screens for a RADIUS server, and the following text explains:

Chapter 8 covers wireless security issues including the use of WPA/WPA2 Enterprise and WPA/WPA2 Personal. WPA/WPA2 Personal doesn't use an 802.1x server.

Extensible Authentication Protocol (EAP)   EAP provides additional methods of authentication by extending the basic capabilities of the operating system. The two built-in EAP methods are Protected EAP (PEAP) and Smart Card Or Other Certificate (see the following list items).

Protected EAP (PEAP)   PEAP uses Transport Layer Security (TLS) to create an encrypted channel between devices for the authentication process. PEAP can be used for 802.11 wireless clients.

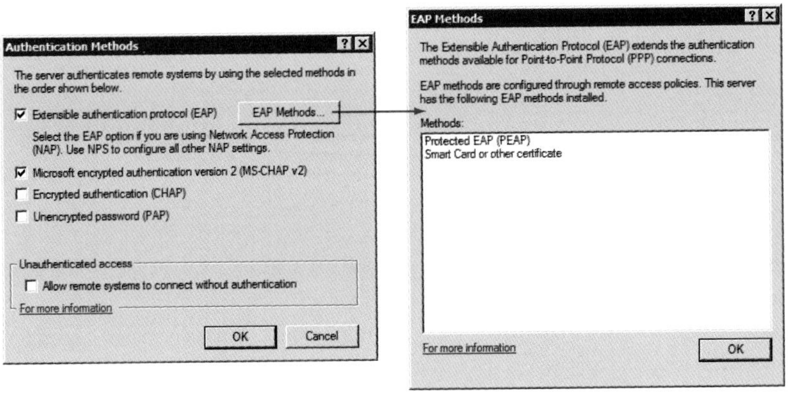

FIGURE 3.12 RADIUS authentication protocols

Smart Card Or Other Certificate Smart cards provide the strongest authentication. Smart cards have certificates embedded in them provided by a trusted certification authority, and they use EAP with TLS (EAP-TLS).

Chapter 11 covers certificates and certification authorities in more depth.

Microsoft Challenge Handshake Authentication Protocol v2 (MS-CHAP v2) Microsoft improved CHAP with MS-CHAP and then improved it again with MS-CHAPv2. For example, it provides mutual authentication between the client and the authentication server. This only works with Microsoft clients.

Challenge Handshake Authentication Protocol (CHAP) This provides compatibility with non-Microsoft clients.

Password Authentication Protocol (PAP) Passwords are sent in clear text. This isn't recommended, because a network sniffer can capture them.

Identifying Unsecure Authentication Protocols

Some older authentication protocols are considered unsecure, and you should avoid using them. The first step in ensuring that these protocols aren't used is identifying them. The following sections identify issues with LAN Manager (LM) and New Technology LAN Manager version 1 (NTLMv1)authentication protocols. NTLMv2 is preferred over both LM or NTLMv1.

LM

LAN Manager (LM) is a very old authentication protocol that is still used by some applications today. The biggest weakness with LM is in how it stores passwords. LM-stored passwords are easily discoverable by hacking tools.

LM first converts the password to all uppercase and then adds null values to extend the password to 14 characters. For example, if a password were eight characters, LM would add six null values. LM then splits the password into two seven-character pieces. Last, it uses weak cryptographic methods to protect these two seven-character pieces and stores the result as an LM hash. Because the result is actually two seven-character pieces, password-cracking tools don't need to crack the entire password. Instead, they just crack each seven-character piece individually. Due to the weak cryptography used, cracking an LM password is very easy.

Support for LM is included in Windows Server 2008 and Windows Server 2008 R2, but it's disabled by default.

> ▶
> Passwords longer than 14 characters can't be stored as an LM hash. Some password policies require 15-character passwords to prevent this vulnerability.

NTLM (NTLMv1)

The New Technology LAN Manager (NTLM or NTLMv1) security protocols were introduced before Windows 2000 for authentication. Although NTLM improved security issues with LM, Microsoft doesn't recommend its use in any applications.

For example, NTLM doesn't provide mutual authentication. In other words, clients are required to authenticate to a server, but clients don't receive verification of the server's identity. Additionally, NTLM doesn't support many of the current cryptographic methods such as Advanced Encryption Standard (AES) for encryption.

Some password crackers (such as Ophcrack) can discover passwords protected with NTLM. NTLM stores the password as an NTLM hash. Even though the NTLM hash is more complex than an LM hash, it can still be cracked.

Additional flaws have been discovered in NTLM, and Microsoft has released updates to fix these. For example, Microsoft Security Bulletin MS10-012 (**www.microsoft.com/technet/security/bulletin/ms10-012.mspx**) documents some discovered flaws with NTLM and outlines the required updates to resolve them.

NTLMv2 is an upgrade to NTLMv1. It provides mutual authentication and is enabled by default in Windows Server 2008 systems. If your organization doesn't have older clients using NTLMv1, it's recommended that you disable NTLMv1.

> ▶
> Chapter 10 covers AES and other encryption methods.

> ▶
> NTLM is enabled by default in Windows Server 2008 and Windows Vista for backward compatibility with legacy clients.

> ▶
> NTLM v2 is more secure than NTLMv1 and is recommended for use in place of NTLMv1.

THE ESSENTIALS AND BEYOND

In this chapter, you learned about the three factors of authentication: something you know (such as passwords), something you have (such as smart cards), and something you are (validated through biometrics). You can use any factor individually or combine two or more for multifactor authentication. Password best practices can be enforced with a password policy, and you can discourage people from guessing passwords with an Account Lockout Policy. Most organizations require administrators to use two accounts and use the Run As Administrator capability to launch applications with administrative permissions when needed. Kerberos is the primary network authentication protocol used in Microsoft domains, and it requires that all computers' clock settings be configured within five minutes of each other. RADIUS can be used for VPNs and to authenticate both wired and wireless clients when configured as an 802.1x server. LM isn't secure and shouldn't be enabled. NTLMv2 is stronger than NTLM; when possible, NTLM should be disabled.

ADDITIONAL EXERCISES

▶ Identify the strength of the following passwords:

  ▶ *password*

  ▶ *Password*

  ▶ *Password1*

  ▶ *Pa$$w0rd1*

  ▶ *Pa$$w0rdPa$$w0rd*

▶ Check your answers here:

  www.microsoft.com/protect/fraud/passwords/checker.aspx

▶ Create a strong password of at least 14 characters that you can remember.

▶ Create a password-reset disk.

▶ Attempt to start an application using the Run As Administrator command.

To compare your answers to the author's, please visit **www.sybex.com/go/ securityessentials**.

REVIEW QUESTIONS

1. What is the difference between identification and authentication?

    A. Nothing. They're the same.

    B. Identification proves an identity.

    C. Authentication proves an identity.

    D. Identification authenticates an individual, and authentication provides authorization.

(Continues)

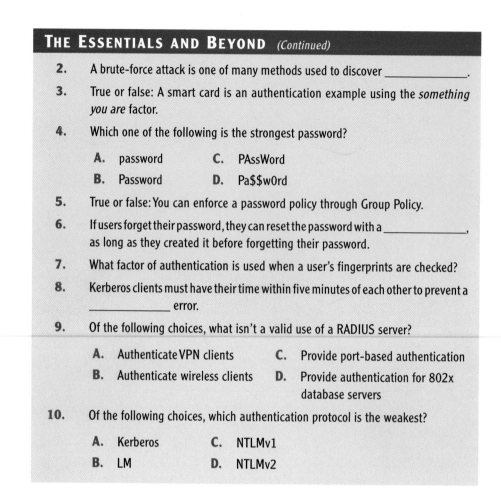

THE ESSENTIALS AND BEYOND *(Continued)*

2. A brute-force attack is one of many methods used to discover _____.

3. True or false: A smart card is an authentication example using the *something you are* factor.

4. Which one of the following is the strongest password?

    A. password   **C.** PAssWord

    B. Password   **D.** Pa$$w0rd

5. True or false: You can enforce a password policy through Group Policy.

6. If users forget their password, they can reset the password with a _____, as long as they created it before forgetting their password.

7. What factor of authentication is used when a user's fingerprints are checked?

8. Kerberos clients must have their time within five minutes of each other to prevent a _____ error.

9. Of the following choices, what isn't a valid use of a RADIUS server?

    A. Authenticate VPN clients   **C.** Provide port-based authentication

    B. Authenticate wireless clients   **D.** Provide authentication for 802x database servers

10. Of the following choices, which authentication protocol is the weakest?

    A. Kerberos   **C.** NTLMv1

    B. LM   **D.** NTLMv2

CHAPTER 4

Securing Access with Permissions

Permissions are the primary method of restricting access to resources in a Microsoft domain. You can assign permissions to New Technology File System (NTFS) drives, shares, Active Directory objects, and the Registry.

Many of the permission concepts are the same with the different resources. For example, each can be configured as Allow or Deny, and if the Deny permission is assigned, Deny always takes precedence. Similarly, all permissions can be assigned to a parent and be inherited by all of the children. For NTFS folders and shares, a child is a file or subfolder, but Active Directory and the Registry also contain child objects. This chapter includes these concepts in the following topics:

▶ **Comparing NTFS permissions**

▶ **Exploring share permissions**

▶ **Identifying Active Directory permissions**

▶ **Assigning Registry permissions**

Comparing NTFS Permissions

Almost all drives used in a Microsoft environment use the New Technology File System (NTFS). NTFS manages the files on the drives, helps maintain file integrity, and provides security.

One of the most important benefits of NTFS is security. You're able to restrict access to any file on an NTFS drive with the use of permissions. The topics in this section identify the different types of permissions and how they interact.

Identifying Basic NTFS Permissions

Only NTFS drives have a Security tab. Simple File Allocation Table (FAT) drives don't have a Security tab.

Figure 4.1 shows the properties page of an NTFS folder named `Study Notes`. Notice that the third tab is labeled Security. This is where you can view the NTFS permissions on any folder or file that has been created on an NTFS volume.

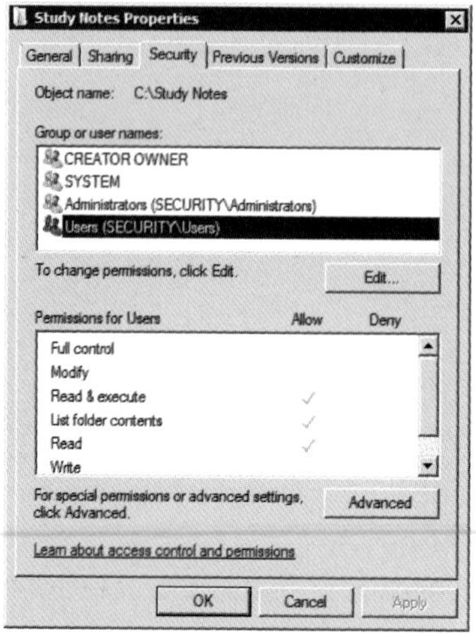

FIGURE 4.1 Viewing NTFS permissions on a folder

In the figure, you can see that the Users group is selected in the top display, and the permissions granted for the Users group are displayed at the bottom. A check box indicates that a specific permission is assigned. If you select a different group or user in the top box, the bottom box shows the permissions assigned.

The Users group is granted Allow permissions for Read & Execute, List Folder Contents, and Read. Any permission can be assigned as either Allow or Deny. Just as you'd think, Allow means a user is granted or allowed the permission, and Deny means the user is denied the permission.

If a user is granted both Allow and Deny permission for any resource, Deny always takes precedence.

Table 4.1 describes these basic NTFS permissions.

TABLE 4.1 Basic NTFS Permissions

Permission	Description
Read	A user can read the contents of a file or folder.
Read & Execute	A user can read the contents of a file or folder, and if it's a program, the user can start (execute) it.

(Continues)

TABLE 4.1 *(Continued)*

Permission	Description
List Folder Contents	This only applies to folders and grants the user permission to list items in the folder and child folders.
Write	This grants the user permission to make changes to the file and save those changes. When granted to a folder, it gives a user permission to add files to a folder. A user can't delete files with the Write permission.
Modify	Users are granted all the Read permissions (Read & Execute and List Folder Contents) and Write permission. Additionally, they can delete files and folders with this permission.
Full Control	This includes all permissions, including the advanced permissions shown in the following section.

The primary difference between Write and Modify is that Modify allows a user to delete files and folders, but Write doesn't. Modify also includes Read.

Several of these basic permissions include other permissions, as shown in Figure 4.2. For example, if a user has Full Control over a file or a folder, they have all the permissions. Similarly, Modify includes the ability to write and delete but also includes Read & Execute, and Read.

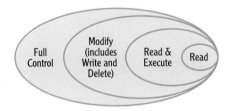

FIGURE 4.2 Relationships between permissions

You may remember the principle of least privilege from Chapter 1, "Understanding Core Security Principles." You should only grant the permissions needed for a user to do their work, and no more. For example, if a user needs to delete files, they'll need Modify permission, but they won't need Full Control permission.

Identifying Advanced NTFS Permissions

Although the basic NTFS permissions are all you'll normally have to manipulate, there are 13 advanced NTFS Permissions you can assign. Many of these permissions are automatically assigned when you assign one of the basic NTFS permissions.

Figure 4.3 shows the advanced permissions assigned to a user (Hunter Jacobsen in the `security.mta` domain) for the Study Notes folder. You can't see all 13 permissions, but you can see most of them in this figure. Hunter was granted Allow for the basic Read permission, which automatically granted him Allow for the four advanced permissions shown in the figure: List Folder / Read Data, Read Attributes, Read Extended Attributes, and Read Permissions.

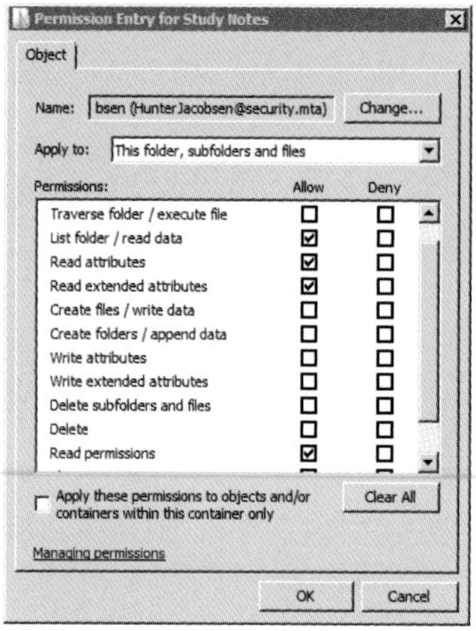

FIGURE 4.3 Viewing advanced NTFS permissions on a folder

You can access the advanced permissions for a folder with the following steps:

1. Launch Windows Explorer by clicking Start ➤ Computer.

2. Right-click over a folder, and select Properties.

3. Select the Security tab.

4. Click the Advanced button.

5. Click Change Permissions.

6. Select a user or group, and click Edit.

The following list explains the 13 advanced permissions. Notice that some of the permission names include a forward slash. The permissions that have different meanings depending on whether the permission is assigned to a folder or a file are explained specifically when they occur:

Full Control   This includes all 13 permissions, including Change Permissions and Take Ownership. Change Permissions and Take Ownership aren't grouped with any other basic permission other than Full Control, but they can be assigned separately.

Traverse Folder / Execute File   For a folder: This allows a user to access child folders even if the user doesn't have access to a parent folder.

For a file: A user can run any executable file.

List Folder / Read Data   For a folder: The user can read the file and folder names within the folder.

For a file: The user can open and read the contents of the file.

Read Attributes   Attributes of files and folders include Read-Only, Hidden, System, and Archive. You can view the values of the Read-Only and Hidden attributes (if you have permission) from the General tab of a file or folder properties page, as shown in Figure 4.4. You can use the attrib command from the command prompt to view all the attributes, as shown on the right in Figure 4.4.

The output of the attrib **command includes the** A, S, H, **and** R **flags, for Archive, System, Hidden, and Read-Only.**

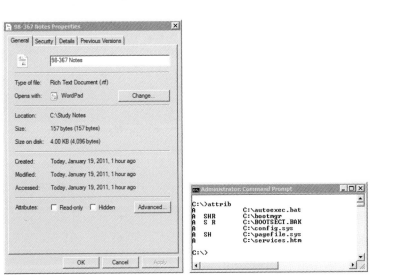

FIGURE 4.4 Viewing basic file and folder attributes

Read Extended Attributes   Many applications support extended attributes. If a file has extended attributes, it includes a Details tab (as you can see in Figure 4.4, next to the Security tab). For example, Microsoft Word includes information such as the author; who last saved the file; when it was last printed; and how many characters, words, and pages the document contains. If the user has this permission, the user can read the extended attributes.

Create Files / Write Data   For a folder: This permission allows a user to create files in a folder, but not delete them.

For a file: This allows a user to modify the contents of a file but not delete the entire file. Note that a user can delete the contents of a file and save an empty file, but a user can't delete the file itself.

Create Folders / Append Data   For a folder: A user can create folders within the folder.

For a file: A user can add data to the end of a file but can't modify any other data in the file.

Write Attributes   A user can change the basic attributes of the file, such as making it a hidden or read-only file.

Write Extended Attributes   A user can change extended attributes of a file.

Delete Subfolders and Files   A user can delete subfolders and files within a folder with this permission. This permission is required to delete folders that contain any files.

Delete   This allows a user to delete a file or an empty folder.

Read Permissions   A user can read the permissions that are assigned to a file or folder with this permission.

Take Ownership   This permission is useful if an employee had exclusive access to the file but left the company. The Administrator account and anyone in the Administrators group has permission to take ownership of a file or folder, even if they don't have read or write permissions. An owner of a file or folder can assign permissions to anyone else.

Table 4.2 shows the 13 advanced permissions that are assigned when any of the basic NTFS permissions are assigned.

The Delete permission doesn't allow a user to delete a folder that has files in it, unless the user also has the Delete Subfolders and Files permission.

▶

Administrators can take ownership of any files or folders. As the owner, they can then modify the permissions.

▶

TABLE 4.2 Advanced NTFS Permissions

Basic Permission	Includes the Following Advanced Permissions
Read	List Folder / Read Data, Read Attributes, Read Extended Attributes, and Read Permissions.
	When assigned to a folder, it includes the List Folder permission.
Read & Execute	List Folder / Read Data, Read Attributes, Read Extended Attributes, Read Permissions, and Traverse Folder / Execute File.
List Folder Contents	List Folder / Read Data, Read Attributes, Read Extended Attributes, and Traverse Folder / Execute File.
	List Folder Contents is available only for folders, not files.
Write	Create Files / Write Data, Create Folders / Append Data, Write Attributes, and Write Extended Attributes.
Modify	List Folder / Read Data, Read Attributes, Read Extended Attributes, Read Permissions, Traverse Folder / Execute File, Create Files / Write Data, Create Folders / Append Data, Write Attributes, Write Extended Attributes, and Delete.
Full Control	This includes all 13 advanced permissions.

Although it's useful to understand that 13 advanced permissions are available, you'll rarely have to manipulate them. Because the basic NTFS permissions automatically assign the relevant advanced permissions, you'll usually only need to manipulate the basic NTFS permissions.

Combining Permissions

You can assign permissions to users or to groups for any file or folder. Most organizations manage permissions by using groups because doing so makes administration much easier.

For example, an organization may have three employees in the Finance department. Each employee needs to have Full Control permissions to budget data, Read permissions to salary data, and Modify permissions to employee data. You can assign these permissions individually, but it's much easier if you place the users in a group and assign permissions to the group instead, as shown in Figure 4.5.

◄

Most organizations use groups to simplify management.

Users can belong to multiple groups. Additionally, it's possible for a user to be a member of different groups that are assigned different permissions. If so, the user is granted the cumulative total of all the permissions.

For example, imagine that a user is a member of the Finance group and the FinanceManagers group. If the Finance group has Read permission to a folder and the FinanceManagers group has Write permission to the same folder, the user is granted both Read and Write permissions to the folder.

When multiple permissions are assigned, users are granted a combination of all the assigned permissions.

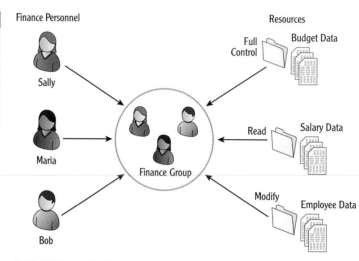

FIGURE 4.5 Using groups to assign permissions

Deny always takes precedence. However, it's recommended that Deny be used sparingly.

One big exception (mentioned earlier) is that if any permission is set to Deny, the user is denied access. In other words, if a user is allowed Read access to a file as a member of one group but is denied Read access as a member of another group, Deny takes precedence. The user is unable to read data in the file.

Permissions can be denied either explicitly or implicitly. When the Deny check box is selected, the permission is explicitly denied. However, if a permission isn't granted, the result is the same, and access is denied.

For example, imagine that the Administrators group (and no one else) is granted Read permission for a file. Anyone who isn't in the Administrators group doesn't have permission to read the file. Access for non-administrators is implicitly denied. When permissions are implicitly denied, it's not necessary to explicitly deny them.

Enabling and Disabling Permission Inheritance

Permissions can be inherited from folders to files and by subfolders within a folder. Inheritance is enabled by default for NTFS drives, but you can disable it. First, it's important to understand how inheritance works.

Consider Figure 4.6. It shows the E: drive with four folders. Budget and Projects are both in the root of the E: drive, and the Audit and Passwords folders (for projects to implement an audit policy and a password policy) are within the Projects folder:

▶ The Finance group is assigned Full Control to the Budget folder.

▶ The IT group is assigned Full Control to the Projects folder.

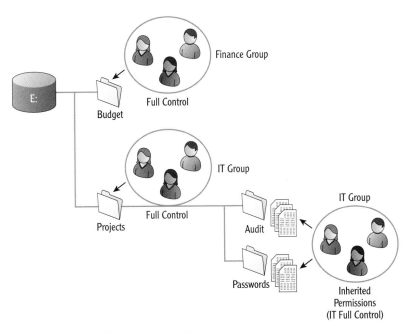

FIGURE 4.6 Inherited permissions

Figure 4.7 shows the same folders in Windows Explorer with the security properties of the Audit folder showing. Notice that the permissions checkmarks assigned to the IT group are all dimmed. Permissions display with dimmed checkmarks when the permissions are inherited. Inherited permissions can't be changed unless inheritance is disabled.

The IT group has Full Control permissions on the Projects folder, so the group inherits Full Control permissions on the Audit and Passwords folders.

Note that inherited permissions apply only to child files and folders, not peers. Both the Budget and Projects folder are at the root of the E: drive, so permissions aren't inherited from one folder to the other. In other words, the Finance group doesn't inherit any permissions to the Projects folder, and the IT group doesn't inherit any permissions to the Budget Folder. These folders don't share a parent/child relationship with each other.

Dimmed settings can be viewed, but they can't be modified unless inheritance is disabled.

Permissions assigned at the drive level are inherited by all root folders on the drive.

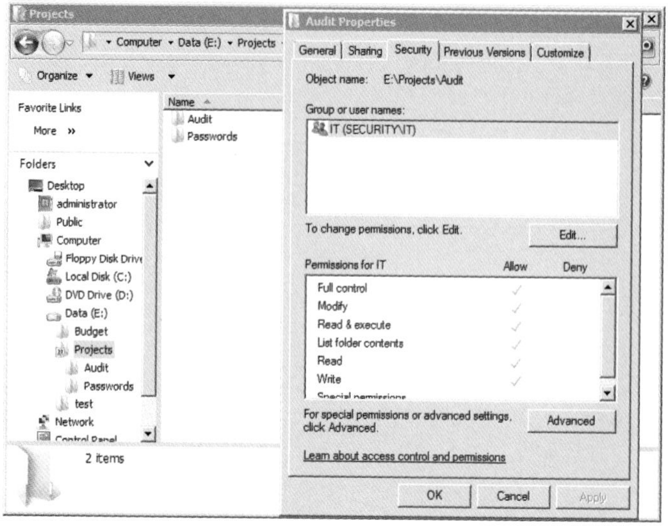

FIGURE 4.7 Windows Explorer showing child folders

Inheritance reduces the administrative workload. After you assign permissions to a folder, you don't need to adjust them every time a file or folder is added. Permissions from the parent are automatically inherited by the child. However, there may be times when you want to disable inheritance. For example, if you want to modify the inherited permissions, you must first disable inheritance. When you attempt to disable inheritance, you're given three choices:

Copy   All inherited permissions are copied and directly applied to the object. However, because they're now directly applied, they're no longer dimmed and can be modified.

Remove   All inherited permissions are removed. This only affects inherited permissions. In other words, if permissions are assigned directly to a folder or file for a user or group, those permissions aren't removed.

Cancel   This cancels the disable-inheritance request and doesn't make any changes.

You can use the following steps to disable inheritance on a Windows Server 2008 system:

1. Launch Windows Explorer by clicking Start ➢ Computer.

2. Browse to the folder where you want to modify inheritance.

3. Right-click the folder, and select Properties. Select the Security tab.

> **Any permission explicitly assigned to an object is retained when you remove inherited permissions.**

4. Click Advanced to access the Advanced Security Settings.

5. Click the Edit button. (On Windows 7, this is called Change Permissions.)

6. Deselect the Include Inheritable Permissions From This Object's Parent check box. A dialog box will appear, and your screen will look similar to Figure 4.8.

7. If you want to copy the permissions so that you modify them, click Copy. If you want to completely remove the inherited permissions, click Remove. If you don't want to make any changes, click Cancel.

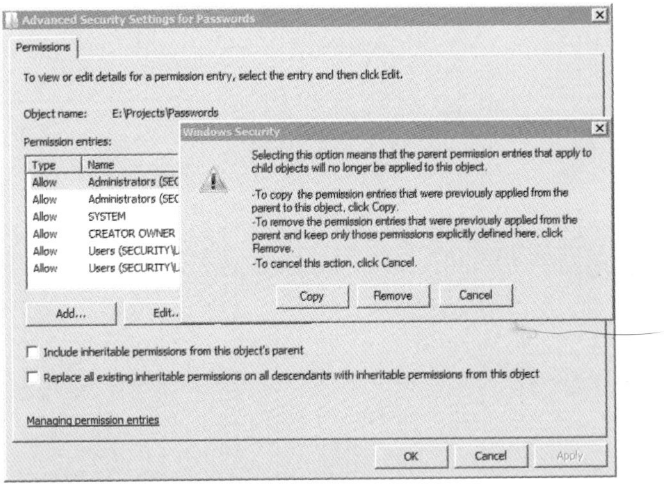

FIGURE 4.8 Removing inheritance

Moving and Copying Files

It's important to understand what happens to explicitly assigned file and folder permissions when you either move or copy a file or folder. There are two simple rules you can remember that identify what happens to the permissions:

▶ If you move a file within the same partition, the explicitly assigned permissions are retained.

▶ Any other time, the permissions are inherited from the new location and the original permissions are lost.

When you're considering these two rules, it's important to understand what a partition is. Any drive letter (such as C: or D:) that you can view in Windows Explorer is a partition.

Permissions are retained when you move a file within the same partition. Any other time you move or copy files, the original permissions are lost.

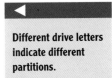

Different drive letters indicate different partitions.

A physical drive can contain one single partition (such as C:), but it can also be divided into multiple partitions (such as C: and D:). If you see that you have two drive letters (such as C: and D:), you know you have two partitions; but it may be two physical drives (with one partition on each) or one physical drive divided into two partitions. When determining what happens to the permissions, you don't need to know if you're moving or copying a file to the same or different physical drives. However, you do need to know if it's a different partition.

Consider Figure 4.9 and Table 4.3. They show the four possibilities of moving or copying files, and the resulting permissions. The first example—in which a file is moved within the same partition—is the only time when the original permissions are retained. Every other time, the original permissions are lost. Permissions are still inherited from the new location.

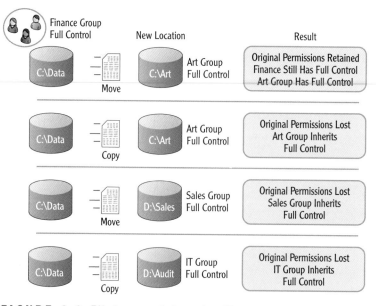

FIGURE 4.9 Effect on permissions when files are moved or copied

In the figure, you can see that the Finance group has Full Control permissions on the C:\Data folder, and no other permissions are assigned. The Art group has Full Control permissions on C:\Art, the Sales group has Full Control permissions on D:\Sales, and the IT group has Full Control permissions on D:\Audit. Files moved or copied into these folders will inherit permissions from these folders, but you should also understand what happens to the original permissions.

TABLE 4.3 Identifying Permissions When Files Are Moved or Copied

Original Permissions	Action	Permissions after Action
Finance group has Full Control.	Move on same partition (C:\Data to C:\Art)	Original permissions are retained. Finance group retains Full Control. Art group inherits Full Control.
Finance group has Full Control.	Copy on same partition (C:\Data to C:\Art	Original permissions are lost. Art group inherits Full Control.
Finance group has Full Control.	Move to different partition (C:\Data to D:\Sales)	Original permissions are lost. Sales group inherits Full Control.
Finance group has Full Control.	Copy to different partition (C:\Data to D:\Audit)	Original permissions are lost. IT group inherits Full Control.

Comparing NTFS and FAT

The FAT filesystem is used to manage files on different types of media. FAT32 is the current version; it uses 32 bits to address files on drives. FAT32 is commonly used on USB flash drives and memory cards used in smaller devices such as digital cameras. Almost any operating system (Microsoft and non-Microsoft) supports FAT32.

FAT32 drives don't support local permissions. You can't protect any files or folders by assigning NTFS permissions to them. If you copy any files or folders to a FAT32 drive from an NTFS drive, all the permissions are lost.

Another limitation with FAT32 is that it doesn't support file sizes 4 GB or larger. If you try to copy a file greater than 4 GB to a FAT32 system, it will give you an error indicating that there isn't enough space. Even if you're copying a 4 GB file to an empty 8 GB USB flash drive, you'll get this error. It's not that there isn't enough space but rather that FAT32 can't handle the large files.

It's possible to reformat FAT32 drives as NTFS drives. You can do this using Windows Explorer by right-clicking the drive and selecting Format. Careful, though—doing so will delete all data on the drive.

> **The biggest limitation of FAT is a lack of security.**

◄

◄

> **You can't copy files larger than 4 GB to a USB flash drive when using FAT32.**

Exploring Share Permissions

Within a network, it's common to share folders on a server or workstation so that users within the network can access the folders. When a folder is shared, users can access the share through mapped drives or by entering the Universal

Naming Convention (UNC) path directly in the Search Programs And Files text box on a Windows Server 2008 R2 or Windows 7 system, or the Start Search text box on a Windows Server 2008 system.

The UNC path has the format of \\servername\sharename. For example, if a share named Projects were available from a server named Success1, the UNC path would be \\Success1\Projects.

The following procedure is one way to create a share:

You can also enter the UNC in the Run box, which you can access by simultaneously pressing the Windows and R keys.

1. Launch Computer Management by clicking Start, typing **Computer** in the Start Search text box, and selecting Computer Management.

2. Expand System Tools and Shared Folders. Select Shares.

3. Right-click Shares, and select New Share.

4. Review the information on the Welcome page, and click Next.

5. Click Browse, and browse to the folder that you want to share. Select the folder, and click OK. Click Next.

6. On the Name, Description, And Settings page, either accept the name or provide a different name. Click Next.

The default permission when creating a share is Read for the Everyone group.

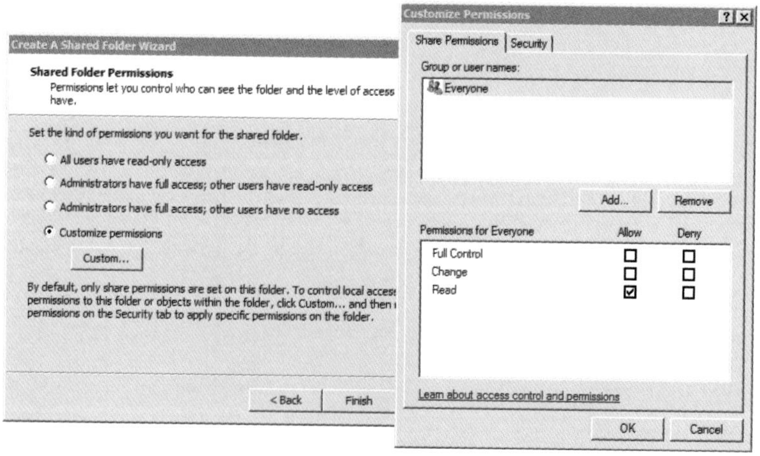

7. The Shared Folder Permissions page allows you to modify the permissions. Select Customize Permissions, and click the Custom button. Your display will look similar to Figure 4.10. You can modify these permissions or accept the default.

8. Click OK. Click Finish. Click Finish again.

FIGURE 4.10 Viewing share permissions

The steps in the next section show how you can add a share with Windows Explorer using the File Sharing Wizard.

Identifying Share Permissions

There are only three share permissions for any share. These permissions apply when a user accesses a share over the network, but they don't apply if the user is accessing the NTFS folder or file from the local filesystem.

Share permissions interact with NTFS permissions. The next section explains how this works. However, for this section, assume that users are accessing a share from a FAT volume without any NTFS permissions. Then, when you assign one of the following three share permissions, only the share permissions apply for users accessing the share over the network:

Read   Users with this permission can read any files or folders within the share.

Change   The Change permission gives users the ability to read, write, modify, and delete files and folders within the share. This is effectively the same as the Modify NTFS permission.

Full Control   Users with this Full Control permission can do anything with files and folders within the share, including change the underlying permissions.

It's also possible to assign permissions using share roles. There are some minor differences in the permission level names in Windows Server 2008 and Windows Server 2008 R2. Windows Server 2008 identifies the permission levels with role names, whereas Windows Server 2008 R2 identifies the permission levels using the permission names. Table 4.4 identifies the different names and the permissions granted.

Share permissions only apply when users access a share over the network.

◄

◄

You can't assign share permissions to files. You assign the permissions to the share, and all files and folders within the share inherit these permissions.

◄

Share permissions don't supersede NTFS permissions. Instead, share permissions inter-act with NTFS permissions.

TABLE 4.4   Share Roles

Role/Permission Level	Permissions	Windows Server 2008	Windows Server 2008 R2
Owner	Full Control	X	X
Co-owner	Full Control	X	
Contributor	Modify	X	
Reader	Read	X	
Read	Read		X
Read/Write	Modify		X

You can use the following steps to create a share using Windows Explorer on a Windows Server 2008 or Windows Server 2008 R2 system. These steps show the permission levels identified as roles:

> **On Windows Server 2008 R2, select Share With ➢ Specific People.**

1. Launch Windows Explorer by clicking Start and selecting Computer.

2. Browse to the folder you want to share.

3. Right-click over the folder, and select Share.

4. Type **Authenticated Users** in the text box, and click Add.

5. Click Reader to the right of Authenticated Users, and change the permission to Contributor. Your display will look similar to Figure 4.11.

> **The Contributor role has the Change permission, which is similar to the NTFS Modify permission.**

   Because this share is being created with the Mary Smith user account, this account is added to the Owner role and is granted Full Control permissions. Also, the HunterJacobsen account in the Security domain was granted Read NTFS permissions to the folder, so the wizard automatically added this account in the Reader role, giving it Read permissions.

> **Windows Server 2008 R2 will only show permission levels of Read or Read/Write. Read/Write is the same as the Change permission.**

6. Click Share. Note that the final display shows the UNC path to the share. Click Done.

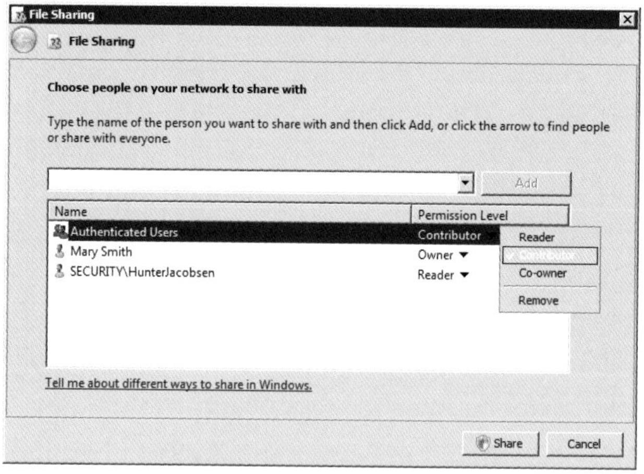

FIGURE 4.11 Creating a share from Windows Explorer

> **Share permissions are cumulative just as NTFS permissions are cumulative.**

If a user is assigned permissions from multiple groups, the user is granted the cumulative total of all the permissions assigned. In other words, if a user was granted Read as a member of the Authenticated Users, and Full Control as a member of the Administrators group, the user has Full Control, which includes Read.

Share permissions can be either explicit or implicit, just like NTFS permissions. For example, if you grant the Sales group Full Control permission to a share but don't grant any permissions to any groups or users, only members of the Sales group have access. Members of other groups aren't explicitly granted access, so they're implicitly denied access.

Combining NTFS and Share Permissions

When users access a share over the network, both the NTFS and share permissions are applied. You can determine the resulting permission with the following three steps:

1. Determine the cumulative NTFS permissions.

2. Determine the cumulative share permissions.

3. Identify which cumulative permission is more restrictive.

For example, imagine that Sally is a member of the IT group and the Finance group, and she is accessing a share named Budget. Permissions are assigned as shown in Table 4.5.

TABLE 4.5   Assigned Share and NTFS Permissions for the IT and Finance Groups

	IT Group Permissions	Finance Group Permissions
NTFS Permission	Full Control	Read
Share Permissions	Change	Read

You can use the aforementioned three steps to determine the resulting permission for Sally when she accesses the share:

1. Determine the cumulative NTFS permissions.
   Full Control, because Full Control includes Read.

2. Determine the cumulative share permissions.
   Change, because Change includes Read.

3. Identify which one is more restrictive.
   Change, because Change is more restrictive than Full Control.

Here's a tricky question. What is Sally's permission if she accesses the folder while logged onto the computer hosting the folder?

Only NTFS permissions apply if a folder is accessed locally.

Because share permissions only apply when a user accesses a share over a network, share permissions don't apply when a folder is accessed locally. The resulting permission is Full Control when accessed locally.

Here's another example (see Table 4.6). See if you can determine the resulting permission before looking at the answer.

TABLE 4.6 Assigned Share and NTFS Permissions with Deny for Sally and the IT and Finance Groups

	IT Group Permissions	Finance Group Permissions	Sally Permissions
NTFS Permission	Modify	Read	Deny Full Control
Share Permissions	Full Control	Change	None assigned

What is the resulting permission if Sally accesses this share over the network? Sally's co-worker (Joe) is also in the IT and Finance Groups. What are his permissions for this Share?

Result for Sally

1. Determine the cumulative NTFS permissions.
   Deny Full Control, because Deny takes precedence.

2. Determine the cumulative share permissions.
   Full Control, because Full Control includes Change.

3. Identify which one is more restrictive.
   Deny Full Control, because Deny Full Control is more restrictive than granting Full Control.

Result for Joe

1. Determine the cumulative NTFS permissions.
   Modify, because Modify includes Read.

2. Determine the cumulative share permissions.
   Full Control, because Full Control includes Change.

3. Identify which one is more restrictive.
   Modify, because Modify is more restrictive than Full Control.

Shares are used in most networks to allow users to share access to files and folders. Occasionally, users are unable to access files that they need through a share. If you can master these three steps to identify permissions, you should be able to identify why a user can't access the share and resolve the problem.

Identifying Active Directory Permissions

Active Directory is a database of objects. For example, it includes user objects to represent users, computer objects to represent computers, and group objects to represent groups. These objects are organized in Active Directory using organizational units (OUs) and simple containers (such as the Users and Computers containers).

As an example, an organization can create different OUs for the different departments. It can have an OU for the Sales department, the IT department, the Finance department, and so on. All user and computer objects for each department are placed in the corresponding OU.

You can modify permissions to these OUs to grant specific users or groups permission to manage the objects in an OU. For example, Help Desk personnel may need to modify objects in the Sales OU, such as resetting passwords for users. You can grant them permissions on the Sales OU to perform the relevant tasks.

Active Directory is hosted on a domain controller, a server running Active Directory Domain Services.

Viewing Active Directory Users and Computers

The primary interface for Active Directory is Active Directory Users and Computers (ADUC). You can access ADUC on a domain controller via the Administrative Tools menu. You can also run ADUC on Windows 7 systems if the Remote Server Administration Tools (RSAT) have been installed.

Figure 4.12 shows ADUC for a domain named security.mta. Some containers and OUs (such as the Users container, the Computers container, and the Domain Controllers OU) are in all domains. Organizations then create additional OUs to meet their needs.

In Figure 4.12, you can see that several additional OUs have been added to the domain: Finance, Human Resources, IT, Production, and Sales. Within the Sales OU, you can see three child OUs and one group named Sales. The use of child OUs is completely up to the discretion of the organization.

RSAT is free and can be obtained from Microsoft's download site.

Groups are represented with an icon of two users. Containers (such as Users and Computers) are plain folder icons. Icons for OUs include an extra icon within the folder.

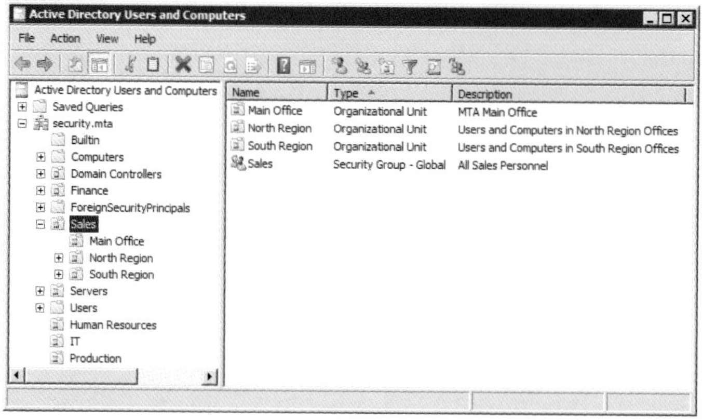

FIGURE 4.12 Active Directory Users and Computers

Comparing NTFS and Active Directory Permissions

If you understand how NTFS permissions work, you already understand a lot about how Active Directory permissions work. Specifically, the following concepts are the same:

Permissions Are Cumulative   If a user is assigned permissions as a member of multiple groups, the user has the cumulative result of all permissions.

Deny Takes Precedence   If the same permission is granted and denied to a user, Deny takes precedence. The user won't have the permission.

Permissions Are Inherited   Permissions assigned to an OU or container are inherited by all objects in the container or OU. This includes child OUs, similar to a subfolder within a folder.

Inheritance Can Be Disabled   Although inheritance is enabled by default, you can disable it. The screens and the process are almost identical in ADUC and NTFS.

As an example of inheritance in Active Directory; consider Figure 4.12 (shown earlier). If you were to grant Full Control permission for a group named SalesAdmins on the Sales OU, the group would also have Full Control permissions on the Main Office, North Region, and South Region OUs.

Viewing Active Directory Permissions

Permissions aren't viewable by default in ADUC. However, you can easily enable them. Within ADUC, select Advanced Features from the View drop-down menu.

Objects will then have a Security tab. You can view the permissions for any object in ADUC by right-clicking the object, selecting Properties, and selecting the Security tab.

Figure 4.13 shows the permissions for the Sales OU. In this figure, you can see that the SalesAdmins group has been granted Full Control permissions to the Sales OU. The SalesAdmins group would typically include individuals who provide regular support to personnel in the Sales department.

Permissions assigned to one OU aren't inherited by peer OUs. For example, even though the SalesAdmins group has Full Control permissions for the Sales OU, group members wouldn't have Full Control for the IT OU or the Human Resources OU.

Inheritance only passes from parent to child containers.

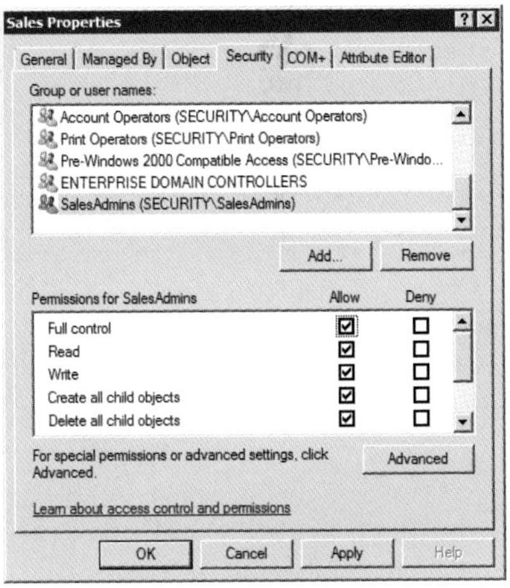

Sales Properties

General | Managed By | Object | Security | COM+ | Attribute Editor

Group or user names:

Account Operators (SECURITY\Account Operators)
Print Operators (SECURITY\Print Operators)
Pre-Windows 2000 Compatible Access (SECURITY\Pre-Windo...
ENTERPRISE DOMAIN CONTROLLERS
SalesAdmins (SECURITY\SalesAdmins)

Add...   Remove

Permissions for SalesAdmins	Allow	Deny
Full control	☑	☐
Read	☑	☐
Write	☑	☐
Create all child objects	☑	☐
Delete all child objects	☑	☐

For special permissions or advanced settings, click Advanced.   Advanced

Learn about access control and permissions

OK   Cancel   Apply   Help

FIGURE 4.13 Active Directory permissions on the Sales OU

The Active Directory permissions are as follows:

Full Control   Just as you'd think, this allows the individual to do anything with the object.

Read   Users with the Read permission can view the object, including the object's properties.

Write   Users with Write permissions can modify any of the properties of the object. This includes renaming the user account and resetting the user password.

Create All Child Objects   This allows a user to create objects within the container. For example, the user can create additional users, computers, groups, and even child OUs.

Delete All Child Objects   Users with this permission can delete any objects within the container.

Generate Resultant Set of Policy (Logging)   This allows the user to use Group Policy tools to determine exactly what Group Policy settings apply to a specific user when logged onto a specific computer. The user must have logged onto the computer at least once for this to work.

Generate Resultant Set of Policy (Planning)   This allows the user to pose "what if" scenarios and determine the resultant Group Policy settings. For example, a user can determine the settings if a user from one OU logged onto a computer in another OU.

Just as NTFS has both basic and advanced permissions, Active Directory has basic and advanced permissions. However, as discussed earlier, NTFS has only 13 advanced permissions. Active Directory has hundreds, if not thousands, of advanced permissions. Thankfully, you don't have to know them all.

Instead, you can use the Delegation of Control Wizard to assign advanced permissions for common tasks when necessary. For example, if you want to allow Help Desk personnel to reset passwords for user accounts in the Sales OU, you can use the Delegation of Control Wizard to do so. You start the wizard by right-clicking over the container where you want to assign the permissions.

Figure 4.14 shows one screen of this wizard. In this screen, the specified group is granted permission to Reset User Passwords And Force Password Change At Next Logon.

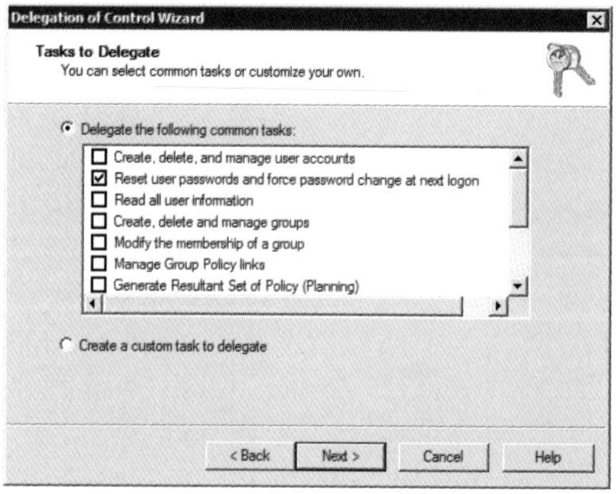

> The Force Password Change permission is related to the User Must Change Password At Next Logon check box on the Reset Password screen shown in Chapter 3 (Figure 3.6).

FIGURE 4.14 Delegating permissions with the Delegation of Control Wwizard

The Delegation of Control Wizard is very powerful as a delegation tool. It includes many built-in templates written for specific tasks to delegate (such as resetting passwords) and can also be extended by adding additional templates available from Microsoft.

Assigning Registry Permissions

The Registry is a database of settings used in Windows. It includes several different groups of settings referred to as *keys* or *hives*. Windows Server 2008 has the following keys that you can access using the Registry editor. Each of these keys has many subkeys, or subtrees:

HKEY_CURRENT_USER   Also known as HKCU, this hive stores the user profile for the user logged onto the local system. The profile includes information such as the environment variables, desktop settings, printers, and more.

HKEY_USERS   Also known as HKU, this hive includes profile information for all user-profile data for all users loaded on the system. It also includes the default profile.

HKEY_LOCAL_MACHINE   Also known as HKLM, this hive stores information about the local computer system including hardware, memory, and device drivers.

HKEY_CURRENT_CONFIG   Also known as HKCC, this hive stores information from the hardware profile used to start up the system.

HKEY_CLASSES_ROOT   Also known as HKCR, this hive includes information about applications and file associations. Data in this hive is derived from information stored in HKLM\Software\Classes and HKCU\Software Classes. If data is stored in both places, the HKCU values take precedence.

Figure 4.15 shows the Permissions page for the HKLM\System key in the Registry Editor. You can access the Permissions display by right-clicking the Registry folder and selecting Permissions. By default, the Administrators group has Full Control permission for all Registry keys.

If you want users to be able to modify certain areas of the Registry, you can add them to the Permissions page for the key and assign the Full Control permission. For example, you may want Help Desk personnel to be able to modify the Registry. If you've assigned other permissions to these users, you've probably already created a Help Desk group. You can then right-click the key (or any subkey within the key) and select Permissions. Click the Add button, add the group, and assign the group Full Control permissions.

◀

You can launch the Registry by clicking Start, typing *regedit* in the Start Search text box, and pressing Enter.

◀

Warning: You can disable your system by misconfiguring the Registry. You should modify settings only when absolutely necessary.

◀

You must assign permissions to the hives separately. It isn't possible to assign permissions to all the hives at the same time.

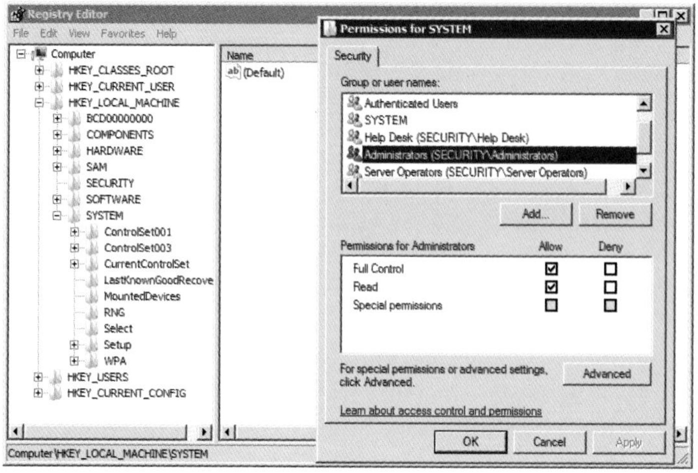

FIGURE 4.15 Viewing permissions in the Registry Editor

Registry permissions aren't inherited by default. If you want an assigned permission to be inherited by all children, you must click the Advanced button and select Replace All Existing Inheritable Permissions On All Descendants With Inheritable Permissions From This Object. Figure 4.16 shows this setting at the bottom of the display.

If you're adventurous, you can also delve into the advanced Registry permissions. However, it's much more common to just use the basic permissions Read and Full Control.

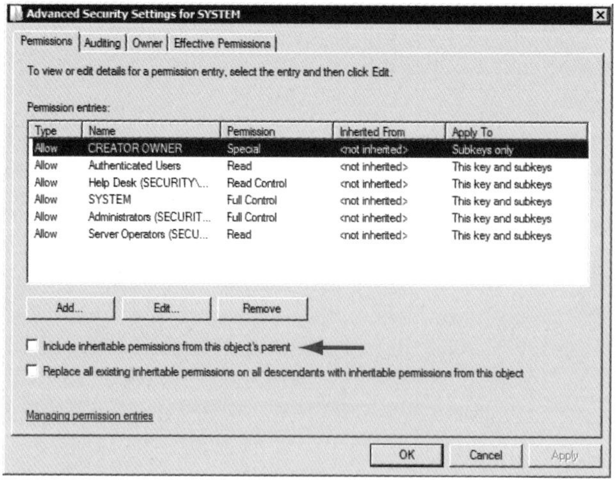

FIGURE 4.16 Enabling permission inheritance in the Registry

THE ESSENTIALS AND BEYOND

In this chapter, you learned about permissions that you can assign to NTFS drives, shares, Active Directory, and the Registry. These permissions share many common characteristics. If a user is assigned multiple permissions, the resulting permission is a combination of all permissions assigned unless a user is denied permissions. Deny always takes precedence, so if a user is granted Allow and Deny for the same permission, the result is Deny. Permissions are inherited by default (except in the Registry), but you can disable inheritance. You can enable inheritance for the Registry. When you move or copy files, the NTFS permissions stay the same if you move the files on the same partition. Any other time (such as when you are copying to the same partition, or moving or copying to a different partition), the permission is inherited from the new location. FAT drives don't support permissions at all; files moved to a FAT drive lose their permissions. Share permissions apply only when a user accesses the share over the network. When you combine share and NTFS permissions, the resulting permission is the more restrictive of the combined share or combined NTFS permissions. The Active Directory Users and Computers tool includes the Delegation of Control Wizard, which you can use to assign permissions to OUs.

ADDITIONAL EXERCISES

▶ Create a folder at the root of a drive, and determine the default permissions.

▶ Create a share. Identify the default permissions.

▶ Identify the tool used to assign permissions in Active Directory Users and Computers.

▶ View the permissions for the HKEY_CURRENT_USER key in the Registry.

To compare your answers to the author's, please visit **www.sybex.com/go/ securityessentials**.

REVIEW QUESTIONS

1. True or false: If a user is granted the basic Read permission for a folder, the user can read both basic and extended attributes.

2. Maria is a member of the Finance group and the Budget group. The Finance group is granted Modify permission for an NTFS folder called Funding. The Budget group is granted Read permission for the same folder. What is Maria's permission to the Funding folder?

   A. Impossible to determine   C. Modify

   B. Read   D. Full Control

(Continues)

THE ESSENTIALS AND BEYOND *(Continued)*

3. True or false: The difference between Modify and Write permissions is that users with Write permission can delete files, but users with Modify permission can't delete files.

4. A user is assigned Allow Full Control to a file as a member of a group. The same user is assigned Deny Full Control as a member of another group. What permission does the user have?

    A. None. Deny takes   **C.** Denied Full Control, but allowed Read.
    precedence.

    B. Allow Full Control.   **D.** Denied Full Control, unless the user is an administrator, in which case Allow Full Control.

5. If a user is granted Full Control permissions for a folder, the user also has Full Control permissions to files in the folder because of _____.

6. Permissions assigned to the C:\Projects folder are Full Control for the IT group. Permissions assigned to the C:\Budget folder are Full Control for the Finance group. You copy the costs.xlsx document from C:\Projects to C:\Budget. What is the permission for this document?

    A. Unable to determine   **C.** Finance group Full Control

    B. IT group Full Control   **D.** Both groups have Full Control.

7. Permissions assigned to the C:\Projects folder are Full Control for the IT group. Permissions assigned to the D:\Budget folder are Full Control for the Finance group. You move the costs.xlsx document from C:\Projects to D:\Budget. What is the permission for this document?

    A. Unable to determine   **C.** Finance group Full Control

    B. IT group Full Control   **D.** Both groups have Full Control.

8. The NTFS permissions assigned to the Budget folder are Full Control for the Finance group. The folder is shared, and the share permissions are Read for the Finance group. What permissions do members of the Finance group have when accessing the share?

    A. Unable to determine   **C.** Full Control

    B. Read   **D.** Unrestricted Read

9. True or false: You can assign permissions for a group giving them the ability to reset passwords for user accounts within a specific OU.

10. True or false: Permission inheritance is enabled by default for all keys in the Registry.

CHAPTER 5

Using Audit Policies and Network Auditing

Auditing provides administrators with an easy method of tracking activity on systems. You can track when users access files, shut down systems, create or modify accounts, and much more. Windows Server 2008 includes nine separate categories of auditing that you can manipulate.

Although Windows Server 2008 audits many events by default, these events may not be enough to meet the needs of your organization. It's important to know what you can audit and how to enable auditing for different events. Of course, when you've enabled auditing, you'll also want to know how to view the audited events. For instance, Microsoft Windows records auditable events in the Security log, and you can use the Event Viewer to view them.

The Microsoft Baseline Security Analyzer (MBSA) provides a different type of auditing. It allows you to audit computers on your network for a wide variety of vulnerabilities. It's a free tool that you can download and install on a single system in your network. You can then use it to perform basic vulnerability scans on any other Windows systems running on the network and audit them for compliance, comparing their status against known security vulnerabilities. This chapter includes all of these topics in the following sections:

▶ **Exploring audit policies**

▶ **Enabling auditing**

▶ **Viewing audit information**

▶ **Managing security logs**

▶ **Auditing a network with MBSA**

Exploring Audit Policies

The AAAs of security refers to authentication, authorization, and accounting. Together they provide accountability.

A secure operating system needs to be able to identify individual users, grant access based on their identities, and track their actions. This starts by implementing practices that reflect the *three As (AAA) of security*: authentication, authorization, and accounting. Figure 5.1 shows how they combine to contribute to reliable accountability within an organization.

FIGURE 5.1 AAA of security

When a user attempts to access a system, the first step is to ensure that users prove who they are or authenticate against the system. Chapter 3, "Understanding User Authentication," covered the three factors of authentication. Chapter 4, "Securing Access with Permissions," covered how permissions provide authorization to different resources. In this chapter, you'll learn how *auditing* tracks a user's activity and provides accounting.

Digital signatures also provide nonrepudiation for email. Chapter 10 covers digital signatures.

Reliable accountability also provides *nonrepudiation*. In short, nonrepudiation prevents someone from denying they took an action. Logging records events in an *audit log* such as who took an action, what action they took, and when. If a user's actions are recorded, the user isn't able to deny taking the action, so the log provides nonrepudiation.

Accounting within a Microsoft Windows environment is relatively easy to implement. You can enable an Audit Policy for an entire domain with Group Policy or for a single server using the Local Security Policy.

Chapter 3 covered the Password Policy and Account Lockout Policy settings.

For example, Figure 5.2 shows the Local Security Policy with the Audit Policy selected. Notice that directly above Local Policies are the Password Policy and Account Lockout Policy. This section covers the details of each of the Audit Policy settings shown in Figure 5.2.

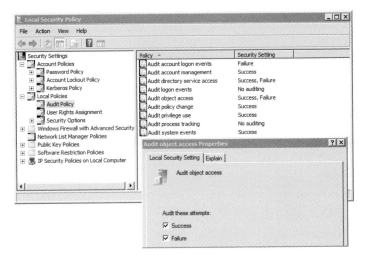

FIGURE 5.2 Audit Policy within Local Security Policy

As you can see, you can enable auditing for both Success and Failure events. For example, Figure 5.2 shows that Success and Failure events are enabled for Object Access. If you enable full Object Access auditing for a folder, and someone deletes a file in the folder, the system creates an entry in the Security log that includes user- and file-specific details. If someone attempted to delete the same file but didn't have permissions to do so, a Failure event would be created in the Security log and would also display the relevant user and file information. This shows that someone attempted an unauthorized action.

> You can enable auditing for Success events, Failure events, or both. You can also disable auditing of any of the policies within the Audit Policy.

WHY MONITOR FAILED EVENTS?

Failed events don't represent actual changes, but many organizations still monitor them. The primary benefit is that logged failed attempts document possible malicious activity.

For example, regular users won't have access to proprietary company data unless they specifically need it. However, if the logs show that a user is repeatedly trying to access this data, it may be cause for alarm. It's worth investigating why this user is attempting to access this data.

Of course, it's also possible that the user needs access to perform their job or a specific function. But in such a case, the user will probably let others know they're having difficulty. A request will likely come to the IT department to modify the permissions for the user.

It's relatively easy to enable these security settings for auditing. The challenge is first thinking through what you want to audit before enabling it. If you enable everything, your logs will become overwhelmed with unneeded details. They'll consume system resources, and it'll be difficult to identify the events that matter. On the other hand, if you don't enable enough, you won't have accounting for important events.

Although most systems have similar security requirements, domain controllers hold all the user accounts and passwords and require higher security. This includes the security requirements for auditing. Table 5.1 introduces the settings that apply to all servers. Table 5.2 introduces the settings that apply to only domain controllers. The tables list the default behavior for these settings. The default behavior isn't the same concept as the default setting. When you first install Windows Server 2008, you can look at these settings and see that they're all set to No Auditing. However, auditing still occurs, based on the default behavior for each setting.

▶

Domain controllers hold a copy of Active Directory Domain Services.

▶

When you first install Windows Server 2008, all of these settings are configured as No Auditing. However, the default behavior still applies.

TABLE 5.1   Audit Settings That Apply to All Servers

Audit Policy Setting	Default Behavior	Comments
Object Access	No events recorded	Records access to any objects such as NTFS files, printers, and Registry keys. However, auditing must also be enabled on the object. If auditing isn't enabled on the object, auditing doesn't occur.
Logon	Successful events recorded	Records when a user logs in locally or when a user accesses a resource over the network. This doesn't include any authentication by a domain controller.
Account Management	Successful events recorded	Records the creation, modification, or deletion of user and group accounts. This includes password changes.
		On a domain controller, it includes the creation, modification, or deletion of computer accounts.
System Events	Successful events recorded on domain controllers	Records system evens such as when a user restarts or shuts down a system. It also records any actions that affect the system security, including the security log.
	Not enabled on member servers	

(Continues)

TABLE 5.1 *(Continued)*

Audit Policy Setting	Default Behavior	Comments
Privilege Use	No events recorded	Records the use of specific user rights. For example, if enabled, it records if a user takes ownership of a file.
Policy Change	Successful events recorded on domain controllers Not enabled on member servers	Records changes to any setting in the User Rights Assignment policies, Audit policies, or Trust policies.
Process Tracking	No events recorded	Records events such as program activation, process exit, and indirect object access.

TABLE 5.2 Audit Settings That Apply Only to Domain Controllers

Audit Policy Setting	Default Behavior	Comments
Account Logon	Successful events recorded on domain controllers	Records when a user or computer authenticates with Active Directory
Directory Service Access	Successful events recorded on domain controllers	Records access to any Active Directory objects (such as users, computers, and groups), but only if auditing is also enabled on the object

These settings don't apply to member servers. A member server is any Windows server that is a member of a domain, but not a domain controller.

The following sections cover the details of the different types of auditing you can enable.

Exploring Object Access Auditing

Object Access auditing can record any time a user accesses or is denied access to an object such as a file, folder, printer, or Registry key. However, it's important to realize that Object Access auditing must be enabled in two separate locations: in the Audit Policy and in the system access control list (SACL) for the object.

By default, Object Access auditing isn't enabled in the Audit Policy.

For example, Figure 5.3 shows the Advanced Security Settings, Auditing tab, and Auditing Entry for a folder named `SecurityProject`. The Auditing tab represents the SACL. In this example, the data contained within the `SecurityProject` folder is valuable, and administrative personnel have decided to record all access from anyone in the Everyone group.

> ▶
>
> **You can audit the use of any NTFS permissions. Chapter 4 covered these same advanced NTFS permissions.**

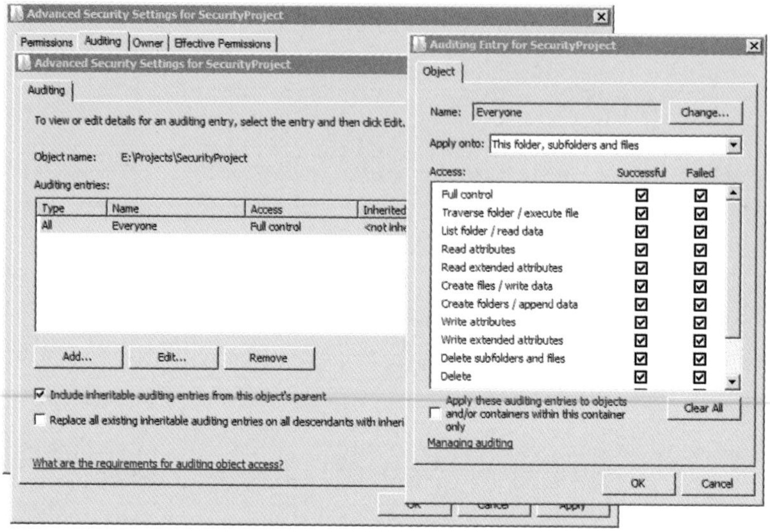

FIGURE 5.3 Auditing configured on an NTFS folder

Notice that each check box for Successful and Failed attempts is selected. If a user reads a file in this folder, it's recorded. If a user attempts to delete a file but fails, the attempt is recorded. An important point is worth repeating, though: If these settings are configured as shown in Figure 5.3, but object access hasn't been configured in the Audit Policy, events won't be recorded. Both the Audit Policy *and* the object's SACL must be configured before logs will be recorded for the resource.

All audited events are recorded in the Security log, and you can view them using the Event Viewer. Figure 5.4 shows the Event Viewer with the Security log selected and an event open. The event shows that the marysmith account in the domain named `SECURITY` accessed the `Top Secret Notes.txt` file in the `C:\Study Notes\SecurityProject` folder.

> ▶
>
> **The "Enabling Auditing" section later in this chapter describes steps to enable Object Access auditing.**

You can't enable auditing for any FAT-based filesystem because a partition formatted using FAT doesn't have auditing capabilities available. Additionally, you can't enable auditing on a share. However, you can enable NTFS auditing for any files and folders within the share. You can also enable auditing for printers and Registry keys.

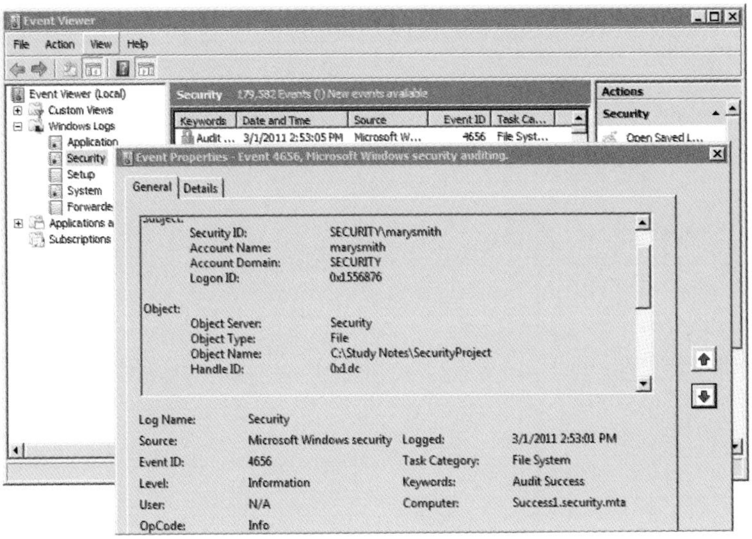

FIGURE 5.4 Event Viewer showing the Security log

Comparing Account Logon and Logon Events

Two account policy audit settings include the word *logon*, and they confuse many people. The two settings are Audit Account Logon Events and Audit Logon Events:

Account Logon   This setting creates an event any time a user or computer authenticates (or attempts to authenticate) with an Active Directory account.

Logon   This setting creates an event when a user logs on locally (also called *interactively*) to a computer or over the network (remotely). For example, if a user logs onto a computer using a local account on the computer (not a domain account), it's a logon event. As another example, if a user accesses a share over the network, it's logged as a logon event on the server hosting the share.

Notice that Account Logon events are only for Active Directory authentication. Any time a user or computer logs on with a domain account, auditing creates an Account Logon event if it's enabled.

On the other hand, when users have accounts on a local Windows server, they aren't authenticated against Active Directory. Instead, the local computer's Security Account Manager (SAM) database authenticates the user. If auditing is enabled, this is recorded as a Logon event.

Any time a user accesses a resource over the network (such as accessing a shared folder or a shared printer), it also creates a Logon event. For example, imagine that Logon events are enabled on a server named Server1 and this server

The default behavior for both Account Logon and Logon auditing is to record Success events.

Account Logon events apply only to domain controllers. Logon events can be recorded on any server.

Domain controllers host Active Directory and don't have a local SAM.

The default behavior for Directory Service Access auditing is to record Success events on domain controllers. It doesn't apply to member servers or clients.

▶

is sharing a folder using a share named Projects. If Sally accesses the share, a Logon event is recorded on Server1. In this case, it doesn't matter if Server1 is a member server or a domain controller—the event is still recorded as a Logon event. Also, it doesn't matter what type of user account (local account or domain account) Sally is using. It will record her access based on whatever account she is using.

Exploring Directory Service Access Auditing

Directory Service Access auditing allows for audit-log generation as a result of any access to Active Directory objects. As a reminder, Active Directory is a large database of objects such as users, computers, groups, and organizational units (OUs). If a server isn't a domain controller, it doesn't host Active Directory, and this setting doesn't apply.

Although it's possible to determine what object the GUID identifies, doing so takes some time and effort.

▶

Directory Service Access auditing is similar to Object Access auditing in that you must enable it in two places. First, you must enable auditing in the Audit Policy setting. Next, you must enable auditing in Active Directory on the specific objects that are to be tracked.

By default, these directory service access events are difficult to interpret. For example, instead of identifying users who make Active Directory modifications using names, the entries often identify objects and properties using globally unique identifiers (GUIDs). For instance, if Sally changed a password for Bob's account, the entry would identify Bob's account as {bf967a9c-0de6-11d0-a285 -00aa003049e2}, which is representative of Bob's user account GUID.

However, Windows Server 2008 introduced some new auditing capabilities with Active Directory Domain Services (AD DS) auditing. If the enhanced features are enabled, it lists the modified account by name. It also includes many more details that are much easier to interpret. You can enable the advanced features by entering the following command on a domain controller at the command prompt with administrative privileges:

You start the command prompt with administrative privileges by right-clicking Command Prompt on the Start menu and selecting Run As Administrator.

```
auditpol /set /subcategory:"directory service changes"
/success:enable /failure:enable
```

You can use the auditpol command to modify the default behavior of the audit policy. The previous syntax shows how to modify Directory Service Access auditing, but the command can be used for much more. Microsoft TechNet includes several web pages that start from here if you're interested:

http://technet.microsoft.com/library/cc731451.aspx

If desired, you can enable only Success events by including /success:enable but not including /failure:enable. Similarly, you can enable only Failure events by including /failure:enable but not including /success:enable. If you later decide you want to turn off the additional auditing, you change enable to disable as in the following command:

```
auditpol /set /subcategory:"directory service changes"
/success:disable /failure:disable
```

Understanding Account Management Auditing

Account Management auditing tracks modifications to accounts and groups on a system. When enabled on a local system, it tracks changes to the local SAM account database. When enabled on a domain controller, it tracks changes to accounts in Active Directory.

Account Management auditing tracks events for the following objects:

User Accounts All additions to, deletions from, and modifications to any user account are tracked.

Groups All additions to, deletions from, and modifications to any group are tracked.

Computer Accounts All additions to, deletions from, and modifications to any user account are tracked.

Understanding System Events Auditing

System Events auditing tracks a variety of system events such as when the system is shut down or rebooted. It also tracks any actions that affect the Security log.

Security logs hold all the audited data. If users are able to clear these entries, the data may be lost, and there may be no record of previous activity. Attackers know this and realize that if they can clear the logs, they can erase traces of their activity. Clearing the log erases all log entries, but the log will continue to log new entries. However, System Events auditing will record that the log was cleared, including who cleared it and when. This entry is included in the log after it's cleared.

As a result, many organizations have processes in place to regularly archive the logs and clear them. For example, an administrator may review and archive the logs every Wednesday. If the audit log shows that it was cleared on another day, it's an indication of a possible problem; an attacker may have tried to clear the log to erase their actions.

If event subscriptions are used, the entire log isn't lost. Event subscriptions forward events from one server to another server. The "Saving Audit Information" section later in this chapter presents more details on event subscriptions.

The default behavior for Account Management auditing is to record Success events on domain controllers.

Computer accounts exist only in Active Directory. You can't add a computer account to the local SAM.

The default behavior for System Events auditing is to record Success events on domain controllers.

Event ID 1102 indicates that the audit log is cleared. Knowing event ID numbers lets you search the logs for specific events. The "Viewing Audit Information" section covers how.

THE IMPORTANCE OF MONITORING REBOOTS

Each time a system is shut down, it's highly vulnerable to unmonitored security events. Because auditing is managed by the operating system, no auditing occurs when the operating system isn't running. However, an attacker can do a lot without launching the operating system.

For example, there are many different bootable disks available that can be used to boot a system. Someone may create a bootable USB or DVD and boot the server with this bootable media. Depending on the operating system included on the bootable media, that person may have access to all data on a system. If an attacker did this, it would be a simple matter to copy all data of interest onto a portable USB drive, or even burn a DVD, depending on what resources are available.

This isn't to say that every server restart indicates an attack. But unscheduled reboots may be worth investigating.

► Understanding Privilege Use Auditing

The default behavior for Privilege Use auditing is no auditing.

Privilege Use auditing records when users exercise specific rights. A *right* is an action that a user is allowed to perform on a system. For example, a user may have the right to change the system time or shut down the system. If Privilege Use auditing is enabled, these events are recorded in the Security log when the user takes the action.

The User Rights Assignment node of Local Security Policy identifies user rights. Figure 5.5 shows a partial listing of these. Notice that these user rights are listed just below the Audit Policy node.

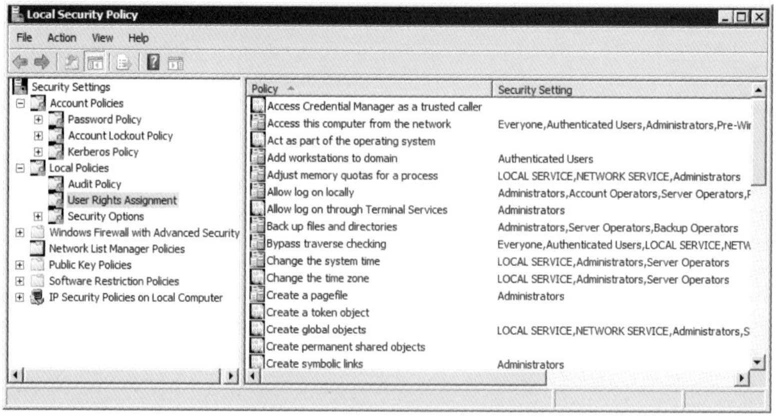

FIGURE 5.5 The User Rights Assignment node of Local Security Policy

However, several rights aren't recorded when exercised by a user, even if Privilege Use auditing is enabled. These events tend to generate many events in the Security log, and they may impede the computer's performance. These rights include the following:

- ▶ Back Up Files And Directories

- ▶ Restore Files And Directories

- ▶ Bypass Traverse Checking

- ▶ Debug Programs

It's possible to modify the Registry to include these events; but in general, doing so isn't recommended.

Understanding Policy Change Auditing

Policy Change auditing records changes to policies. This includes any changes to the audit policies, user rights assignment policies, and trust policies. For example, event ID 4704 indicates that a user right was assigned. Event ID 4719 indicates an audit policy was changed.

The default behavior for Policy Change events is to record Success events on domain controllers.

Understanding Process Tracking

Process Tracking can be useful when you're troubleshooting problems with applications. It records events related to programs, applications, and processes. It's probably the audit setting administrators use the least. On the other hand, developers often find value with this setting when debugging applications.

The default behavior for Process Tracking events is no auditing.

Enabling Auditing

When you've identified what settings you want to configure and which objects you want to audit, you can configure the system to begin the audit-log collections. You can enable auditing for a local system by modifying the Local Security Policy. If you want to enable auditing for several systems in a domain, you can do so via Group Policy.

The following steps show how to enable auditing locally for any Windows Server 2008 server:

1. Click Start ➢ Administrative Tools ➢ Local Security Policy. If prompted by User Account Control (UAC), click Continue.

2. Expand Security Settings ➢ Local Policies, and select Audit Policy.

3. Double-click any of the audit settings.

4. Select Success and/or Failure, as desired. Click the Explain tab to view information about the setting.

5. Click OK.

You can configure settings for as many Audit Policy choices as desired.

You can use the following steps to enable auditing via Group Policy for a domain. These steps will enable auditing for all systems in the domain:

1. Click Start ➢ Administrative Tools, and select Group Policy Management. If prompted by UAC, click Continue.

2. Expand Forest ➢ Domains and your individual domain.

3. Right-click Default Domain Policy, and select Edit.

4. Expand Computer Configuration ➢ Policies ➢ Windows Settings ➢ Security Settings ➢ Local Policies, and select Audit Policy.

5. Double-click any of the audit settings.

6. Select the Define These Policy Settings check box. Your display will look similar to Figure 5.6. Select Success or Failure, as desired. Click the Explain tab to view information about the setting.

7. Click OK.

> **The Default Domain Policy applies to all computers in the domain.**

FIGURE 5.6 Configuring auditing with Group Policy

You can configure settings for as many Audit Policy choices as desired. Although the steps enable the Audit Policy, you'll need to take additional steps to complete the configuration and begin capturing log entries for certain policies such as Object Access auditing and Directory Service Access auditing. The following sections show how to complete the configuration.

Enabling Object Access Auditing

You can enable auditing for any file or folder on an NTFS drive. However, remember that this is a two-step process. You must first enable Object Access auditing via the Audit Policy (as shown in the previous section) and then enable auditing on the individual folders or files.

You can enable auditing only on NTFS drives. You can't enable auditing on FAT or FAT32 drives.

The following steps show how to enable Object Access auditing for a folder stored on a Windows Server 2008 server:

1. Launch Windows Explorer by clicking Start and selecting Computer.

2. Browse to the folder you want to audit. Right-click the folder, and select Properties.

3. Select the Security tab.

4. Click Advanced, and select the Auditing tab.

5. Click Edit, and then click Add.

6. Type in the name of the user or group you want to audit. If you want to audit all access, type the name **Everyone**. After typing the username or group, click OK.

7. Select the access that you want to audit. For example, if you want to audit any attempts to delete data, select the Successful and Failed check boxes for both Delete Subfolders And Files, and Delete. Your display will look similar to Figure 5.7.

8. Click OK to add the Auditing entry.

9. Click OK three more times to confirm the changes.

If desired, you can test these settings by creating, modifying, and deleting files in the folder. You can then launch the Event Viewer, select the Security log, and view the events.

Inheritance works the same for auditing as it does for permissions. Auditing entries are inherited by default from the parent to the child. In other words, if you enable auditing on a folder, auditing is enabled in all files and folders within the folder by default.

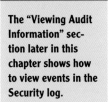

The "Viewing Audit Information" section later in this chapter shows how to view events in the Security log.

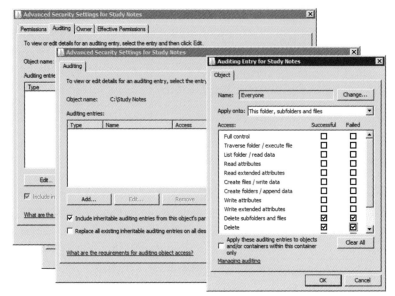

FIGURE 5.7 Configuring auditing on an NTFS folder

Enabling Directory Service Access auditing is a two-step process, similar to the way Object Access auditing is a two-step process.

Enabling Directory Service Access Auditing

If you have enabled Directory Service Access auditing in the Audit Policy, you also need to identify which objects you want to audit within Active Directory, and select the specific actions you want audited. You make these selections in Active Directory Users and Computers. Although some Directory Service Access auditing is enabled by default, it's very limited.

When Advanced Features is enabled, you can view the Security tab of any Active Directory object.

The following steps show how to enable auditing users in the Users container in a domain. You can use the same steps to enable auditing in any OU or container:

1. Click Start ➤ Administrative Tools, and select Active Directory Users And Computers. If prompted by UAC, click Continue.

2. Select View ➤ Advanced Features.

3. Expand the domain. Right-click the Users container, and select Properties.

Active Directory includes some auditing by default, so you may see some entries here.

4. Select the Security tab. If the Security tab doesn't appear, ensure that Advanced Features is selected.

5. Click the Advanced button.

6. Select the Auditing tab.

7. Click the Add button.

8. Type in **Everyone**, and click OK. Doing so adds the Everyone group to the Auditing tab.

9. Change the Apply Onto setting from This Object And All Descendant Objects to Descendant User Objects. Doing so changes the permissions list to just permissions affecting user objects.

10. Scroll down, and select the check boxes for both Successful and Failed to the right of Reset Password. Your display will look similar to Figure 5.8.

11. Click OK to confirm the Auditing Entry dialog box.

12. Click OK to dismiss the Advanced Security Settings dialog box.

13. Click OK to dismiss the properties page for the Users container.

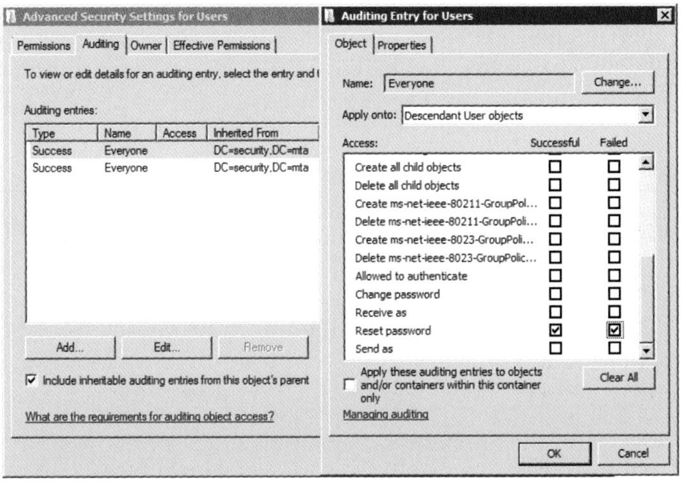

FIGURE 5.8 Configuring Directory Service Access auditing in Active Directory Users and Computers

You may want to take an additional step. If you want to take advantage of the additional AD DS auditing capabilities, you need to enable them. You can do so as follows:

1. Click Start, right-click Command Prompt, and select Run As Administrator. If prompted by UAC, click Continue.

2. Enter the following command at the command prompt:

   ```
   auditpol /set /subcategory:"directory service changes"
   /success:enable /failure:enable
   ```

   This command enables logging of additional details for both success and failure events for any directory service changes. You can do much

AD DS auditing capabilities can be configured to log entries with user-friendly details. For example, users are identified in the logs with user names instead of with account GUIDs.

more with this command, but this configuration change is enough for many administrators.

Of course, if you've enabled auditing, you'll want to look at the logged events. The next section shows how to examine the log files being generated by your auditing settings.

Viewing Audit Information

Auditing events and information are stored and made available in the Event Viewer as part of the Security log. One challenge with the Security log is that it can get quite large. However, you can search for specific events if desired instead of browsing the log manually.

You can use the following steps to launch the Event Viewer, view the Security log, and filter the entries:

1. Click Start ➢ Administrative Tools ➢ Event Viewer. If prompted by UAC, click Continue.

2. Expand Windows Logs, and select Security. Your display will look similar to Figure 5.9. Note the number of events in your log. The figure shows that 90,388 events are in the log.

3. Double-click any of the entries to view the contents. Note the event ID of the event. Click Close.

4. Right-click Security, and select Filter Current Log.

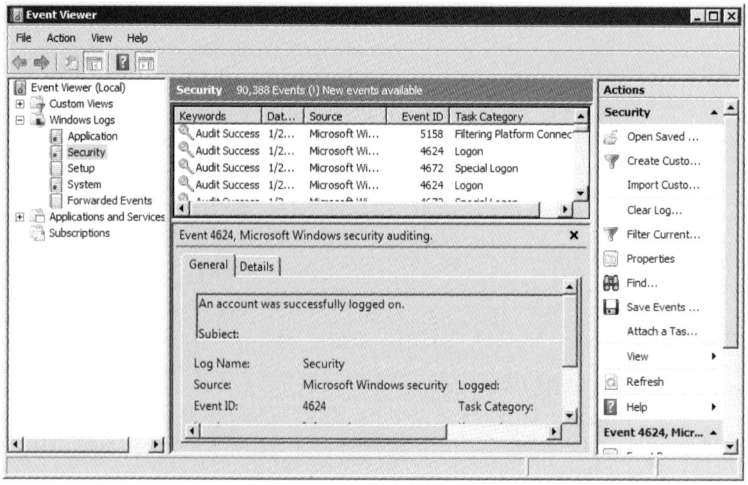

FIGURE 5.9 Viewing the Security log in Event Viewer

5. On the Filter Current Log page, change All Event IDs to the number of the event you noted previously. Your display will look similar to Figure 5.10.

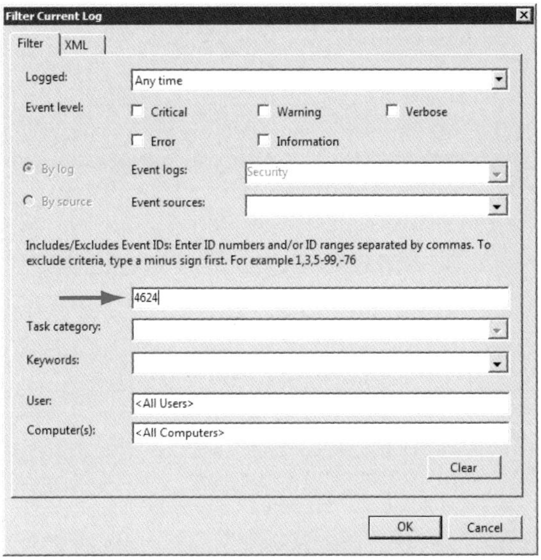

FIGURE 5.10 Filtering the Security log in Event Viewer

Notice that you can also filter the display to show ranges of events (such as 4620-4650), or multiple events (such as 4624, 4801).

6. Click OK. The log now shows only the events specified in the filter.

7. Right-click Security, and select Clear Filter. The log now shows all the events.

There are literally thousands of event IDs, and you can't remember them all. However, some resources are available on the Internet to help. For example, Derek Melber put together an excellent list in this article:

```
www.windowsecurity.com/articles/Event-IDs-Windows-Server-2008
-Vista-Revealed.html
```

Managing Security Logs

Security logs require some basic administrative maintenance tasks. If you want to keep the logs, you need to regularly save or archive them. Additionally, you may want to adjust the maximum size of the logs and indicate whether older events should be overwritten.

For example, Figure 5.11 shows the properties page for the Security log. The image shows that the size of the log file has been configured for 131072 KB (about 130 MB).

Figure 5.11 shows the default settings for the Security log. If left unmanaged, the log won't fill up the hard drive but instead will overwrite events when it reaches the maximum size.

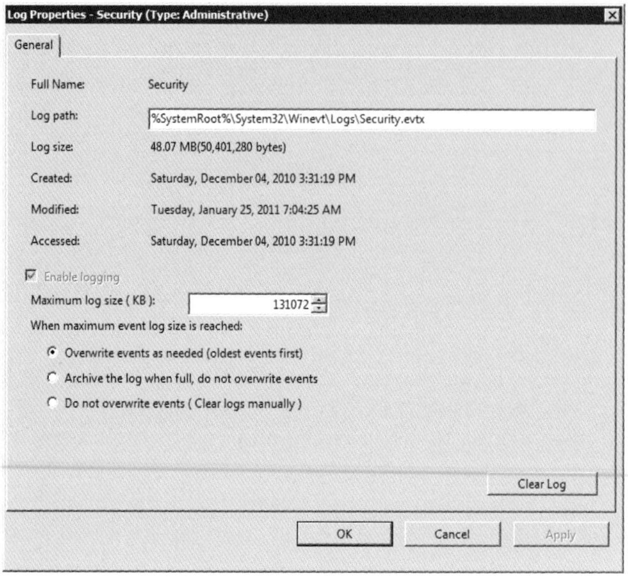

FIGURE 5.11 Viewing the Security log properties

If the log fills up, you have three options. Each of these options has tradeoffs:

Overwrite Events As Needed (Oldest Events First)   If you never clear the log, this option ensures that the hard drive never fills up. However, older recorded events are lost. This is the default setting.

Archive The Log When Full, Do Not Overwrite Events   This setting automatically creates an archive of the log and clears the running log. If the archived logs aren't deleted from the server, the logs will consume the hard-drive space.

Do Not Overwrite Events (Clear Logs Manually)   This option stops logging events when the log becomes full. Newer activity isn't recorded. With this setting enabled, an attacker could generate innocent activity to fill the logs and then perform malicious activity that wasn't recorded.

It's best to manage these logs by regularly archiving and clearing them, either manually or through an automated process. It's also best to set the maximum size of the log to significantly larger than is normally needed. For example, if the log normally grows to 10 MB in size during a week, you can set the maximum size to 100 MB. If you have malicious activity, you'll be certain that it's recorded.

Saving Audit Information

If security is a concern, you should regularly archive audit logs. If you don't, you won't have a record of what has happened over time. Auditing may be occurring, but the events will be overwritten on a regular basis.

You can save the Security log in the Event Viewer by right-clicking the log and selecting Clear Log. You'll be prompted to give the log a name and save it to any location desired. You can then copy the saved log to another server or include it in the server's backup plan.

A great feature that is available on Windows Server 2008 is the ability to forward events to other systems using event subscriptions. For example, if you're tasked with managing three file servers, you can configure an event subscription to forward events from each of these computers to a single computer. This way, you only have to monitor events on a single computer, instead of on all the computers.

Figure 5.12 shows how an event subscription works. Events are first recorded on one or more source computers; then the events are forwarded to a collector computer. You can view these events in the Event Viewer of the collector computer in the Forwarded Events section of Windows Logs.

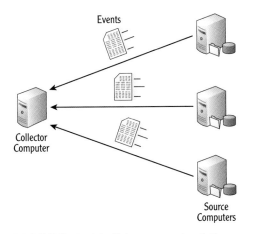

FIGURE 5.12 Using event subscriptions

You can adjust how often events are forwarded. For example, you can configure the subscription so that events are forwarded every 10 minutes.

Administrators enable Windows Remote Management on both source and collector computers for Event Subscriptions by executing the winrm qc command from the command line.

A benefit of an event subscription is that you're automatically creating an archive of the log. The source computer holds the original log. After the events are forwarded, the collector computer holds another copy of the events.

Securing Audit Information

If it's important to ensure that the audit logs are available when you need them, and in their original form, then you need to secure them. You can take several steps to secure audit logs. The steps you take depend on the long-term value of the logs.

The following list identifies some common measures taken to protect audit logs:

Create Backups   A backup of the log is a copy that can be restored if necessary. If you've archived the logs, you can include the log location as part of the server's normal backup plan.

Store the Logs on Another Server   Logs stored on another server (such as with an event subscription) provide a copy that you can access when needed. You can also back up the logs from the other server.

Store the Logs on Write-Once Media   For example, you can use Write Once Read Many (WORM) DVDs. The goal is to ensure that the historical log files aren't rewritten.

Protect the Logs with Permissions   Ensure that only authorized personnel have access to the logs. The permissions to access archived logs may be more restrictive than the permissions granted to view the original logs.

Enable Auditing on the Archived Files   You can track any access to the archived logs by enabling auditing on the log files. This records any access and modifications to the logs.

Some laws dictate extreme measures to protect audit logs. For example, nuclear facilities require detailed auditing of key data. All access is logged, and the logs are kept for years. Although the previous examples give some insight into how logs can be protected, these methods won't all apply in every circumstance.

> It's important to realize that just clearing and archiving the log doesn't create a backup. If the hard drive where the archive is stored fails, the archived log is lost.

Auditing a Network with MBSA

The Microsoft Baseline Security Analyzer (MBSA) is a free tool provided by Microsoft. It checks computers for a wide assortment of known vulnerabilities to ensure that systems are secure. It then provides a report listing all the issues it discovered. As an administrator, you can investigate each of the issues and take steps to resolve them.

Many organizations implement compliance auditing to ensure that their systems comply with basic security requirements. For example, an organization may create a written security policy defining what systems or data it wants to protect. The company may then use various technologies to implement the protection requirements. Later, it will likely continue to update the systems to ensure that the organization is still in compliance.

> MBSA provides basic compliance auditing. It verifies that systems are in compliance with basic security standards.

You can use MBSA to check a single computer or a range of computers. For example, you can run it against all the computers in a domain or all the computers within a specific IP address range.

Figure 5.13 shows the selection page you'll see if you choose to scan multiple computers. As configured, it will scan all the computers in the IP address range 192.168.1.10 through 192.168.1.100.

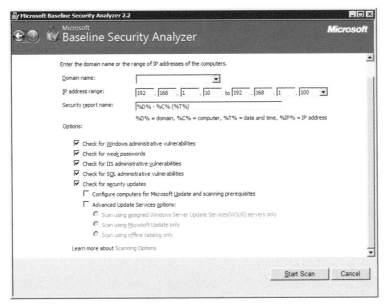

FIGURE 5.13 Starting an MBSA scan

You can select and deselect different options depending on what you want to check. By default, the scan performs checks in the following areas:

Administrative Vulnerabilities   This check scans for common security issues. For example, it checks to ensure that the Guest account is disabled, each drive is using NTFS, and only a limited number of users are in the Administrators group.

Weak Passwords   Each account on the target system is checked for blank or weak passwords. You can disable this when running MBSA on a domain controller to reduce the amount of time it will take to complete.

IIS Administrative Vulnerabilities   If Internet Information Services (IIS) is installed, this checks for known issues with IIS. If IIS isn't installed, these checks aren't run even if the check box is selected.

SQL Server is used to manage databases. MSDE is not used on Windows Server 2008.

SQL Administrative Vulnerabilities   If SQL Server or the Microsoft Data Engine (MSDE) is installed, this checks for known issues with each of them. If SQL Server isn't installed, these checks aren't run even if the check box is selected.

Security Updates   MBSA first connects to the Windows Update site and downloads an XML file that includes a listing of all current security updates. It then checks the system against this XML file to determine what updates have been installed and whether any updates are missing.

Internet access is required to download the XML file.

In addition to checking systems for these issues, you can also configure the MBSA to configure computers for Microsoft Update. In other words, if the clients aren't configured for automatic updates, you can change the setting so that they will be configured after the scan is complete.

The following two sections show where to get MBSA, how to install it, and how to run it.

Installing MBSA

Be sure you download the version for your architecture (x86 for 32-bit systems and x64 for 64-bit systems).

You can download MBSA from the Microsoft downloads site (**www.microsoft.com/ downloads**) by searching on MBSA. Select the newest version that matches your system.

After you've downloaded MBSA, you can use the following steps to install it:

1. Browse to where you saved the file, and double-click it.

2. Review the information on the Welcome screen, and click Next.

3. Review the license terms, click I Accept The License Agreement, and click Next.

4. Click Next to accept the default location.

5. Click Install. If prompted by UAC, click Continue.

6. When the installation completes, click OK.

That's it. You're now ready to start auditing computers in your network for known vulnerabilities.

Running MBSA

You can also choose to run MBSA against multiple computers by clicking Scan Multiple Computers.

After you install MBSA, it's relatively easy to run. You can use the following steps to run it against your local computer and check for known vulnerabilities:

1. Click Start ➢ All Programs, and select Microsoft Baseline Security Analyzer. If prompted by UAC, click Continue.

2. Click Scan A Computer.

3. Review the security options that are selected. If desired, you can modify the options. Click Start Scan.

4. When the scan completes, you can view the results. Figure 5.14 shows part of an example report.

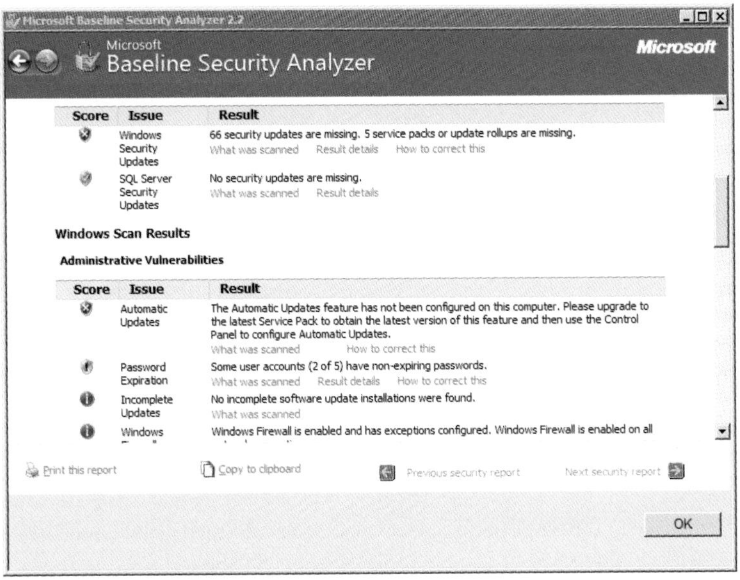

FIGURE 5.14 Viewing an MBSA report

Of course, after you've run a report and identified security issues with a system, the next step is to investigate the issues. For example, in the displayed report, this system is seriously out of date, with many security updates, service packs, and roll-ups missing. You would resolve this by investigating to determine if there is a reason why the updates are missing. If not, you'd resolve the issue by installing them.

THE ESSENTIALS AND BEYOND

In this chapter, you learned about the built-in auditing capabilities of Microsoft Windows Server 2008 systems. The Audit Policy contains nine categories of auditing. The majority of auditing settings need to be enabled in only the Audit Policy. However, two settings (Object Access and Directory Service Access) must be enabled in two places. You first enable the settings in the Audit Policy. Next, you enable auditing on the individual object that you want to audit. On NTFS systems, you enable Object Access auditing for any individual folder or file using the Security tab. For Active Directory objects, you enable Directory Service Access

(Continues)

THE ESSENTIALS AND BEYOND *(Continued)*

auditing on the Active Directory object such as a container or an OU. MBSA is a free tool you can download and use to perform security-compliance checks on Microsoft systems in your network. It includes the ability to perform scans on single computers or groups of computers. MBSA provides an easy-to-read report that details vulnerabilities.

ADDITIONAL EXERCISES

▶ Create a folder named SensitiveData, and enable Object Access auditing to record all access to the folder.

▶ Add files to the SensitiveData folder. Modify the files and delete them. View the audited entries.

▶ Filter the Security log so that you can view only events with an event ID between 4000 and 5000.

▶ Enable auditing so that you can record changes to the Security log. Archive the system log. View the entry that shows the log was cleared.

To compare your answers to the author's, please visit **www.sybex.com/go/ securityessentials**.

REVIEW QUESTIONS

1. What are the three As (AAA) of security?

    A. Authentication, authorization, and accounting

    B. Authentication, accountability, and accounting

    C. Accountability, access control, and accounting

    D. Authorization, access control, and auditing

2. True or false: If you want to audit all access to a folder, all you have to do is enable Object Access auditing in the Audit Policy.

3. Which Audit Policy selection records any time a user logs onto a local system?

    A. Logon Events

    B. Account Logon Events

    C. System Events

    D. Process Tracking

4. Which Audit Policy selection records modifications to Active Directory?

    A. Privilege Use

    B. Account Management Events

    C. Directory Service Access

    D. Policy Change

5. If you want to ensure that an audit-log entry records each time a system is shut down, you should enable Successful entries for _____ auditing.

(Continues)

THE ESSENTIALS AND BEYOND (Continued)

6. What tool can you use to view audited events?

7. Which of the following choices can be used to automatically collect events on a single server from multiple servers?

   A. Process Tracking Events auditing   C. Automatic archiving

   B. MBSA   D. Event subscriptions

8. True or false: You can secure audit logs with WORM media.

9. Where can you get MBSA?

10. True or false: MBSA can detect weak passwords for accounts on Microsoft systems.

CHAPTER 6

Protecting Clients and Servers

It's important to understand the different steps you can take to protect clients (end-user computers) and servers. Some common techniques apply to both, whereas other techniques apply to only the clients or only the servers. User Account Control (UAC) is a built-in mechanism that is used to separate administrative actions from regular user actions on both clients and servers. Additionally, it's important to keep every system in an organization up to date, in order to protect the environment against newly discovered potential vulnerabilities.

Also consider that users can use offline folders to store data accessed from shares. Occasionally, you may want to protect this offline data by encrypting offline folders. And you can protect clients by using software-restriction policies to control what applications run.

You can add a layer of protection for servers by placing them in virtual local area networks (VLANs) and by ensuring that the server isn't running services that have conflicting security goals. Read-only domain controllers (RODCs) are a new type of domain controller that can protect and further restrict Active Directory in branch offices. Every Active Directory environment must include a server running the Domain Name System (DNS) service. Because DNS is so critical to any Active Directory environment, you should take steps to provide additional security within DNS. This chapter includes these concepts in the following topics:

▶ **Understanding User Account Control**

▶ **Keeping systems updated**

▶ **Protecting clients**

▶ **Protecting servers**

▶ **Exploring DNS security issues**

Understanding User Account Control

User Account Control (UAC) provides a very basic level of protection to systems by separating privileges needed for standard tasks and privileges needed for administrative tasks. An administrative account includes the built-in Administrator account and any other accounts that are in the Administrators group. When a user logs on with an administrative account, the user is assigned two access tokens. One token is used for the regular user account activities and is also used to launch the Desktop. The second token is utilized for administrative purposes. The goal is to prevent unauthorized changes to a computer by restricting the instances when administrative credentials are available.

When the user performs basic tasks such as creating documents or working with email, the regular token is used. However, when a user attempts to perform a task requiring administrative privileges, the user will see a dialog box similar to Figure 6.1. If the user clicks Continue, the administrative token is used to perform the administrative task.

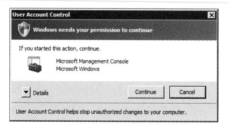

FIGURE 6.1 UAC prompting for approval to execute a task

An important point about UAC is that the administrator token is used only to perform the single approved task. If the user wants to perform another administrative task, the UAC dialog box is presented again for approval. This prevents malware from taking advantage of the elevated privileges token in order to perform other unapproved tasks.

UAC also goes into action if a non-administrative user attempts to take an action requiring administrator privileges. Non-administrators don't have an administrative token, so they won't be able to simply click Continue. UAC will give the non-administrator the opportunity to provide administrative credentials, as shown in Figure 6.2. This functions in a fashion similar to the Run As Administrator feature described in Chapter 3, "Understanding User Authentication."

FIGURE 6.2 UAC prompting for
administrator credentials

The user can click
Use Another Account
and enter the
credentials of an
account with appro-
priate permissions.

This is useful when Help Desk personnel need to assist end users. For example, suppose Bob (an end user) is having problems, and Sandy (the Help Desk
professional) is helping Bob. Sandy wants to look at the Event Viewer, but Bob's
account doesn't have privileges to do so. Sandy can launch Event Viewer without
logging Bob off the system. UAC will show a display similar to Figure 6.2, Sandy
can enter her credentials, and Event Viewer will launch.

Understanding the Dimmed Desktop

When UAC prompts you to continue or provide administrator credentials, it dims
the Desktop. The only activity you can perform in the dimmed Desktop (also called
the secure Desktop) is respond to the UAC prompt.

The dimmed Desktop prevents malicious software from overriding UAC. UAC
waits for manual intervention, and during this time, application activity is sus-
pended. Although it's possible to disable the dimmed Desktop, doing so isn't recommended. If it's disabled, malicious software can trigger and respond to UAC
and approve an action without any user interaction.

The dimmed desktop
is also known as
the secure desktop.
For example, Group
Policy settings use
the term secure
desktop.

Modifying User Account Control

You can modify the behavior of UAC on Windows 7 and Windows Server 2008 R2
via the Control Panel. Figure 6.3 shows the User Account Control Settings page.
You can access this page from the Control Panel by typing **user account control**
in the Search Control Panel text box and selecting Change User Account Control
Settings.

Windows Vista and
Windows Server
2008 give you only
the option of turning
UAC on or off.

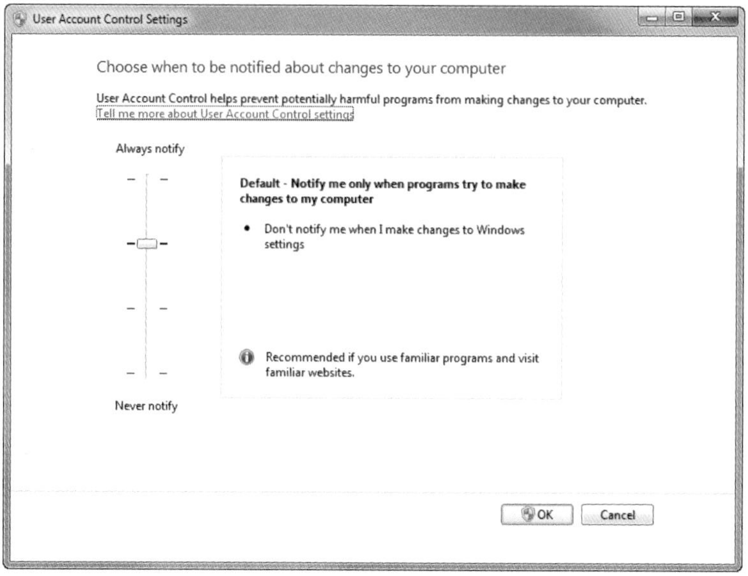

FIGURE 6.3 User Account Control Settings page

The following settings are available:

Always Notify Me When   This setting provides notifications when a program tries to install software or make changes to your computer. The setting is recommended if you routinely install new software or visit unfamiliar websites. This is the default behavior for Windows Vista and Windows Server 2008 (but not Windows 7 and Windows Server 2008 R2).

Default - Notify Me Only When Programs Try To Make Changes To My Computer
This setting notifies you when programs try to make changes to your computer that require administrator permissions. It doesn't notify you when you make changes to the Windows settings as long as you have administrative permissions. It's recommended if you use familiar programs and visit familiar websites, such as only your company's websites, or legitimate websites such as **www.msn.com.** This is the default setting for Windows 7 and Windows Server 2008 R2.

Notify Me Only When Programs Try To Make Changes To My Computer (Do Not Dim My Desktop)   This is similar to the default setting for Windows 7 and Windows Server 2008 R2 except that the Desktop isn't dimmed. Because the Desktop isn't dimmed, malicious software can respond to UAC without any user interaction. This setting is provided as an option for systems with limited resources (such as older processors or minimum memory) that take a long time to dim the Desktop. However, it isn't recommended, because security is weakened.

Never Notify We When   This setting turns off UAC. It isn't recommended and is included only as an option for older applications that don't work with UAC at all. For example, if an application was written for Windows 2000 or Windows XP (before UAC was developed), it may not be compatible with UAC. You can disable UAC to run such a program, but doing so weakens the computer's overall security.

Keeping Systems Updated

An important step in protecting all systems (clients and servers) is ensuring that they're up to date. The reason is that bugs and security flaws are regularly discovered in operating systems and applications. As they're discovered, these flaws are often resolved, and they're addressed as part of system updates. The entire process of discovery and resolution of security flaws includes several steps:

1. Flaw Discovered   The flaw may first be discovered by security personnel or by hackers. Many professional security personnel regularly examine software and discover vulnerabilities. Attackers also try to discover any flaws they can exploit, and many attackers share this information with other attackers.

2. Vendor Notified   Most vendors (including Microsoft) have confidential channels where security professional can privately report the flaw. Sometimes these flaws are reported publically in written articles, which also notify attackers at the same time as vendors. Other times, suspicious activity is noticed, and the vendors discover the flaws on their own.

3. Vendor Develops and Tests a Solution as an Update   The vendor then creates a fix in the form of an update. Because any change can cause problems, this update is tested before release. The amount of time this takes depends on the seriousness of the flaw. Some updates take as long as six months before they're released. Other updates are released within a month.

4. Vendor Makes Update Available   Microsoft makes security updates available on Patch Tuesday, the second Tuesday of every month, via the company's update site. The updates released on this day include all of the updates that have been tested by Microsoft.

5. Updates Downloaded and Installed   Clients can then download and install the system update. Ideally, this is done automatically. For example, Microsoft

Chapter 1 introduced the importance of keeping systems updated in the "Hardening a Server" section.

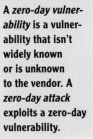

A *zero-day vulnerability* is a vulnerability that isn't widely known or is unknown to the vendor. A *zero-day attack* exploits a zero-day vulnerability.

Patches addressing serious flaws may be released *out of band*, on a day other than Patch Tuesday. This is rare and occurs only for serious vulnerabilities.

releases updates via Windows Update (and Microsoft Update). Systems configured with Automatic Updates can automatically download and install the updates onto the system. Of course, the update only resolves the vulnerability if downloaded and installed. If it isn't installed, the system remains vulnerable. Worse, more attackers now know about the vulnerability because it's advertised in the update (see the sidebar "Reverse-Engineering Updates").

REVERSE-ENGINEERING UPDATES

Some attackers wait for Patch Tuesday to see the released patches. They then decompile and analyze the code to discover what it's doing. As they discover the vulnerability that the code is correcting, they also discover the original weakness. This entire process is known as *reverse engineering*, and it can be applied to almost any software, including system updates.

Because many systems aren't updated right away, or at all, the attacker can now develop an attack to exploit the vulnerability. As long as systems remain unpatched, they remain vulnerable.

There are several options to keep systems updated. The most common method uses Automatic Updates, but organizations can also use more advanced server technologies, such as Windows Server Update Services (WSUS) or System Center Configuration Manager (SCCM), to keep their systems updated.

Updating Systems with Automatic Updates

You can configure individual systems with *Automatic Updates*. When you enable Automatic Updates, the system will periodically check the Microsoft Update site for system updates. It then takes specific actions depending on the configuration.

Figure 6.4 shows the Automatic Updates page on a Windows 7 system. You can view this screen by launching the Control Panel, typing **updates** in the Search Control Panel text box, and selecting Turn Automatic Updating On or Off. As configured, it will check the Microsoft update site periodically; and when updates are available, it will automatically download them. With the settings displayed in Figure 6.4, at 3 a.m. the system will install any updates that have been downloaded.

Microsoft classifies updates as Important, Recommended, and Optional. Table 6.1 explains the differences.

F I G U R E 6 . 4 Controlling how updates are applied

T A B L E 6 . 1 Update Types

Update Type	Explanation
Important	Affects security, privacy, and reliability of the system. Microsoft recommends installing these updates automatically, as shown in Figure 6.4.
Recommended	Addresses noncritical problems. Doesn't address fundamental issues with the computer or Windows software, but can enhance a user's computing experience. These updates can be installed automatically by selecting the Recommended Updates check box, as shown in Figure 6.4.
Optional	Can include updates, drivers, or new software from Microsoft. You can only install these manually.

Updates can be
security updates
or critical updates.
Security updates
are fixes for security
vulnerabilities.
Critical updates
address non-security-
related bugs.

If Microsoft Update is selected (as shown in Figure 6.4), the updates will include those addressing Microsoft software in addition to the Windows operating system. If this check box isn't selected, only updates for the operating system are included.

You can select one of four settings for the installation of updates (in the Important Updates section):

Install Updates Automatically (Recommended)   Updates are automatically downloaded and installed based on the schedule. This is the setting used in most organizations.

Download Them But Let Me Choose Whether To Install Them   If you want to know exactly when updates are installed, you can use this option. You're notified when updates have been downloaded and are ready for installation.

Check For Updates But Let Me Choose Whether To Download And Install Them
If you have limited Internet bandwidth, use this to control when updates are downloaded. You're notified when updates are available for download.

Never Check For Updates (Not Recommended)   The system doesn't check for updates at all. You can still download and install updates manually by choosing Start ➢ All Programs ➢ Windows Update. You might want to use this for an isolated system that will be manually updated.

Updating Systems with WSUS or SCCM

> In an endless reboot cycle, the system restarts, and before the user can log on, the system restarts again. This continues until the system is turned off.

It's important to realize that even though Microsoft does do testing, it can't test every possible hardware and software configuration. The worst-case scenario occurs when a patch fixes one problem but creates another problem. Unexpected outcomes may result, such as forcing the system into an endless reboot cycle.

If this happens to one or two systems, it's inconvenient and requires troubleshooting to get the system back to being operational. However, if this happens to a large number of machines, such as 500 computers in an organization, the result can be catastrophic. In this case, not only are 500 employees unable to perform regular work, but the IT staff has a crisis on their hands that they must remediate.

> SCCM can do much more than deploy updates. For example, it can also deploy applications to clients and deploy full operating-system images.

Many organizations take control of updates by centrally administering and distributing them in order to prevent similar scenarios from occurring. Two Microsoft tools are available to organizations:

Windows Server Update Services (WSUS)   *WSUS* is available as a free download. You can install it on a Windows server and use it to manage updates to clients in the organization.

System Center Configuration Manager (SCCM)   *SCCM* is an add-on server product. It's not free but has significant enhancements over WSUS. The primary advantage is that you can schedule when updates are deployed to clients with WSUS.

Although WSUS and SCCM have significant differences, the basic functions are the same. Consider Figure 6.5. The server retrieves updates from the Microsoft update site using a synchronization process. An administrator then approves updates to test clients for testing and can later deploy the updates to all clients on the internal network.

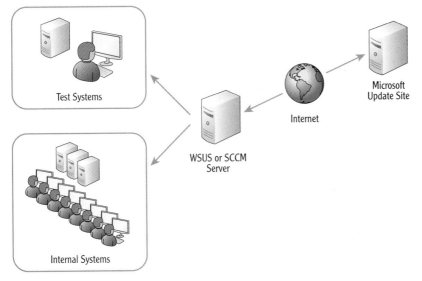

Test Systems

Internet

Microsoft
Update Site

WSUS or SCCM
Server

Internal Systems

FIGURE 6.5 Using WSUS or SCCM to deploy updates

The big difference is the ability for you to control which updates are approved and deployed. If testing identifies a problem with an update, only one or two test systems are affected. This is much easier to manage than walking into work one day to discover that all of your systems have crashed.

Using Group Policy to Configure Clients

You've seen how Group Policy can help manage security in a network. Chapter 3 showed how to configure a Password Policy for a single system or all systems within a domain with Group Policy. Chapter 5, "Using Audit Policies and Network Auditing," showed how to configure an Audit Policy with Group Policy. You can also use Group Policy to configure automatic updates.

The key Group Policy settings are shown in Figures 6.6 and 6.7. Both settings are available in a domain-based Group Policy in the following location: Computer Configuration ➢ Policies ➢ Administrative Templates ➢ Windows Components ➢ Windows Update.

A significant benefit of Group Policy is that you can configure a setting once and have it apply to many or even all clients in your network.

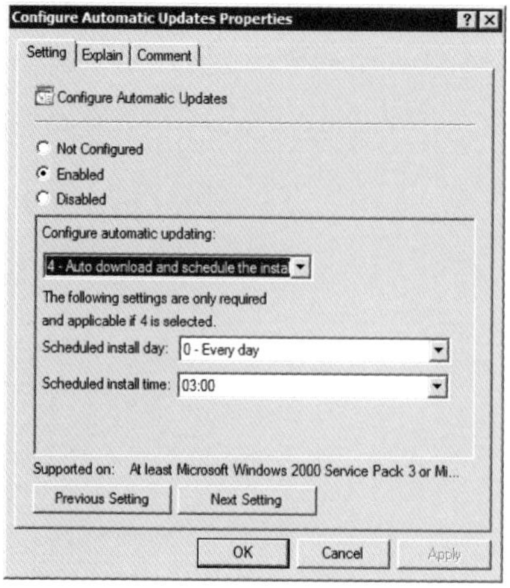

FIGURE 6.6 Configuring automatic updates with Group Policy

Figure 6.6 shows the configuration page to automatically download and schedule the installation of system updates. Figure 6.7 shows the page that reconfigures the systems to retrieve updates from an internal WSUS server (named wsus1 in this example) instead of from the Windows Update site.

Protecting Clients

The previous sections covered both clients and servers, but some issues apply to only clients. For example, users may enable and use offline folders on client machines, but offline folders aren't used the same way on a server. Similarly, some administrators want to prevent users from running specific software on client systems, and they can do so with software-restriction policies. This section explains what offline folders are, how they can be encrypted, and why you may want to consider the use of software-restriction policies.

Understanding Offline Folders

Chapter 3 introduced shares and share permissions. As a reminder, a share is a folder on a server that has been shared and is available to users on the network. Users can access a share via mapped drives or directly by entering a Universal Naming Convention (UNC) path in the Start Search text box.

A UNC path has the format
`\\servername\sharename`.

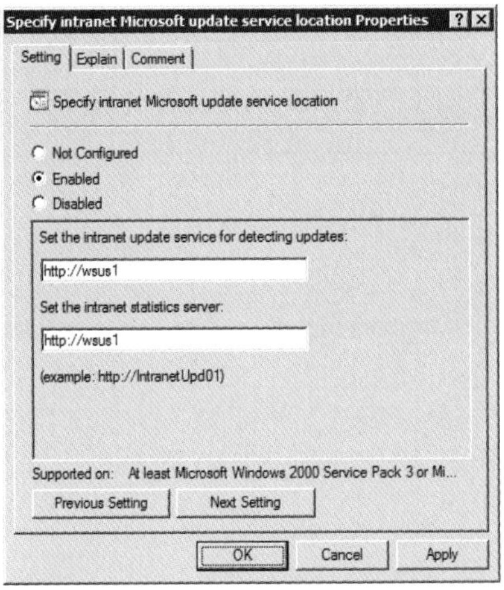

FIGURE 6.7 Configuring clients to receive updates from a WSUS server with Group Policy

When users are connected within a network, they can access shares in the network as long as they have been assigned permissions to the share. For example, Sally may regularly access the \\File1\Sales share (located on the File1 server in the network) while connected at work. However, when she travels to a customer's location, she's no longer connected to her work network, and she doesn't have access to the Sales share.

Offline folders allow a user to have access to shared data while disconnected from the network. A user specifies which files to cache on the local machine, and then these files are stored in a special folder on the local machine called Offline Folders. If the user is connected to the network, the copy on the share is used. If the user isn't connected, the cached copy is used.

When a system reconnects to the network, it checks to see if any of the files in the Offline Folders folder have been changed. It then synchronizes the copies. If the file in the share has changed, it's downloaded to the client. If the file changed on the client, it's uploaded to the share (if the settings allow). If both copies changed, the user is notified and can then decide how to handle the conflict.

You can manage offline files on a Windows 7 system using the offline folders configuration page. You can access this from the Control Panel, by entering offline in the Control Panel Search text box, and selecting Manage Offline Files.

A cached copy of the file is a copy stored on the user's local hard drive in the Windows\CSC folder.

Some offline settings allow files to be only downloaded to the client. In this case, changes made on the client computer can't be uploaded to the server.

Encrypting Offline Folders

Chapter 1 presented confidentiality as one of the three elements of the security triad (also called the CIA triad or the AIC triad). Confidentiality protects data from unauthorized disclosure. Although permissions provide basic protection, some data requires additional protection such as encryption to protect against loss of confidentiality.

It's possible to encrypt data stored on NTFS drives with Encrypting File System (EFS). Only authorized personnel are able to open EFS-encrypted files.

It's important to understand the basics of how this works, though. If an authorized person opens an encrypted file, it's automatically decrypted so the user can read it. That's fine on a local system; but look at Figure 6.8 to see the effect if an encrypted file is stored on a share. When the user accesses the file, it's decrypted by the server and sent over the network in clear text.

> Chapter 10 covers encrypting NTFS files and folders with EFS. EFS is built into NTFS.

> It's possible to encrypt data going across the network. Chapter 7 introduces Internet Protocol Security (IPsec). IPsec can encrypt data on the network.

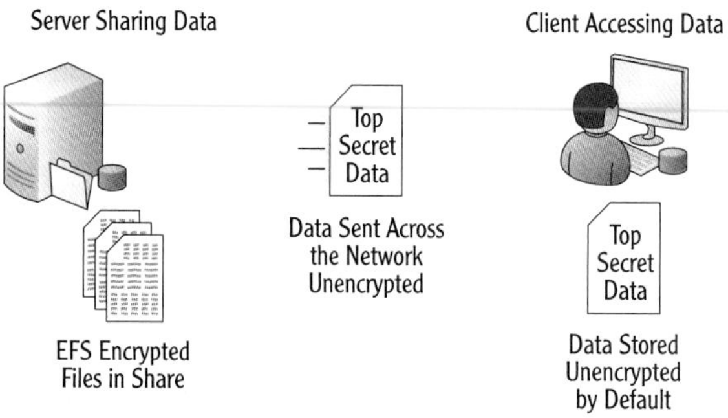

Server Sharing Data

Client Accessing Data

Top Secret Data

Data Sent Across the Network Unencrypted

Top Secret Data

EFS Encrypted Files in Share

Data Stored Unencrypted by Default

FIGURE 6.8 Accessing an encrypted file from a share

Additionally, if the user is using offline files, the decrypted version of the file is cached by default. This may present a security risk, especially if the user takes the computer outside of the work environment. If the computer is stolen, the thief can potentially gain access to unencrypted data. However, it's possible to encrypt offline files. Figure 6.9 shows the Offline Files properties page with the Encryption tab selected. As mentioned previously, you can access this page from the Control Panel by entering **offline** in the Control Panel Search text box and selecting Manage Offline Files.

If the files aren't encrypted, you simply click the Encrypt button to encrypt all offline files. Doing so encrypts files stored in the offline folders cache. Additionally, any new files added to the cache are encrypted.

Although this explanation stresses the protection of data identified as secret that is stored in encrypted format on the server, these aren't requirements. For example, even if the data isn't encrypted on the server, you can still choose to encrypt it on client systems that are using offline folders.

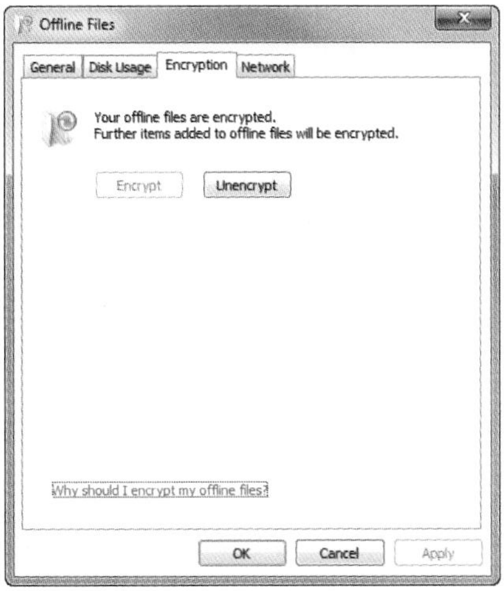

FIGURE 6.9 Encrypting offline files

◄

Files are encrypted with EFS. If EFS is disabled or offline, files are stored on a non-NTFS drive; the Encrypt button doesn't appear.

The security risks to a laptop computer carried around by a mobile user are much greater than the risks to a server. Laptop computers are stolen every day. However, it's much rarer for a thief to break into a place of business and steal a server from a locked server room.

Using Software-Restriction Policies

Another tool administrators have available to protect clients is software-restriction policies. Software-restriction policies are a group of rules that you can use to prevent certain software from running on a system, or to allow only specific software to run.

◄

Software-restriction policies are supported in Windows Server 2008 and Windows 7 systems.

Software-restriction policies provide several different options for identifying applications. You start by defining a default security level, and then you create exceptions to the default. For example, you could define a default security level of Unrestricted (meaning that any software can run) and then define exceptions to identify what software is blocked.

Figure 6.10 shows Local Security Policy with Software Restriction Policies open. By default, this node is empty. However, if you right-click Software Restriction Policies and select New Software Restriction Policies, the policies are created. The following text explains each of these rules:

Disallowed   This rule blocks all software from running. You then create exceptions in the Additional Rules section to identify what software can run. For example, a kiosk computer in a public location could have this rule set with an exception to allow a specific application to run. The rule would block all other applications.

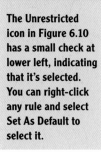

The Unrestricted icon in Figure 6.10 has a small check at lower left, indicating that it's selected. You can right-click any rule and select Set As Default to select it.

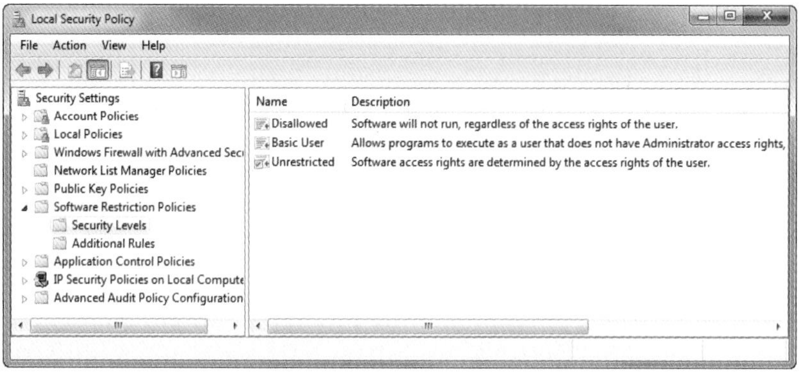

FIGURE 6.10 Viewing software restriction policy security levels

Basic User This allows only programs that need basic user rights to run. Programs requiring administrative permissions are blocked.

Unrestricted This is the default rule. This rule allows all software to run (as long as the user has permissions) except for software identified as an exception.

Exceptions are defined in the Additional Rules section. You can define multiple exceptions.

After defining the default rule, you can then define the exceptions to the rule. For example, Figure 6.11 shows three rules created as exceptions to the default rule. Exceptions can be in any of the categories shown in Table 6.2.

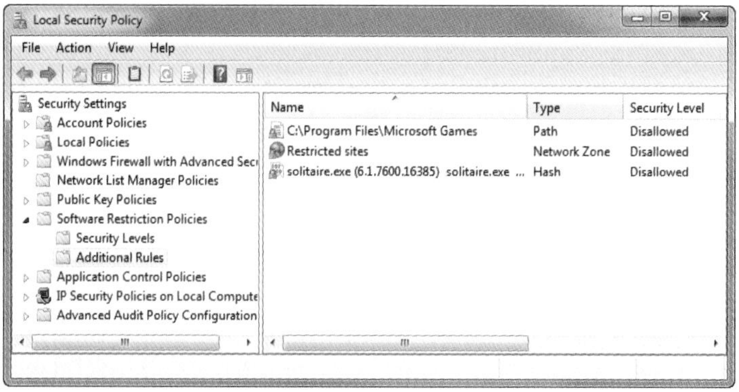

AppLocker and software-restriction policies aren't compatible with each other. You can run one or the other, but not both.

FIGURE 6.11 Software exceptions created as additional rules

A more advanced use of software restriction is AppLocker. AppLocker is similar to software-restriction policies but also allows you to control what programs users can run based on group membership. Although software-restriction policies work with Windows XP and newer operating systems, AppLocker works only with Windows Vista and Windows 7 desktop operating systems.

TABLE 6.2 Software-Restriction Policy Additional Rules

Rule Type	Comments
Path	You can identify any path, such as `C:\Program Files\Microsoft Games` (as shown in Figure 6.11), to block execution of any programs located in the folder and subfolders. Alternately, you can specify a program by using the full path to the program, such as `C:\Program Files\Microsoft Games\Solitaire\Solitaire.exe`, which will prevent Solitaire from running from that location.
Network Zone	This identifies the zones in Internet Explorer: Internet, Local Computer, Local Intranet, Restricted Sites, and Trusted Sites. Figure 6.11 has a rule blocking applications in the Restricted Sites location.
Certificate	This identifies an application that has been digitally signed by a certificate. This is a reliable way to identify the application. However, to use this rule you need to have a certificate provided by the vendor that created the application.
Hash	A hash rule creates a hash of the file to identify it. Figure 6.11 includes a hash of the `solitaire.exe` program. Before an application starts, the system re-creates a hash of the program and compares it to the hashes in the hash rule. If it matches, the application is blocked. Even if the file is moved to a different location, the hash rule will block its execution.

◄

A *hash* is a number created from a hashing algorithm. As long as the file is unchanged, the hashing algorithm always creates the same hash.

Protecting Servers

Just as some protections apply directly to clients, others apply directly to servers. It's important to realize that these additional protections are in addition to the other steps already mentioned for both servers and clients.

For example, Chapter 1 stressed the importance of hardening a server. Hardening a server includes reducing the attack surface, keeping the system updated, enabling the firewall, and installing antivirus software. This chapter has expanded on ways to keep systems (including servers) updated. Some other methods you can consider to protect servers are included in the following sections.

Using Separate VLANs

▶ VLANs are covered in depth in *Microsoft Windows Networking Essentials* (Wiley, 2011), which covers exam 98-366.

A virtual local area network (VLAN) is a managed LAN that can be created on a Layer 3 switch. It offers improved security, increased performance, and the ability to add clients to a network segment regardless of the physical location. With this in mind, you can use a VLAN to separate your servers from your clients.

For example, Figure 6.12 shows two VLANs configured with a switch. The VLAN on the left is for the clients, and the VLAN on the right is for the servers.

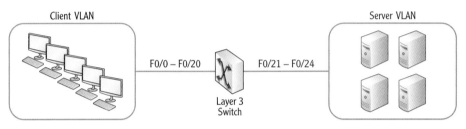

Client VLAN   Server VLAN

F0/0 – F0/20   F0/21 – F0/24

Layer 3
Switch

FIGURE 6.12 Using VLANs to separate servers

The VLAN provides improved LAN security by limiting broadcast traffic from the servers to specific ports. As shown, broadcast traffic from the servers would reach only ports F0/21 through F0/24. It wouldn't reach any of the clients in the client VLAN.

Separate VLANs can also improve performance of each VLAN segment because each VLAN is a separate broadcast domain. Broadcast traffic in the client VLAN doesn't affect the traffic in the server VLAN.

Separating Services

▶ DNS provides name resolution, resolving names to IP addresses. A server running DNS is required in a Microsoft domain.

A Windows Server 2008 server can host multiple roles. For example, it's common to have a domain controller also host a DNS service. Similarly, it's common to have a file server also act as a print server.

However, you want to avoid combining services that compete with each other in security requirements. For example, a domain controller hosts Active Directory and includes internal information, such as user accounts, groups, computer accounts, and so on. But a web server hosting an Internet site may be accessed anonymously by anyone in the world with Internet access. It's not wise to include both of these on the same server because they have dramatically different security contexts.

Windows Server 2008 supports 16 roles, as shown in Figure 6.13. Windows Server 2008 R2 also supports the Hyper-V role for virtualization, for a total of 17 roles.

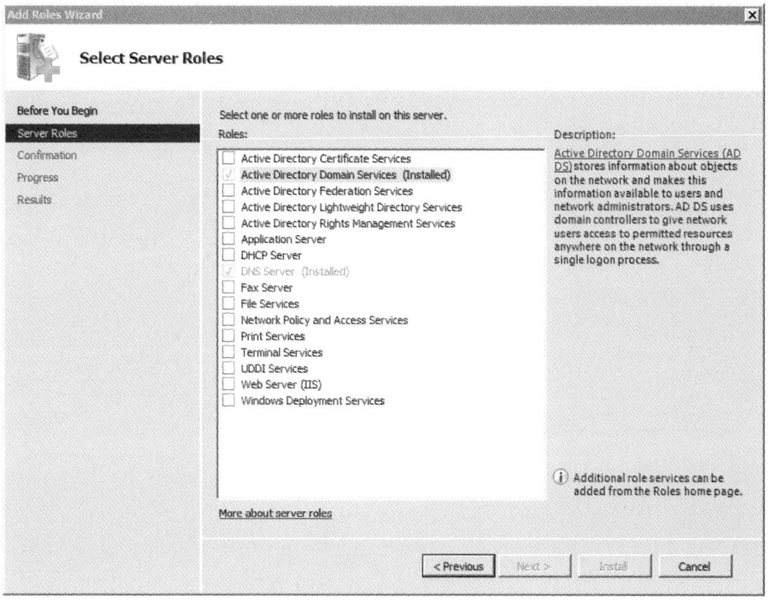

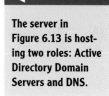

The server in Figure 6.13 is hosting two roles: Active Directory Domain Servers and DNS.

FIGURE 6.13 Roles in Windows Server 2008

The following are some guidelines you can use that identify which services you may consider combining and which you should keep separate:

Active Directory Services   It's acceptable to combine Active Directory services with one another. Active Directory Domain Services (AD DS) is the primary role for a domain and some other Active Directory services such as Active Directory Certificate Services (AD CS) expand the capabilities of Active Directory. Additionally, it's recommended to host DNS on the domain controller and enable Active Directory–integrated (ADI) DNS.

Chapter 11 presents some basics on Active Directory Certificate Services.

Application Server   An application server hosts a server application such as Microsoft's Forefront Threat Management Gateway, or Microsoft Exchange Server for email. Forefront is a security family of products. If you're using Forefront as a network firewall, you shouldn't include another role that serves data, such as a web server. However, some elements of Microsoft Exchange require a web server. You need to identify the purpose of the server application and avoid security conflicts.

DHCP and DNS   It's acceptable and common to combine the DHCP and DNS roles, but this isn't required. Both provide networking services. If you install DNS on a domain controller, you can create Active Directory–integrated DNS zones and enable secure dynamic updates.

Network Policy and Access Services   Services in this role provide protection and shouldn't be combined with any of the Active Directory roles. You can use this role to host a virtual private network (VPN) server. You can also use this role for Network Access Protection (NAP) to inspect clients for basic security before granting them access to a network.

> **Chapter 7 covers NAP in more depth.**

Fax Server, File Services, Print Services   These roles can be combined. The exception is if one of the roles is handling sensitive data. For example, if a file server is hosting sensitive research and development data requiring extra protections, you may choose to store the sensitive data on a different server. It depends on the value of the data.

Terminal Services (Remote Desktop Services on Windows Server 2008 R2)
Terminal Services (renamed Remote Desktop Services in Windows Server 2008 R2) hosts applications and/or Windows Desktops for remote users. You shouldn't install this role on a server hosting any Active Directory roles.

UDDI Services   Universal Description, Discovery, and Integration (UDDI) is used to share information about web services within an intranet or on an extranet. It's common to host this on a web server, but it shouldn't be combined with Active Directory roles.

> **When you use Server Manager to add additional roles, it will provide a warning if the roles aren't recommended together.**

Web Server (IIS)   If the web server is used to host a website for Internet access, it's usually best to limit the server to only the Web Server (IIS) role. However, a web server used internally may host additional roles. For example, an internal web server could also include the File Services and Print Services role. Some other roles—such as the Active Directory Rights Management Services—use and require this role.

Windows Deployment Services (WDS)   WDS deploys images of operating systems to systems within the network. It's common to include DHCP on a WDS server but it isn't recommended that you include any Active Directory roles on the WDS server.

You probably noted a theme in the previous descriptions. Active Directory roles often include the most sensitive data, and it's best to ensure that the Active Directory roles aren't added to servers that can be accessed publically.

Using Read-Only Domain Controllers

Traditional domain controllers in a domain all hold the same data, and the data can be changed on any of these domain controllers. However, *read-only domain controllers (RODCs)*, introduced in Windows Server 2008, don't include some sensitive data recognized as "secret" in Active Directory. Additionally, changes can't be written to the database copy that is stored on an RODC.

Using an RODC can be very useful in branch offices that don't have the same level of physical security as an organization's primary location. If the domain controller is stolen from a less secure branch office, the loss doesn't compromise sensitive secrets of the domain.

Branch offices are often separated from the main offices of a corporation by a WAN link. At times, WAN links may be slow or considered unreliable. If a domain controller isn't deployed in the remote office, and the WAN link to the main office becomes unavailable, this can affect the user's ability to log onto the domain and access network resources in the remote office. By placing a domain controller in the remote office, you can increase productivity of workers by allowing them to authenticate even if there are slow or unreliable WAN links to the main office.

Before Windows Server 2008, administrators had to weigh the benefits and risks of placing a domain controller in a remote office. If they placed a traditional domain controller in the remote office, they could improve productivity for these users. However, if the domain controller was stolen, it had the potential to compromise the entire domain. By deploying an RODC instead, administrators no longer have to sacrifice security and can effectively mitigate some of the risk associated with remote-office domain controller deployments.

Each RODC has a password replication policy (PRP) that you can configure. The PRP identifies the accounts whose passwords can be stored on the RODC. For example, if the branch office includes 10 users with regular user accounts, you can modify the PRP so that it will include the passwords for these 10 users. When each of these users first logs on, the RODC checks the credentials with a regular domain controller across the WAN link. If the user authenticates successfully, the RODC caches the password for the user. The next time the user logs on, the cached password on the RODC is used to validate the logon; and if the logon attempt is successful, the user is logged on without authentication traffic having to traverse the WAN link.

However, if a user who isn't identified in the PRP attempts to log on, the RODC will validate the password with a domain controller in the main site, but it won't cache the password. The request is authenticated via the WAN link to a regular domain controller each time the user attempts to log on.

Sensitive data in Active Directory includes account passwords. Passwords of administrator accounts aren't stored on an RODC.

Most organizations protect their servers, including their domain controllers, in locked server rooms. Branch offices often don't have the luxury of a separate secure server room.

The PRP applies to a single RODC. Every RODC can have a different PRP.

Domains that support RODCS include the following two special groups.

▶

The Allowed RODC
Password Replication
Group applies to all
RODCs in the domain.

Allowed RODC Password Replication Group   Users added to this group automatically have their passwords cached on each RODC in the domain. This is different from the PRP, which affects only a single RODC. This group is empty by default.

Denied RODC Password Replication Group   This group includes several other groups, such as the Enterprise Admins and Domain Admins groups. Users in this group (or any of the member groups) will never have their passwords cached on an RODC.

▶

If a user is in both
these groups, deny
takes precedence.
Their passwords
won't be cached on
the RODC.

Exploring DNS Security Issues

The *Domain Name System (DNS)* service is an integral part of a Microsoft domain. The primary purpose of DNS is to resolve host names to IP addresses and to identify servers running specific services.

▶

DNS is covered
in more depth in
*Microsoft Windows
Networking Essentials*
(Wiley, 2011), which
covers exam 98-366.

Three important DNS records you should be familiar with for the 98-367 exam are listed next:

A (Host) Records   An *A record* includes information used to resolve a host name to an IP address. A DNS client queries the DNS server with a host name. The DNS server looks for the A record and returns the corresponding IP address. In this context, a host is a device with an IP address. A host is commonly a computer, but it can also be a router, a firewall, or any other device with an IP address.

▶

AAAA records
provide the same
service for IPv6.
An AAAA record
resolves a host name
to an IPv6 address.

PTR (Pointer) Records   A *PTR record* is used to provide reverse lookups. A client can query a DNS server with an IP address, and if the PTR record exists, the DNS server returns the name of the host. PTR records are optional on DNS servers. If they don't exist, the DNS server can't perform reverse lookups, but DNS still works for name-to-IP address resolution.

SRV (Service) Records   *SRV records* identify computers running specific services. For example, when a user logs onto a domain, the client computer queries DNS for SRV records identifying domain controllers in the user's domain.

▶

SPF records help
protect against email
spoofing.

SPF (Sender Policy Framework) Records   *SPF records* identify the specific systems authorized to send email for a domain. They're published in public DNS servers and available for any mail server to query. For example, the wiley.com domain could have three mail servers used to send and receive email. They would publish an SPF record to identify these three servers. The SPF records provide validation for email and help prevent email spam by checking for email spoofing.

In general, spoofing refers to an effort to impersonate or masquerade as someone or something else. In email spoofing, the spoofed email looks like it's from a legitimate source, but is actually sent by a spammer. In IP spoofing, the source IP address is changed so that the data looks like it came from one IP address (such as a trusted IP), but it actually originated from an attacker.

Protecting Against Email Spoofing with SPF Records

Spammers often send out thousands of emails with a spoofed source address. The spammer may alter the From and Reply-to fields in the email header, but the actual source IP address is still included.

The source address rarely identifies the attacker. For example, Chapter 2, "Understanding Malware and Social Engineering," presented information about botnets controlled by attackers. Computers in botnets often send out spam when directed by the attacker. These emails are difficult to trace to the actual attacker. However, an SPF record can help identify spoofed email.

Imagine that an email server receives an email with a spoofed From field indicating that it came from someone at wiley.com. Embedded within the email is the source computer's IP address. The email server queries a public DNS server for an SPF record for wiley.com. The SPF record identifies the mail servers authorized to send email from wiley.com. If the email was received from a server that isn't included in the SPF record, the email is considered spoofed and is ignored or discarded.

An important point is that legitimate organizations with email servers must submit SPF records to public servers. If an SPF record doesn't exist for an organization, attackers can use this domain name more easily to spoof email. Carrying the earlier example further, if there isn't an external SPF record for the wiley.com domain, spammers can use spoof email from wiley.com. Legitimate email servers won't be able to use an SPF record in order to determine if mail appearing to come from wiley.com is valid or spoofed.

> ◀
>
> **A legitimate organization doesn't spoof email, so it's common for an email server to discard spoofed email.**

Understanding Dynamic Updates

On the Internet, DNS records are typically created manually. Someone actually puts their hands on a keyboard and enters the data to match up the host name with an IP address. Because external IP addresses are often assigned statically and they rarely change, manual DNS record creation and maintenance works fine on the Internet.

However, on internal Microsoft networks, a client can get a different IP address each time it turns on, due to Dynamic Host Configuration Protocol (DHCP). Manually creating DNS records for large numbers of internal clients just isn't manageable. Instead, the clients can be allowed to use *dynamic updates* to create or update their DNS records.

The process starts with DHCP. Most internal networks use DHCP to assign IP addresses and other TCP/IP configuration information to clients as soon as they turn on.

After DHCP assigns an IP address to a Microsoft system, the system then automatically uses dynamic update to create the DNS record. Figure 6.14 shows the overall process:

> DHCP is covered in more depth in *Microsoft Windows Networking Essentials* (Wiley, 2011), which covers exam 98-366.

1. When the client turns on, it exchanges data with DHCP to obtain TCP/IP configuration information. For example, DHCP assigns an IP address and a subnet mask, and it can also assign a default gateway and the address of the DNS server.

2. The client then communicates with DNS to create an A record based on the client's host name and the assigned IP address.

> Each of these steps has more depth. However, it's important to understand the big picture. Dynamic update means that the DNS records are updated dynamically.

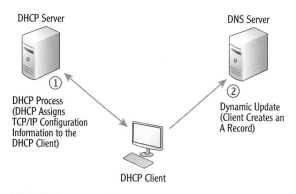

FIGURE 6.14 Dynamic update process

Using Secure Dynamic Updates

Although dynamic update streamlines the creation of records on DNS, many organizations want to secure the process. *Secure dynamic updates* provide two primary benefits.

First, only authenticated clients can create records in DNS. Computers in a domain authenticate with Active Directory. If the computer can't authenticate, the record isn't created. Additionally, you can assign permissions to DNS zones. This gives administrators greater control over the zone data.

Figure 6.15 shows the Properties page for a DNS zone. Notice that Type is Active Directory-Integrated. Notice also that Dynamic Updates is set to Secure Only. This means that only secure dynamic updates are allowed. Regular dynamic updates (not secure dynamic updates) will be blocked.

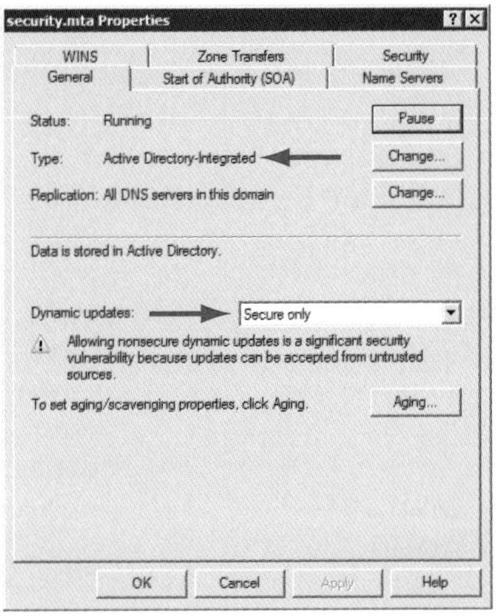

FIGURE 6.15 Dynamic update process

This brings up two very important points to remember if you're interested in configuring secure dynamic updates:

The DNS Zone Must Be an Active Directory–Integrated (ADI) Zone   Active Directory manages an ADI zone, reducing administration. Overall, this makes DNS easier to maintain. If it isn't an ADI zone, you won't have the option of selecting Secure Only for Dynamic Updates.

DNS Must Be Installed on a Domain Controller   You can only create an ADI zone if DNS is installed on a domain controller. If DNS is running on a member server, you can only create primary and secondary zones, but not an ADI zone. In other words, if a server isn't hosting Active Directory, you can't create an Active Directory–integrated zone on the server.

Microsoft documentation consistently recommends installing DNS on a domain controller. Because Active Directory relies on DNS so much, this makes a lot of sense. Additionally, Microsoft consistently recommends converting DNS zones to ADI zones.

The Essentials and Beyond

In this chapter, you learned about some common techniques used to protect both clients and servers. User Account Control separates administrative actions from regular user actions and helps protect against malware. You can configure automatic updates for your systems to ensure that they stay updated; or, if you want more control, you can use WSUS or SCCM to deploy updates. WSUS is free, and SCCM is an add-on server product. Offline folders give users access to shared data even when they aren't connected to the network. You can encrypt data in offline folders to provide an added layer of protection. You can also use software-restriction policies to restrict what software runs on a client. Some techniques used to protect servers include using separate VLANs, ensuring that services don't have competing security requirements, and using RODCs. DNS SPF records protect against spam by detecting email spoofing attempts. If you use ADI zones for DNS, you can also implement secure dynamic updates.

Additional Exercises

▶ Identify the current settings for User Account Control on your system.

▶ Determine if your system is using Automatic Updates.

▶ Configure your system to encrypt offline folders.

▶ Determine if software-restriction policies are defined locally on your system.

To compare your answers to the author's, please visit **www.sybex.com/go/ securityessentials**.

Review Questions

1. What causes the Windows 7 Desktop to dim when a user attempts an action requiring administrative approval?

2. True or false: If files are encrypted on a server using EFS, they're automatically encrypted when a user uses offline folders.

3. Which of the following can't be used to update a system?

    A. Automatic Updates   **C.** SCCM

    B. WSUS   **D.** DNS

4. True or false: You can use Group Policy to configure all computers in a domain to use automatic updates.

5. True or false: After Microsoft has released security updates, clients are no longer vulnerable to the exploits that the updates resolve.

(Continues)

THE ESSENTIALS AND BEYOND *(Continued)*

6. What kind of DNS record resolves an IP address to a host name?

   A. A record   **C.** SPF record

   B. PTR record   **D.** MX record

7. You want to deploy a domain controller to a branch office. However, the branch office has very little physical security. What should you do?

   A. Don't deploy the domain controller.

   B. Deploy DNS with the domain controller, and use secure dynamic updates.

   C. Deploy a read-only domain controller (RODC).

   D. Remove Administrator accounts before deploying the domain controller.

8. True or false: You should separate DNS from Active Directory Domain Services for enhanced security.

9. True or false: You should separate Terminal Services from Active Directory Domain Services for enhanced security.

10. True or false: You can enable secure dynamic updates only on DNS servers installed on a domain controller.

Protecting a Network

Attackers are out there constantly trying to attack networks. Some use common well-known methods, and others are trying to learn and exploit new methods. It's important to have a basic understanding of the different types of attacks used today and some common methods you can employ to protect a network.

Network-based firewalls are commonly used by organizations with Internet access. They provide network isolation for the internal network. There are many different firewall choices; however, many organizations use hardware-based firewall appliances that provide multiple layers of protection.

Network Access Protection (NAP) is a new technology in Windows Server 2008 used to inspect clients for health. Administrators can define what a healthy client is, and NAP can provide basic protection by isolating or refusing access to unhealthy clients.

You can use different protocol security methods to provide additional network protection. For example, protocols such as IPsec can encrypt traffic to ensure confidentiality. This chapter includes these concepts in the following topics:

▶ **Identifying common attack methods**

▶ **Exploring firewalls**

▶ **Exploring Network Access Protection**

▶ **Identifying protocol security methods**

Identifying Common Attack Methods

Attackers use several well-known methods to attempt to breach networks. Actual attacks are constantly evolving. Although individual attacks will vary, they usually fall into one of the common attack methods discussed in this section.

Many organizations deploy Intrusion Detection Systems (IDSs) to detect and mitigate active attacks. At the very least, an IDS can detect and report the attack to administrators. IDSs that are more sophisticated can respond to attacks and take steps to protect the network environment and block the attack.

For example, an active IDS may detect an attack from a specific IP address and change the Access Control List (ACL) on a router to block all traffic from this computer.

The following sections describe some general attack methods. It's important to remember that attackers continuously modify their attack methods. At the same time, security professionals continuously modify their protection methods. Attackers discover new vulnerabilities and launch new attacks. Security professionals create and implement new protection methods. Attacks and protection methods are constantly evolving.

As a result, an attack that was successful yesterday may no longer be successful today. However, some of the same attack methodologies are still used in an attempt to breach network environments.

Denial of Service

A *denial of service (DoS)* attack is any attack on a system designed to prevent the system from providing a service. For example, a web server serves web pages to Internet clients. A DoS attack against a web server attempts to prevent it from serving web pages to requesting clients.

DoS attacks can be carried out in a variety of ways. Some DoS attacks attempt to consume a system's basic resources, such as its processing power or memory. While the system is processing the DoS attack, it doesn't have enough resources to process legitimate requests. Worse, a DoS attack may cause a system to crash.

A common DoS attack is a *SYN flood* attack. To understand how the attack works, it's important to understand how the TCP handshake process works (see Figure 7.1). In the Figure, Joe's computer is establishing a session with a server.

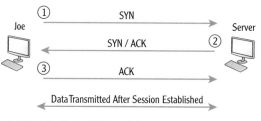

FIGURE 7.1 TCP handshake process

Joe's computer starts by sending a packet with the synchronize (SYN) flag set. When the server receives the packet, it responds with another packet with both

---

Changing the ACL on the router is also known as implementing a *packet filter*.

A flag is simply a single binary bit set to a 1. For example, the SYN flag is set by setting a specific bit in the TCP packet to a 1.

the SYN and ACK (acknowledges) flags set. Joe's computer then completes the three-way handshake by sending a third packet with the ACK flag set.

At this point, both computers have an established TCP session. They both have assurances that the other computer is operational, and they're able to communicate with it. Data is transmitted between the two computers after the session is established.

However, in a SYN flood attack, the attacker withholds the third packet. Imagine Joe extending his hand to shake hands with you: you reach out to shake his hand, but at the last second Joe pulls his hand away.

Worse, in a SYN flood attack, the attacking computer continues to send SYN packets. Whereas you or I may stop extending our hand to someone who consistently pulls theirs away, a server will continue to try to complete these sessions unless it recognizes them as an attack.

A SYN flood attack can initiate hundreds of TCP sessions on a computer. If the attack isn't stopped, it can consume the server's resources, preventing the server from responding to legitimate requests. In some situations, a SYN flood attack can cause a system to crash.

Distributed Denial of Service

A *distributed denial of service (DDoS)* attack is a DoS attack initiated from multiple clients. For example, if thousands of computers send a simple ping request to a server on the Internet, the server can get overwhelmed trying to answer these requests. While trying to answer all the pings, the server is much slower in responding to legitimate requests.

A botnet can include thousands or even millions of clones or zombies. A botnet controller can direct these systems to launch an attack against a specific system at a specific time. For example, each of these systems can be instructed to launch a SYN flood attack against a system at the same time.

Sniffing Attack

A sniffing attack captures and analyzes traffic transmitted over a network. Attackers use protocol analyzers (also called *sniffers* or *packet sniffers*) to capture the traffic. If the traffic isn't encrypted, the attacker can potentially view the information being transmitted, because it's captured in clear text. Although the process can be tedious, a determined attacker can gain a significant amount of data from a sniffing attack.

It's also possible for an attacker to connect a sniffer to a router or switch via a wireless access point (WAP). The sniffer captures the traffic, and the WAP trans-

A SYN flood attack is also called an *IP half-scan attack* because instead of the attacker sending two packets (the SYN and ACK packets), it sends only one (the SYN packet).

◄

◄

Most IDSs can recognize SYN flood attacks and block them.

Many systems on the Internet block ping requests to block this type of attack. However, many other types of DDoS attacks are possible using other protocols.

◄

◄

Chapter 2 introduced the concept of botnets. Botnets are controlled by attackers, and the zombies are the controlled computers in the botnets.

◄

Sniffing attacks are also called *eavesdropping* attacks. The attacker listens in, or eavesdrops, on the conversation.

mits it wirelessly. The attacker can sit in a company's parking lot with a laptop computer, receive the wireless transmissions, and analyze them.

Microsoft Network Monitor is an example of a sniffer. It can be used for legitimate troubleshooting purposes, and it's also used by attackers to capture and analyze traffic. Figure 7.2 shows Network Monitor open with a saved capture.

Network Monitor is covered in *Microsoft Windows Networking Essentials* (Wiley, 2011), which covers exam 98-366. It includes steps to download, install, and run Network Monitor.

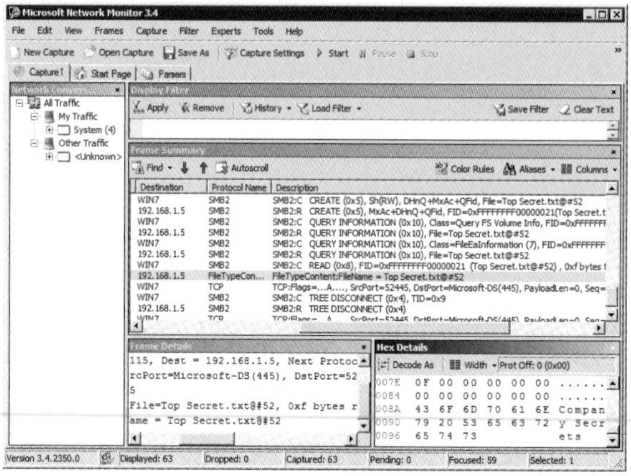

FIGURE 7.2 Network Monitor capturing company secrets

In Figure 7.2, a user accessed a file named Top Secret.txt over the network. The file included the text "Company Secrets." One of the captured packets used to access this file is selected in the Frame Summary section. The Frame Details section provides additional details on the packet. The Hex Details section shows the actual text ("Company Secrets") in the file.

One of the ways to protect against this type of attack is to use strong physical security. Switches and routers should be protected in a locked wiring closet or server room to prevent attackers from accessing them.

Chapter 9 discusses some common security methods used within organizations.

Capturing FTP and Telnet Traffic

Protocols such as File Transfer Protocol (FTP) and Telnet send data across the network in clear text. If an attacker is able to capture FTP and Telnet transmissions, they can read the data using a sniffer like Network Monitor. This includes usernames, passwords, and any other data sent in the transmission.

However, it's possible to secure transmissions by encrypting the traffic. For example, both FTP and Telnet can be secured with Secure Shell (SSH) or Internet Protocol Security (IPsec).

In addition to strong physical security, you can encrypt data to protect it as it traverses the network. For example, IPsec can encrypt data going across the wire. IPsec is covered later in this chapter.

Sniffers can be run in one of two modes: nonpromiscuous mode or promiscuous mode:

Nonpromiscuous Mode The sniffer captures only data sent directly to or from the system capturing the traffic. Each frame transmitted includes a source and destination IP address. If neither of these matches the IP address of the computer collecting the capture, then the frame isn't recorded. In other words, the sniffer won't capture unicast traffic sent to and from other systems. Microsoft Network Monitor runs in this mode by default but can be switched to promiscuous mode.

Promiscuous Mode The sniffer captures any traffic that reaches the interface card of the system capturing the traffic, regardless of the source and destination IP addresses. Most sniffers can operate in promiscuous mode. Although older versions of Microsoft Network Monitor don't operate in promiscuous mode, the current version does.

Spoofing Attack

A *spoofing attack* is any attack where the attacker attempts to impersonate or masquerade as someone or something else. In an IP-spoofing attack, the source IP address may be modified to make a packet look like it came from somewhere else.

As an example, a *local area network denial (LAND) attack* spoofs the source address within a TCP SYN packet. More specifically, it changes the source IP address so that it's the same as the destination address. The result is that a successful LAND attack causes a system to repeatedly reply to itself.

Port Scan

A port scan attempts to discover what ports are listening on a system. Ports 0 to 1023 are well-known ports used for specific protocols. For example, port 80 is the well-known port for HTTP. If a port scan discovers port 80 open, the attacker knows that HTTP is very likely running on the system. If HTTP is running, it's very possible this is a web server.

The attacker will take additional steps to verify that HTTP traffic is being accepted and then try to determine what web server is running. For example, it could be a Microsoft web server running Internet Information Services (IIS), or it could be a Linux system running Apache's Web Server.

Encryption helps preserve confidentiality of data. Unauthorized personnel aren't able to read encrypted data.

Network Monitor refers to promiscuous mode as P-mode.

Chapter 6 introduced spoofing in the context of email spoofing and how SPF records can help prevent against email spoofing.

It's possible to use a well-known port for a different protocol. The open port doesn't prove the associated protocol is running, but it does give a good hint.

Table 7.1 provides a review of many of the commonly used ports. For a full list of commonly used ports, you can look at the web page hosted by the Internet Assigned Numbers Authority (IANA) here: `www.iana.org/assignments/port-numbers`.

TABLE 7.1 Commonly used ports

Port	Protocol	Comments
20, 21	FTP	File Transfer Protocol.
22	SSH	Secure Shell.
23	Telnet	Can be secured with SSH.
25	SMTP	Simple Mail Transfer Protocol. Used to send email.
110	POP3	Post Office Protocol. Used to receive email.
143	IMAP4	Internet Message Access Protocol. Used when email is stored on the server.
80	HTTP	Hypertext Transfer Protocol. Used for web pages.
443	HTTPS	Secure HTTP. Common uses Secure Sockets Layer (SSL) for encryption.
53	DNS	Domain Name Service. Used to resolve names to IP addresses, IP addresses to names, and more.
88	Kerberos	Network authentication protocol used by Microsoft Active Directory.
389	LDAP	Lightweight Directory Access Protocol. Language used to communicate with Active Directory.
636	SLDAP	Secure LDAP. LDAP communications encrypted with SSL or Transport Layer Security (TLS).
137, 138, 139	NetBIOS	Commonly used in Microsoft networks to access file servers. Not used on the Internet.
161, 162	SNMP	Simple Network Management Protocol. Used to manage network devices such as routers and switches.

(Continues)

Ports and protocols are covered in *Microsoft Windows Networking Essentials* (Wiley, 2011), which covers exam 98-366.

TABLE 7.1   *(Continued)*

Port	Protocol	Comments
3389	Remote Desktop Services	Used to connect to systems remotely in a Microsoft network.
1701	L2TP	Layer 2 Tunneling Protocol. Used to establish virtual private network (VPN) connections.
1723	PPTP	Point-to-Point Tunneling Protocol. Used to establish VPN connections.

Exploring Firewalls

One of the primary methods of controlling traffic in and out of a network is with a firewall. Firewalls filter traffic using different techniques. Some of the basic types of firewalls are as follows:

▶ Packet-filtering (stateless)

▶ Stateful-filtering

▶ Content-filtering

▶ Application-layer-filtering

A packet-filtering firewall filters packets based on IP addresses, ports, and some protocols. If you want to allow traffic through a firewall from only specific computers, you can create rules using these computers' IP addresses. Similarly, you can create rules to allow or block traffic based on ports. For example, the well-known port for HTTP is port 80. By blocking port 80, you block HTTP traffic.

One of the problems with a packet-filtering firewall is that it can examine packets only individually. It can't identify whether the traffic is part of an ongoing conversation. The vulnerability is that an attacker can insert malicious traffic that meets the packet-filtering rules but hasn't been requested by the client.

In contrast, a stateful-filtering firewall filters traffic based on the state of network connections. It can monitor traffic streams and determine if traffic is a part of an ongoing connection. If a packet isn't part of a known connection, a stateful firewall can block it.

◀

Firewalls are also covered in *Microsoft Windows Networking Essentials* (Wiley, 2011), which covers exam 98-366.

◀

Advanced firewalls can combine all of the filtering methods in a single firewall.

Stateless firewalls are typically faster than stateful firewalls. However, stateful firewalls can detect unauthorized traffic interjections and malicious attacks.

◀

▶

Chapter 2 mentioned how content-filtering firewalls can block some malware.

Content-filtering firewalls can block traffic based on the content. For example, malware is often delivered via spam, embedded as a zip file or another type of attachment. The content filter can detect undesirable content and block or remove it. Content filtering is often done on email servers to filter spam and unwanted attachments.

An application-layer filtering firewall filters traffic based on an application or service. The firewall has a separate component for each application protocol (such as HTTP or FTP) that it filters. These firewall components examine the traffic using that protocol to allow and block certain types of traffic. For example, HTTP Get commands (which allow retrieval of documents or files) could be allowed, whereas Put commands (which post documents or files) could be blocked. In practice, software-based application-layer filters are CPU-intensive and used sparingly. On the other hand, hardware-based application-layer filtering firewalls provide better performance.

A hardware-based firewall is a dedicated security device. It's more efficient and provides more comprehensive protection than a software-based firewall.

▶

Comparing Hardware-Based and Software-Based Firewalls

Windows Server 2008 and Windows 7 include built-in software-based firewalls. A *software-based firewall* is an additional feature of the operating system. In contrast, most network firewalls are *hardware-based firewalls*. A hardware-based firewall is a dedicated security device that provides network security and helps to isolate a network from unwanted traffic. It has software running within it, but the software is completely dedicated to security.

▶

The host-based Windows firewall in Windows 7 and Windows Server 2008 is installed and enabled by default.

You may also hear the terms *host-based* and *network-based firewalls*. The firewalls built into host operating systems (such as Windows 7 and Windows Server 2008) are host-based firewalls. Dedicated hardware firewalls are typically network-based and provide protection for a network rather than just a single host or a single computer.

For example, Figure 7.3 shows a hardware-based firewall placed at the boundary between the Internet and an intranet. In the figure, all traffic into or out of the network goes through the network-based hardware firewall. Additionally, each server and desktop computer has a software-based firewall enabled.

Many vendors sell firewall appliances. A firewall appliance simplifies the complexity of the firewall. It's a dedicated hardware device that an organization can purchase, plug in, and begin using without much configuration.

The word *appliance* is meant to evoke an image of a simple-to-use household appliance like a microwave oven. You don't have to understand how a microwave oven works to use it. You put a bag inside and press some buttons, and a minute or two later you're munching popcorn.

Similarly, you don't have to understand the complexity of a firewall appliance to use it. You plug it in and enter some basic configuration (or accept the defaults), and it starts protecting your network. Firewall appliances are simple to operate, but you shouldn't underestimate their capabilities. They can efficiently filter a wide assortment of traffic with minimal administrative intervention.

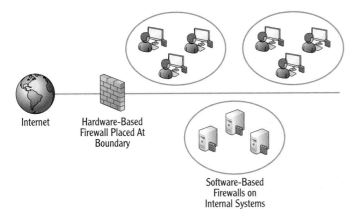

Internet   Hardware-Based
            Firewall Placed At
            Boundary

Software-Based
Firewalls on
Internal Systems

FIGURE 7.3 Hardware-based vs. software-based firewalls

FIREWALLS AND DEFENSE IN DEPTH

When you're using firewalls, it isn't a choice of whether to use a host-based firewall to protect individual systems or to protect a network with a network-based firewall. Instead, most organizations use both. This is part of a defense-in-depth strategy.

Although the goal of a network-based firewall is to block unwanted traffic from entering the network, traffic can still get in through other methods. For example, if a user unknowingly brings in malware on a USB flash drive, the network-based firewall won't detect it. If the malware has a worm component that attempts to locate and infect computers on the network, the host-based firewalls provide a layer of protection for these computers.

Comparing UTMs and SCMs

Firewalls continue to improve in capabilities and functionality. A common trend with firewall appliances is to bundle multiple capabilities within a single hardware firewall. Two recent additions to the firewall scene are *secure content management (SCM)* firewalls and *unified threat management (UTM)* firewalls.

▶

Spam is the primary delivery method of malware. By reducing spam, malware risks are also reduced.

SCM appliances are primarily focused on filtering email and web-based traffic. They examine email and filter out spam and email attachments that may contain malware. Some can also work as proxy servers.

A proxy server acts on behalf of the client computers in the internal network to retrieve web content from the Internet. Proxy servers reduce usage of Internet bandwidth by caching retrieved data. When one user retrieves data from the Internet, the proxy server caches the data. When another user requests the same data, the proxy server sends the data from cache instead of retrieving it from the Internet again. Most proxy servers can block access to restricted websites based on an organization's security policy. Additionally, most proxy servers can check and validate content to block malware.

▶

Microsoft's Forefront Threat Management Gateway is an example of a UTM firewall.

Although an SCM can provide excellent protection for email and proxy services, the UTM expands this to include much more. UTM firewalls provide several layers of protection. For example, the Microsoft Forefront family includes the Microsoft Forefront Threat Management Gateway (TMG). The Microsoft Forefront TMG combines several benefits, including the following, into a single product:

▶

NAT is explained in more depth in the "Isolating a Network with NAT" section later in this chapter.

Routing Features   The routing component can provide basic routing between the internal network and the Internet. The router includes packet-filtering capabilities and also includes network address translation (NAT) to translate private and public IP addresses.

Firewall Security Features   The firewall element inspects and filters traffic to protect against attacks and malicious software. It provides anti-malware protection, content filtering, stateful filtering, and application-layer filtering.

Intrusion-Detection Features   The intrusion-detection element identifies and blocks many common attacks. For example, it can detect and block IP half-scan attacks (SYN flood attacks), port scans, and more.

Network Performance Features   Web-caching capabilities reduce Internet bandwidth usage via proxy server caching. When one user retrieves data from the Internet, Forefront TMG caches the data. When another user requests the same data, Forefront TMG sends the data from cache instead of retrieving it from the Internet again.

Remote-Access Features   The VPN component provides internal network access for remote clients.

In summary, the SCM focuses primarily on filtering email and other web-based content. A UTM is much broader in scope. Additionally, because a single vendor provides the UTM, the components complement and work with each other even when providing security for different components. A UTM often uses similar or unified interfaces, reducing the time required to learn the different elements.

Providing Remote Access via a VPN

A VPN provides access to an organization's private internal network via a public network such as the Internet. Clients first connect to the Internet and then connect to the VPN server. Traffic to and from a VPN server is protected using tunneling protocols such as PPTP, L2TP, and SSTP. Additionally, clients must authenticate before being granted access to the internal network.

Although the service provided by a VPN is highly valuable to organizations, it does present significant risks. Most VPNs employ several security methods to ensure that unauthorized users aren't able to use the VPN and access the internal network. Integrating the VPN solution with other firewall features in a unified solution helps minimize the risks.

Isolating Servers on Perimeter Networks

Many organizations host servers that are accessible to the Internet. If these servers are placed directly on the Internet, they're highly vulnerable to attackers. If they're placed directly on an organization's internal network, allowing access to these Internet-facing servers increases risks to other resources on the internal network.

To help mitigate these risks, organizations use *perimeter networks* to protect Internet-facing servers. A perimeter network is a network that is protected from the Internet but also isn't directly on the intranet. For example, Figure 7.4 shows a perimeter network protecting a web server, a VPN server, and an email server. This is sometimes called a *back-to-back configuration*.

The external firewall provides a layer of protection from the Internet for the servers in the perimeter network. The internal firewall provides additional protection to all the systems on the internal network. Clients that are granted access to servers in the perimeter network are typically blocked from accessing resources on the internal network.

The web server in Figure 7.4 host websites accessible from the Internet. The email server sends and receives email via the Internet.

An *Internet-facing server* is any server accessible from the Internet.

A perimeter network is also called a *demilitarized zone (DMZ)*.

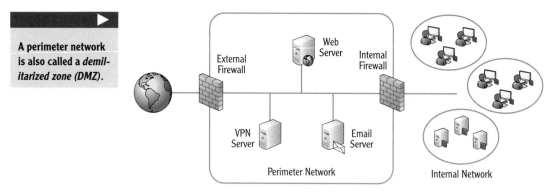

FIGURE 7.4 Perimeter network

Perimeter networks are typically created using two hardware-based firewalls, as shown in Figure 7.4. However, it's also possible to create a perimeter network with a single firewall, as shown in Figure 7.5.

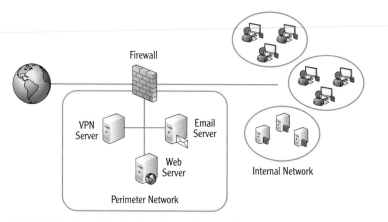

FIGURE 7.5 Single firewall creating a perimeter network

Vendors often provide configuration best practice documents to assist you in the initial configuration of a complex firewall.

In Figure 7.5, the single firewall has three network interface cards (NICs). One NIC is connected to the Internet, one NIC is connected to the perimeter network, and the third NIC is connected to the internal network. This type of configuration is often referred to as a *three-pronged* or a *three-legged* firewall configuration.

A single firewall perimeter network is less expensive because only a single hardware firewall is needed. However, it's more complex and sometimes harder to configure. The complexity adds to the possibilities for errors. If it's not configured correctly, the benefits of the firewall can be completely circumvented. Additionally, it represents a single point of failure for security: If it fails, an attacker can access the perimeter network and the intranet.

Using Honeypots

A *honeypot* is a server set up to entice attackers. It looks like a live production server and appears to be holding actual data. However, its purpose is only to attract attackers. Administrators intentionally lock down a honeypot partially (or even sloppily), making it easy for attackers to get in.

Honeypots provide two primary benefits. First, they lure attackers away from live networks. While attackers are poking around on the honeypot, they aren't attacking the live network. Second, a honeypot allows security personnel to record and observe the attackers and learn more about the attacking methodologies in use.

Honeypots are often placed in the perimeter network. Although it's possible to place a honeypot in an internal network, it's less likely that it will be discovered and attacked in an internal network.

◀

A *honeynet* is a group of two or more servers emulating a live network. Honeynets are often hosted in virtual networks by a single physical server.

Isolating a Network with NAT

Addresses on internal networks use private IP addresses defined by RFC 1918. These addresses aren't assigned to any computers on the Internet but are assigned to computers on internal networks. The private IP ranges are as follows:

- ► 10.0.0.1 0 through 10.255.255.255
- ► 172.16.0.1 0 through 172.31.255.255
- ► 192.168.1.1 0 through 192.168.255.255

In contrast, all IP addresses on the Internet are public IP addresses. If you're using a firewall between the Internet and your internal network, you need to translate these addresses between private and public. Most firewalls include a routing component that supports *network address translation (NAT)*.

NAT translates private IP addresses to public IP addresses, and translates public ones back to private. NAT helps isolate the internal computers because these computers have private IP addresses and aren't directly accessible through the Internet.

Exploring Network Access Protection

Windows Server 2008 includes *Network Access Protection (NAP)* as part of the Network Policy and Access Services server role. NAP can inspect each client attempting to connect to a network and determine if it meets certain requirements before allowing it to connect. Unhealthy clients are isolated or denied network access, whereas healthy clients are granted access.

NAP includes four primary capabilities that work together to ensure that only healthy clients connect. They're as follows:

- ▶ Health-state validation
- ▶ Limited access for unhealthy clients
- ▶ Automatic remediation for unhealthy clients
- ▶ Periodic compliance checking for healthy clients

An administrator defines characteristics of a healthy client, such as ensuring that the firewall is enabled, all current updates are installed, and anti-malware software is installed and up to date. NAP inspects the clients when they try to connect. Healthy clients are granted access, and unhealthy clients are disconnected or quarantined based on the NAP policy.

Quarantined clients only have access to a restricted network that includes remediation servers. The remediation servers in the restricted network include the resources needed for the clients to comply with the health policy. For example, a remediation server may have the updates that the clients need installed to be considered healthy.

Some remediation steps are simple, such as enabling and configuring a firewall, or connecting to a specific server in the restricted network to download and install updates. You can configure the NAP policy for automatic remediation. This allows NAP to modify and update unhealthy clients without user intervention.

After a client has been validated as healthy, NAP periodically checks the client to ensure that it remains in a healthy state. For example, if a NAP policy requires a client to have the firewall enabled, but the user disables the firewall while connected, the NAP policy will detect the change. Depending on the remediation policy procedures, the client could be disconnected completely, have access restricted to the remediation server's network, or be automatically reconfigured for compliance.

Understanding NAP Components

Several components of a NAP solution work together. They're detailed here:

NAP isn't supported on clients before Windows XP Service Pack 3.

System Health Agents   Windows XP Service Pack 3, Windows Vista, and Windows 7 have System Health Agents (SHAs) that regularly run in the background and check the status of a client. These SHAs identify the status of the computer, such as whether antivirus software is installed and up to date, whether the system is using Automatic Updates, whether the system has the firewall enabled, and more. The SHAs report the status in the form of a Statement of Health. A system will have multiple SHAs checking different components, and each SHA creates a separate Statement of Health. Windows Server 2008 servers don't have SHAs, so they can't be NAP clients. However, Windows Server 2008 R2 servers can be NAP clients.

System Health Validators   Administrators define a healthy state for a client in a Windows Security System Health Validator (SHV) on a NAP server. For example, Figure 7.6 shows the Windows Security SHV for a Windows Vista system. NAP includes a built-in SHV, and you can create additional SHVs to check for different requirements based on the needs of the organization. An SHV is then used to define the requirements for a health policy.

◀

Different clients have different enforceable capabilities. For example, you can enforce the installation of spyware protection on Windows 7 and Windows Vista, but not on Windows XP Service Pack 3.

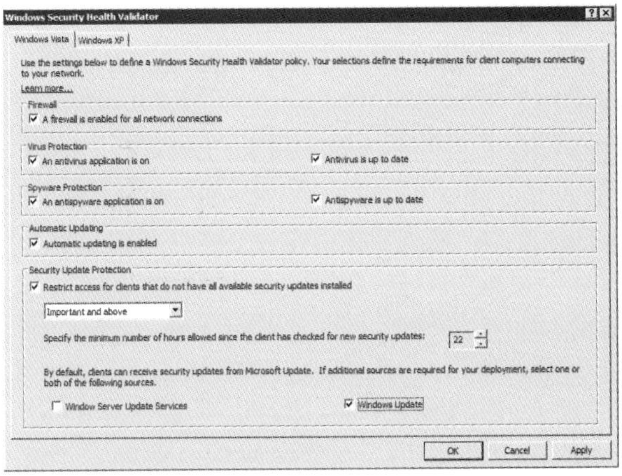

FIGURE 7.6 SHV for NAP

Health Policy   Health policies are created on a health server. They identify what SHVs to use for the different clients in the environment. They also define the response for nonhealthy clients. For example, the health policy can be configured for monitoring only, or to isolate clients and limit access. In a monitoring-only environment, client health is reported and logged, but clients access isn't restricted. This allows administrators to determine the effect of a health policy before enforcing it.

System Statement of Health   The NAP server collects the individual Statements of Health from clients and compares them against the requirements identified in the health policy. It then compiles these into a single System Statement of Health for each client. This System Statement of Health identifies whether the client is in compliance with the health policy or not.

Health Registration Authority A separate component of NAP is the Health Registration Authority (HRA). If a client meets the requirements in a health policy, the HRA retrieves a health certificate for the client.

Health Certificate The health certificate is used by the client to gain access to network resources. If a client doesn't have a health certificate, the health policy may restrict clients to a restricted network.

Restricted Network If the health policy is enforced, clients can be quarantined to a restricted network that includes remediation servers. For example, a remediation server can deploy updates for the operating system or deploy and update anti-malware software.

You can add the Network Policy And Access Services role to a Windows Server 2008 server. This role includes all the components to support a NAP solution.

Evaluating Client Health with VPN Enforcement

One way you can use NAP is to validate the health of VPN clients using VPN enforcement. Look at Figure 7.7 as you follow along with this description.

The NAP health policy server and Health Registration Authority components can be on the same server.

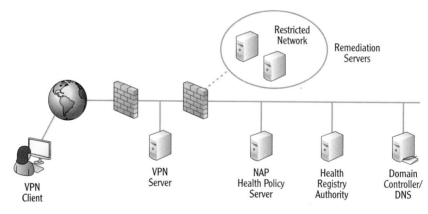

FIGURE 7.7 NAP used for VPN enforcement

The VPN client connects to the Internet and then uses a tunneling protocol (such as SSTP) to connect to the VPN server. The client then passes credentials (such as a username and password) to the VPN server to authenticate. The VPN server validates these credentials with a domain controller. Up to this point, there's no difference between a regular VPN server and a VPN server using NAP.

A NAP server configured with VPN enforcement then takes additional steps. It queries the NAP health policy server for the health requirements documented in the SHV (shown in Figure 7.6). It also queries the client to create a System Statement of Health. The information is passed to the HRA; and if the client meets the requirements, the HRA obtains a health certificate for the client. The client is then granted access to the network.

Unhealthy clients' access can be limited to the restricted network until they meet the health requirements.

Using Other NAP Enforcement Methods

VPN enforcement is valuable to many organizations to ensure that VPN clients are healthy before connecting, but you can also use NAP to enforce other requirements. The three other enforcement methods are as follows:

DHCP Enforcement   Dynamic Host Configuration Protocol (DHCP) issues TCP/IP configuration information such as an IP address, a subnet mask, and so on. You can use NAP to validate a client's health prior to issuing this TCP/IP information. Doing so prevents unhealthy clients from accessing the network with DHCP-assigned IP addresses.

> **IPsec can provide confidentiality, integrity, and authentication for data transmissions.**
> ◄

IPsec Enforcement   IPsec can require computer authentication before transmitting traffic, and it can also require encryption of transmitted traffic. IPsec enforcement allows you to verify that clients can communicate with IPsec and are configured to do so. If the client's IPsec policy is compliant with the NAP IPsec health policy, the HRA obtains a health certificate on behalf of the client.

> ◄
> **You can use 802.1x enforcement to control routing within a network. This provides isolation for subnets and prevents access to the isolated networks by unhealthy clients.**

802.1x Enforcement   802.1x is an authentication protocol that can provide port-based access control for network devices such as managed switches, routers, and wireless access points. You can use 802.1x enforcement to control access through these network devices. For example, clients with health certificates can be granted full access. Clients without health certificates can have their access limited to only specific ports, and only specific networks. The network devices must be compatible with 802.1x.

Identifying NAP Requirements

NAP has some specific requirements. Some requirements are directly related to the clients, and others are directly related to the servers.

Clients don't have to be members of a domain for NAP enforcement.

Client operating systems supported by NAP are Windows XP (with at least Service Pack 3), Windows Vista, and Windows 7. These clients include the SHAs that report the client's health with Statements of Health. SHVs running on the NAP server identify the differences between the operating systems to create a separate System Statement of Health.

Several server components must be running on Windows Server 2008 or Windows Server 2008 R2 to support NAP. The components and their roles and services are identified in Table 7.2.

TABLE 7.2   NAP server requirements

NAP Component	Roles and Services
Network Access Protection health policy server	Network Policy And Access Services, Network Access Protection
HRA server	Network Policy And Access Services, HRA service, web server (IIS)
Virtual Private Network (VPN) enforcement server	Network Policy And Access Services, Routing And Remote Access Services
DHCP enforcement server	Network Policy And Access Services, DHCP role

The HRA can include a certification authority (CA), or certificates can be issued by a CA running on a different operating system. The CA can be running a Microsoft or non-Microsoft operating system. Remediation servers can be running any version of the operating system needed to provide the remediation service.

When you're using 802.1x enforcement, only managed switches can be used. Unmanaged switches don't support the configuration requirements for port-based authentication.

Identifying Protocol Security Methods

Several protocol security methods are available to increase security. One of the steps you can take is to encrypt data as it traverses the network, to protect it from sniffing attacks. Additionally, DNS has improved protocol security in the form of security extensions that you can use to increase DNS security. The following sections cover some common methods.

IPsec

Internet Protocol Security (IPsec) is an encryption protocol used to provide secure communications between two computers over a network. It can provide confidentiality, integrity, and authentication for these communications.

You can use IPsec for mutual authentication between both computers in the network session. You can also use IPsec to encrypt data before it's transmitted and to prevent sniffing attacks.

IPsec includes two primary mechanisms:

Authentication Header (AH)   AH is used to provide authentication and integrity. Both systems in the IPsec transmission use authentication methods to prove who they are. Additionally, each packet is hashed, and the hash of the packet is placed in the AH field and sent with the packet. The hash provides integrity for the packet. IPsec uses this hash to determine whether the received packet has been modified.

Encapsulating Security Protocol (ESP)   ESP encrypts the data and provides confidentiality. Encrypted data captured with a sniffer isn't readable. AH is also used when ESP is used to provide authentication and integrity for the data.

You can assign IPsec policies to individual computers or to multiple computers with Group Policy. Figure 7.8 shows the IP Security Policies node within the Default Domain Policy on a Windows Server 2008 domain controller. The three IPsec policies are the default policies, but none of them are assigned by default:

A *sniffer* is a protocol analyzer that can capture traffic transmitted over the network. The attacker can read data transmitted in clear text, but it can't read encrypted data.

A *hash* is simply a number. It's calculated at the source and destination, and if the hashes are different, it shows that the data has lost integrity.

These default IPsec policies aren't available by default through the Local Security Policy on Windows Server 2008. They're available by default only in a domain Group Policy object.

F I G U R E   7 . 8 IPsec default policies in Group Policy

Client (Respond Only)   Computers with this policy can establish IPsec sessions. However, these clients never initiate an IPsec session.

Secure Server (Require Security)   Computers with this policy assigned always require IPsec sessions. When a session is initiated, the computer with this policy requests an IPsec session. If the other system is unable to establish an IPsec session, the communication session is ended.

Server (Request Security)   Computers with this policy always attempt to establish an IPsec session. However, if the other system is unable to establish an IPsec session, the communication can still continue. Systems with this policy can successfully establish IPsec sessions with any other system having an IPsec policy assigned.

As an example, you may have a financial server holding proprietary data that you want to protect. Any time users access data on this server over the network, you want to ensure that the data is encrypted with IPsec. You can assign the Secure Server (Require Security) policy to the financial server.

You would also assign the Client (Respond Only) IPsec policy to any system that will connect to the financial server. When a client connects to the financial server, the IPsec policy on the server attempts to initiate an IPsec session with the client. If the client has the Client (Respond Only) IPsec policy or the Server (Request Security) IPsec policy, it can respond and create an IPsec session.

Systems with the Client (Respond Only) policy can also connect to other systems that don't require IPsec. If these other systems don't have an IPsec policy, IPsec isn't used. Even if the other systems are also assigned the Client (Respond Only) IPsec Policy, then IPsec isn't used because the Client (Respond Only) policy will never initiate an IPsec session.

You can also fine-tune the IPsec policies so that IPsec is used only for specific traffic. For example, if you want to ensure that FTP traffic is encrypted but other traffic isn't, you can add a filter for the IPsec policy to encrypt only FTP traffic.

▶

IPsec incurs additional overhead, so using IPsec can load down a system. Administrators must balance the need for security with the need for performance.

Comparing Tunneling Protocols

As a reminder, a VPN provides access to a private network over a public network such as the Internet. Because the Internet is a public network and susceptible to sniffing attacks, it's not safe to transmit private data in clear text over the Internet. Instead, VPNs allow for the use of tunneling protocols to protect data as it traverses the Internet.

These tunneling protocols encapsulate and encrypt the traffic destined for the internal network. The three primary tunneling protocols used on Windows Server 2008 servers that function as VPN servers are as follows:

Point-to-Point Tunneling Protocol (PPTP)   PPTP is an older tunneling protocol and has some vulnerability issues, but it's still used in many applications on Microsoft networks. It uses Microsoft Point-to-Point Encryption (MPPE) to encrypt data in the tunnel.

Layer 2 Tunneling Protocol (L2TP)   L2TP is a standard used by many vendors such as Microsoft, Cisco, and others. It commonly uses IPsec (expressed as L2TP/IPsec) to encrypt the data. One of the problems with IPsec is that it can't pass through a device using NAT because NAT corrupts IPsec packets.

Secure Socket Tunneling Protocol (SSTP)   SSTP is a newer tunneling protocol that was introduced in Windows Server 2008. It uses Secure Socket Layer (SSL) for encryption, which is the same encryption protocol used to encrypt HTTP (as HTTPS).

> **NAT translates private IP addresses to public IP addresses, and public back to private. NAT is included on many network-based firewalls.**

Figure 7.9 shows a VPN connection with a VPN client connecting to a VPN server over the Internet to access the organization's internal resources.

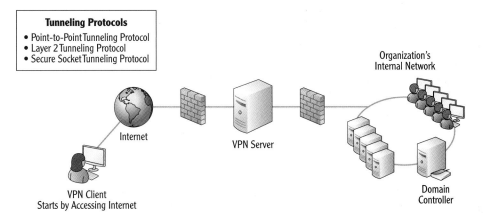

FIGURE 7.9 VPN connection

DNSSEC

The Domain Name System (DNS) service is used to resolve names to IP addresses and to identify servers running specific services. It's a required service in Microsoft domains and on the Internet. While DNS is highly efficient and reliable, it doesn't have much security built in.

> **Chapter 11 describes the use of certificates and digital signatures.**

DNS Security Extensions (DNSsec) is a group of specifications that provide extra security for DNS. It provides the following three primary benefits:

Origination Authentication of DNS Data   DNS records are digitally signed. These digital signatures provide authentication between DNS servers.

Data Integrity   Hashing is used with the DNS records to verify the record hasn't been modified. This helps prevent DNS cache-poisoning attacks.

Authenticated Denial of Existence   This is a special record type called NSEC3 that indicates a record doesn't exist for a queried name. However, instead of including the name directly, the NSEC3 record hashes and encrypts the response. It protects against zone-enumeration attacks where an attacker attempts to enumerate, or list, all the records within a zone.

DNSSEC was implemented on several DNS key servers on the Internet in 2010. It's also supported on Microsoft DNS servers, including DNS servers hosted on Windows Server 2008 and Windows Server 2008 R2.

THE ESSENTIALS AND BEYOND

In this chapter, you learned about some common attack methods. DoS attacks attempt to prevent a system from providing a service, and DDoS attacks are DoS attacks coming from multiple systems simultaneously. Other attacks include sniffing attacks, spoofing attacks, and port scans. Network-based firewalls are typically hardware-based and provide isolation for a private network. A UTM appliance includes protection on multiple levels, and an SCM appliance is typically focused on email content. NAP can inspect clients to ensure that they meet administrator-defined health requirements; unhealthy clients can be isolated in a restricted network. Some protocols can be configured to provide additional security. IPsec can encrypt traffic transmitted on the wire within a network. VPNs use tunneling protocols such as PPTP, L2TP, and SSTP with encryption to protect VPN traffic. DNSSEC is an extension of DNS that provides additional security by digitally signing DNS records.

ADDITIONAL EXERCISES

▶ The ping of death is a type of DoS attack. Use the Internet to research and identify what it is.

▶ Identify the well-known usage for ports 137, 138, and 139.

▶ Draw a diagram of a perimeter network that can protect an Internet-facing server.

▶ Identify when DNSSEC was deployed to root DNS servers.

To compare your answers to the author's, please visit **www.sybex.com/go/ securityessentials**.

(Continues)

THE ESSENTIALS AND BEYOND (Continued)

REVIEW QUESTIONS

1. True or false: A DDoS attack comes from a single computer.

2. An attacker is capturing and analyzing network traffic with a protocol analyzer. What type of attack is this?

3. A _____ attack is a specific type of spoofing attack. It spoofs the source address within a TCP SYN packet and causes the system to repeatedly reply to itself.

4. You want to allow both LDAP and secure LDAP traffic through a firewall. What ports need to be opened?

   A. 161 and 162   C. 389 and 636

   B. 389 and 3389   D. 80 and 443

5. True or false: A hardware-based firewall is typically more efficient than a software-based firewall.

6. An organization plans to host a web server accessible from the Internet. Where should the web server be placed to provide the best protection?

   A. In the intranet   C. On a firewall

   B. On the Internet   D. In a perimeter network

7. What type of firewall provides combined protection for multiple threats and can include firewall security features, routing features, and VPN components?

   A. SCM   C. Stateful firewall

   B. UTM   D. Packet-filtering firewall

8. Of the following choices, which client(s) can NAP inspect and isolate? (Choose all that apply.)

   A. Linux   C. Windows Vista

   B. Windows XP SP3   D. Windows 7

9. Sensitive data is transmitted on your network from a server. You want to ensure that this data is encrypted. What would you use?

   A. SSTP   C. IPsec

   B. PPTP   D. L2TP

10. What is used to digitally sign DNS records?

CHAPTER 8

Understanding Wireless Security

Wireless networks have become quite popular in recent years. They're relatively inexpensive and don't require you to run cables for connectivity. Instead, you simply set up a wireless access point or wireless router and configure it, and wireless clients can connect to the network.

However, security for wireless networks had a rough start. If you don't use up-to-date technologies, your wireless networks will be highly vulnerable to attacks. Although you can't make your wireless network 100 percent secure, there are several things you can do to increase its security. The most important step you can take to implement wireless security is employ a wireless encryption technology such as WPA or WPA2; and you can further enhance protection by using WPA-Enterprise or WPA2-Enterprise.

This chapter presents some basics about wireless devices and networks and then covers different elements of wireless security in the following topics:

► **Comparing wireless devices**

► **Comparing wireless security methods**

► **Configuring wireless routers**

► **Configuring Windows 7 for wireless**

Comparing Wireless Devices

802.11 wireless standards are covered in more depth in *Microsoft Windows Networking Essentials* (Wiley, 2011), which covers exam 98-366.

►

Wireless networks use one of four primary wireless standards, and many devices support multiple standards. Table 8.1 shows the common wireless standards in use today.

TABLE 8.1 IEEE 802.11 Wireless Standards

IEEE Standard	Speed	Base Frequency
802.11a	54 Mbps	5 GHz
802.11b	11 Mbps	2.4 GHz

TABLE 8.1 *(Continued)*

IEEE Standard	Speed	Base Frequency
802.11g	54 Mbps	2.4 GHz
802.11n	300 Mbps	2.4 GHz or 5 GHz

Another term for speed is data rate. The data rate is the total speed of the connection and the throughput is usually lower than the data rate.

The Speed column in Table 8.1 shows the maximum speed possible with these standards. However, various types of interference can potentially reduce the achievable throughput speeds. Also, IEEE 802.11n can reach speeds even greater than 300 Mbps in some configurations. IEEE 802.11n uses multiple antennas in a multiple input multiple output (MIMO) configuration to increase throughput, and it can reach speeds as high as 600 Mbps.

The security methods you choose aren't dependent on the 802.11 standard. In other words, it doesn't matter if you're using 802.11g or 802.11n when you're deciding what security methods to use. But each of your devices needs to support a compatible standard. Similarly, each of your devices needs to support common security algorithms and protocols, which are discussed later in this chapter.

Before jumping into wireless security, it's important to understand the different types of wireless devices you'll find in a network. In general, you'll see only three wireless types of devices: wireless adapters, wireless access points, and wireless routers.

Wireless Adapters

Computers with wireless capabilities have wireless adapters. Many mobile computers have built-in wireless adapters that give them native wireless support. You can buy wireless network-adapter modules and install them in desktop computers. There are also USB wireless adapters available: You simply plug in the USB adapter and configure it, and you have wireless connectivity.

Many other devices include wireless capabilities, including phones such as the Windows Phone 7, iPhone, and Droid; and gaming systems such as Xbox 360 and Wii. Even some eBook readers such as the Kindle include wireless capabilities.

Of course, you need to connect to something. In a large organization, you'll likely connect to a wireless access point. However, in mobile hotspots and smaller organizations, you'll probably connect to a wireless router.

Wireless Access Points

A wireless access point (WAP) provides connectivity for wireless clients to wired devices. It bridges the wireless clients to the wired network and gives them access to resources in the wired network. WAPs include the following components:

▶ At least one interface connecting it to a wired network

▶ A transceiver that allows the WAP to transmit and receive wireless transmissions

▶ Bridging software to bridge the wireless and wired segments

Figure 8.1 shows a WAP in an organization. Wireless clients can connect to the WAP to access wired resources within the network.

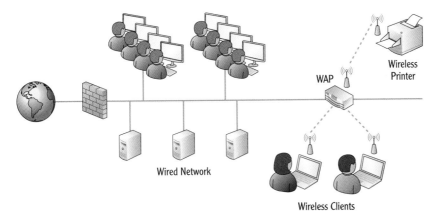

FIGURE 8.1 Wireless access point bridging wireless clients

WAPs have at least one wired interface connecting them to a wired network. Wireless networks that use a WAP operate in infrastructure mode.

Larger organizations can use multiple WAPs. Doing so extends the range of the wireless network and allows clients to roam within the network without losing connectivity.

It's also possible to connect wireless clients directly to each other without a WAP in ad hoc mode.

Wireless Routers

Smaller organizations often use wireless routers. A wireless router combines the capabilities of WAP with the capabilities of a router. For example, Figure 8.2 shows a wireless router in a small network.

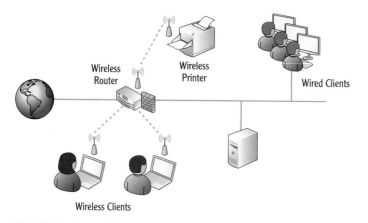

FIGURE 8.2 Wireless router in a small network

In the figure, you can see that the wireless router provides access to the Internet for all users in the network. The router often also provides basic firewall capabilities.

Wireless routers include physical ports, and wired clients connect directly into these physical ports using standard twisted-pair cable. The WAP component of the wireless router provides access for the wireless clients to the wired network.

Most wireless routers include additional capabilities, such as network address translation (NAT) and Dynamic Host Configuration Protocol (DHCP). The DHCP component issues TCP/IP configuration information to clients, including IP addresses, subnet masks, the address of the default gateway (usually the wireless router), and an address for a Domain Name System (DNS) server. The NAT component translates internal private IP addresses to external public IP addresses, and public IP addresses back to private IP addresses.

Comparing Wireless Security Methods

The Wi-Fi Protected Access (WPA and WPA2) protocols provide the primary security for wireless networks today. However, there are different flavors of WPA and WPA2 that you should understand. Also know that an older protocol called Wired Equivalent Privacy (WEP) has significant weaknesses and shouldn't be used at all. But because WEP is still used by so many unsuspecting users, it's important to understand its weaknesses and flaws.

Understanding Encryption Keys

Different wireless security methods use keys, so it's important to understand some basics about encryption keys. Wireless security uses *symmetric encryption*, which means that a single key is used to encrypt and decrypt data.

Chapter 10 covers the use of symmetric keys and asymmetric keys in more depth.

Encryption uses an algorithm and a key. The algorithm is a mathematical formula that scrambles, or ciphers, the data. The key provides randomness so that the data is scrambled differently when different keys are used. Although the algorithm stays the same all the time, the key should change regularly. Additionally, the key must stay secret. If not, anyone can decrypt the data.

As an example, consider a basic rotation algorithm based on the alphabet. Here's the algorithm:

Encryption   Move X spaces forward.

Decryption   Move X spaces backward.

In this case, the key is X. Suppose the key has a value of 3. You can then encrypt the word *Success* by rotating each letter forward three spaces. *S* becomes *V*, *u* becomes *x*, *c* becomes *f*, and so on. When each letter in *Success* is rotated three letters forward, the encrypted value is *Vxffhvv*.

The encrypted value can be decrypted using the same key of 3 to rotate the letters backward. *V* is rotated backward three spaces to get *S*, *x* is rotated backward three spaces to get *u*, and so on. If an attacker intercepts the text *Vxffhvv*, it isn't easy to read. However, if the attacker knows the algorithm and knows the key, decryption is simple.

Security is compromised when encryption keys aren't kept secret and when the keys are frequently reused.

Today's encryption algorithms aren't as simplistic as rotating forward or backward, but most of them are well documented. Anyone can use the Internet to look up the algorithms for any of the wireless security methods described in this chapter. However, as long as the encryption keys remain secret and are changed often, attackers can't decrypt the encrypted data.

WEP isn't recommended for use. Most WEP-capable hardware will support WPA. New hardware supports WPA2.

Wired Equivalent Privacy

Wired Equivalent Privacy (WEP) is a security protocol intended to provide wireless clients with privacy equivalent to that of wired clients. Unfortunately, WEP has several problems. Attackers can easily hack into networks protected with WEP.

Some of the problems with WEP include the following:

Weak Encryption   WEP uses a stream cipher named RC4 to encrypt data in combination with reused keys. Attackers can crack this combination using widely available software. A stream cipher encrypts data as part of a data stream. In contrast, block ciphers (used with WPA and WPA2) encrypt data in blocks of specific sizes. Block ciphers are much stronger than stream ciphers.

Poor Key Management   WEP doesn't have a secure channel to transmit encryption keys. Instead, encryption keys are transmitted in clear text at the beginning of a session, allowing an attacker to discover the keys. Additionally, subsequent encryption keys are predictable, reused, and not changed often.

Attacker Tools Widely Available   Attackers can easily locate and download tools from the Internet. These tools allow attackers to crack WEP-protected wireless networks.

> Attackers can use a wireless sniffer to capture data and quickly discover the WEP encryption keys. It's then a simple matter to decrypt and read the data.

When the problems with WEP were discovered, WPA was quickly developed and released as an interim replacement. Later, WPA2 was adopted as a permanent replacement for WEP.

Wi-Fi Protected Access

> Wireless hardware manufactured today supports WPA and WPA2 by default. Only older hardware needed upgrades to support WPA.

Wi-Fi Protected Access (WPA) is a security certification used for wireless transmissions. It was introduced as an interim replacement for WEP after the problems with WEP were discovered. One of the goals of WPA was to provide a software solution without requiring newer hardware than WEP was using. In contrast, WPA2 often requires different hardware.

Even though WPA doesn't require different hardware than WEP, it does require different firmware. Existing WEP wireless devices can be modified with firmware upgrades by flashing the BIOS so that it will support WPA. After the upgrade, the WEP hardware supports WPA.

> Many current versions of WPA support both TKIP and Advanced Encryption Standard (AES; see the "Understanding AES" sidebar).

One of the major improvements WPA provides over WEP is encryption and key protection. WPA uses the Temporal Key Integrity Protocol (TKIP) as the security algorithm. Encryption keys aren't sent out in clear text, and they're changed often, correcting two security issues with WEP. TKIP regularly changes the keys without requiring the user to change their passphrase.

Although WPA is significantly more secure than WEP, it has its faults. Attackers have cracked it, and WPA2 is recommended for use instead of WPA at this point. The designers of WPA realized that WPA wouldn't be a permanent solution, but that wasn't the goal—the goal was to last until WPA2 could be developed and released.

WPA and WPA2 each provide two modes of protection, such as WPA-Personal and WPA2-Personal, and WPA-Enterprise and WPA2-Enterprise. The "Wi-Fi Protected Access Version 2" section covers the differences between Personal and Enterprise modes.

UNDERSTANDING AES

AES is a strong, efficient symmetric encryption algorithm used in many different scenarios. In addition to being used with WPA and WPA2, it's also used to encrypt Kerberos transmissions, encrypt hard drives with BitLocker, and encrypt USB flash drives with BitLocker To Go. These are just a few examples. It's been adopted by the U.S. government for a wide assortment of purposes.

Symmetric encryption means it uses the same key to encrypt the data that it uses to decrypt it. In other words, symmetric encryption uses a single key. In contrast, *asymmetric encryption* uses two keys (known as a *public key* and a *private key*).The public and private keys are created as matching pairs.

AES has different strengths. AES-128 uses 128-bit keys, AES-192 uses 192-bit keys, and AES-256 uses 256-bit keys. Larger keys increase the strength of the encryption but may negatively impact performance.

Wi-Fi Protected Access Version 2

Wi-Fi Protected Access version 2 (WPA2) is a permanent replacement for WEP and certifies that devices or software are compliant with IEEE 802.11i. It uses AES by default but is also backward compatible with WPA and can use TKIP. WPA2 is stronger than WPA and recommended for wireless networks today.

One significant difference between WPA and WPA2 is that WPA2 supports Federal Information Processing Standards (FIPS) 140-2 by default. FIPS is a set of standards developed by the United States government, and FIPS 140-2 defines cryptography standards. For example, Figure 8.3 shows the Advanced Settings page for a wireless connection on a Windows 7 system, and how it can be used to enable FIPS compliance. If the security type were set to WPA-Personal instead of WPA2-Personal, the Advanced Settings button wouldn't be available and FIPS couldn't be enabled.

As mentioned previously, both WPA and WPA2 can be used in either Personal mode or in Enterprise mode. *WPA-Personal* and *WPA2-Personal* modes use the same preshared key (PSK) or passphrase for all wireless devices. Personal mode is used in small organizations and by home users.

WPA2 is backward compatible with WPA. If your hardware supports WPA2, it supports WPA.

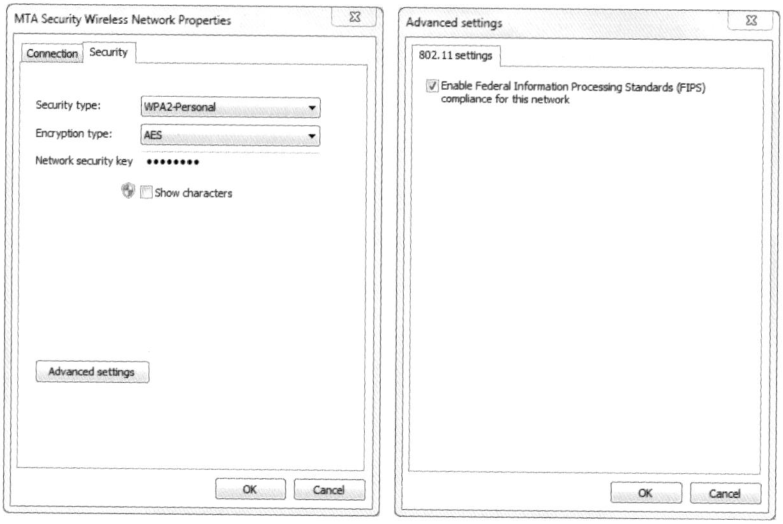

FIGURE 8.3 Enabling FIPS standards for a wireless connection

> **WPA-Enterprise and WPA2-Enterprise use an 802.1X authentication server and provide stronger security than WPA-Personal and WPA2-Personal do (with just a PSK).**

WPA2-Enteprise and *WPA2-Enterprise* modes use an 802.1X server for authentication. Large organizations use Enterprise mode to increase security. Clients have to authenticate individually with an 802.1X server; and after they authenticate, the 802.1X server distributes encryption keys to them. Enterprise mode includes the elements shown in Figure 8.4 and described here:

Supplicant The supplicant is the wireless client requesting access to the network.

Authenticator The WAP acts as the authenticator and prevents access to supplicants until they're authenticated by an authentication server.

Authentication Server The server verifies the credentials of wireless clients. You can configure a Windows Server 2008 server running the Network Policy and Access Services role as an 802.1X Authentication server.

Extended Authentication Protocol

When using WPA-Enterprise and WPA2-Enterprise, you use an 802.1X server for authentication. A Windows Server 2008 server supports multiple authentication methods when configured as an 802.1X server. The Extensible Authentication Protocol (EAP) provides the framework to create multiple additional authentication methods. These protocols provide additional security for the authentication process. For example, Chapter 3, "Understanding User Authentication," introduced several EAP protocols in the RADIUS topic, including Protected EAP (PEAP) and EAP-Transport Layer Security (EAP-TLS). As a reminder, smart cards use EAP-TLS.

If you want to ensure that all wireless users authenticate with a smart card, you can use an 802.1X authentication server with EAP-TLS.

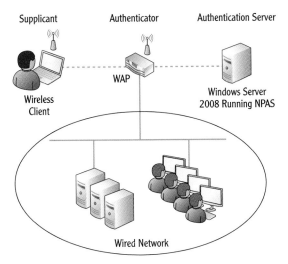

FIGURE 8.4 802.1X authentication

The two primary EAP methods supported by Windows Server 2008 802.1X servers are as follows:

EAP-TLS   Extensible Authentication Protocol Transport Layer Security uses certificates for authentication. EAP-TLS is a well-respected and established standard for authentication. It supports authentication with smart cards.

PEAP   Protected EAP provides a layer of protection by encapsulating and encrypting the authentication channel. PEAP can use smart cards with certificates for authentication, or passwords. When passwords are used, PEAP uses EAP with Microsoft Challenge Handshake Protocol version 2 (EAP-MSCHAPv2).

Other EAP methods continue to appear for 802.1X servers. As the technologies mature and gain popularity, updates may add these additional EAP protocols to Windows Server 2008 products configured as 802.1X servers.

Viewing Windows 7 Wireless Settings

Windows 7 supports several different security settings for wireless including WPA, WPA2, and both Personal and Enterprise modes. Figure 8.5 shows the security types you can select for a wireless connection on a Windows 7 system.

Steps later in this section show how you can access this screen on a wireless-enabled Windows 7 system.

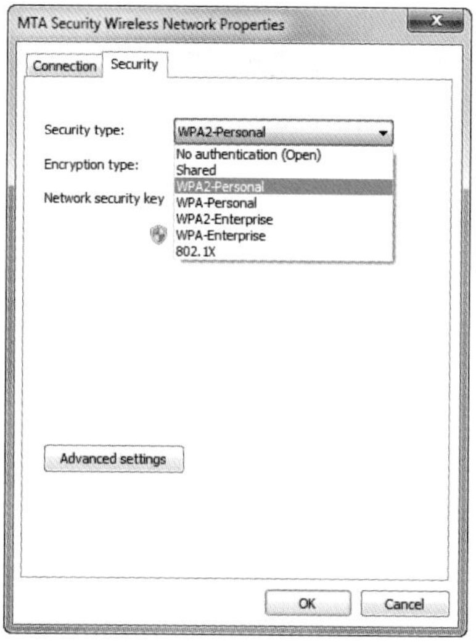

FIGURE 8.5 Wireless security choices on Windows 7

You may notice that the names of the selections in Figure 8.5 differ slightly from the wireless security methods listed previously. For example, you don't see a setting for WEP. However, if you have to go backward to WEP, you can do so. The list describes each of these selections:

No Authentication (Open)   This setting doesn't use any encryption, and instead transmits data in clear text, or in the open. Many public hotspots use this to provide free wireless access.

Shared   Shared uses WEP. The wireless device is configured with a PSK that must be the same on the wireless devices in order for them to connect to the wireless network.

This shared key is also called the network security key; WEP uses it for encryption. An attacker can eavesdrop on a wireless transmission, crack the WEP encryption, and discover the shared key.

WPA-Personal / WPA2-Personal   WPA-Personal and WPA2-Personal use a PSK, but they're both much more secure then WEP. The PSK is the same for all users in most wireless networks. However, some wireless routers support multiple PSKs. For example, the Cisco Valet wireless router uses one PSK for most devices and allows you to create other PSKs (called *passwords*) to share with guests without giving out your primary PSK.

WPA-Enterprise / WPA2-Enterprise   WPA-Enterprise and WPA2-Enterprise use an 802.1X authentication server. The 802.1X server authenticates clients before granting access to the wireless network.

802.1X   This choice is for WEP networks that support 802.1X servers. The 802.1X server provides authentication. Just as with other WEP choices, it isn't recommended today. As a reminder, WPA-Enterprise and WPA2-Enterprise use an 802.1X server. However, this menu choice in Windows 7 is used only if a client is using WEP with an 802.1X server.

The following steps show how to view the security settings for a wireless-enabled Windows 7 system. If your Windows 7 system doesn't have wireless capabilities, you won't see wireless menu choices:

1. Click Start ➢ Control Panel.

2. Type **Network** in the Search Control Panel text box, and select Network And Sharing Center. If your system supports wireless connections, it will have a selection titled Manage Wireless Networks, as shown in Figure 8.6.

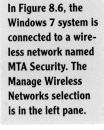

In Figure 8.6, the Windows 7 system is connected to a wireless network named MTA Security. The Manage Wireless Networks selection is in the left pane.

F I G U R E   8 . 6 Viewing the Network And Sharing Center on a wireless-enabled Windows 7 system

3. Click Manage Wireless Networks.

4. Right-click the wireless connection, and select Properties. If necessary, select the Security tab. Your display will look similar to Figure 8.7. In the

figure, the security type selected is WPA2-Personal with AES encryption, but your wireless connection may be using something different.

5. Click the Connection tab. Your display will look similar to Figure 8.8. In the figure, the connection is set to automatically connect whenever the wireless network is in range.

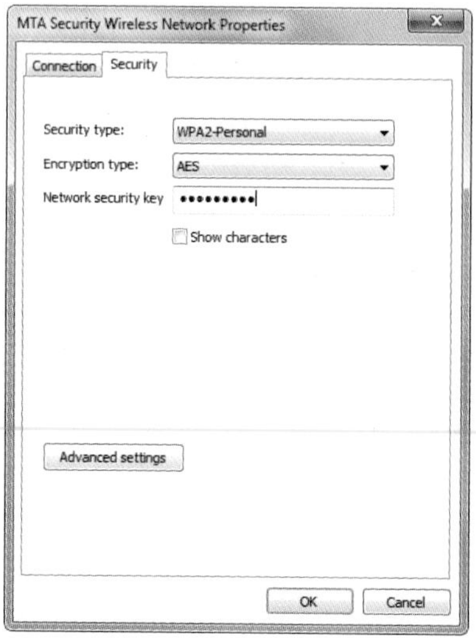

FIGURE 8.7 Viewing the Security tab of a wireless connection properties page

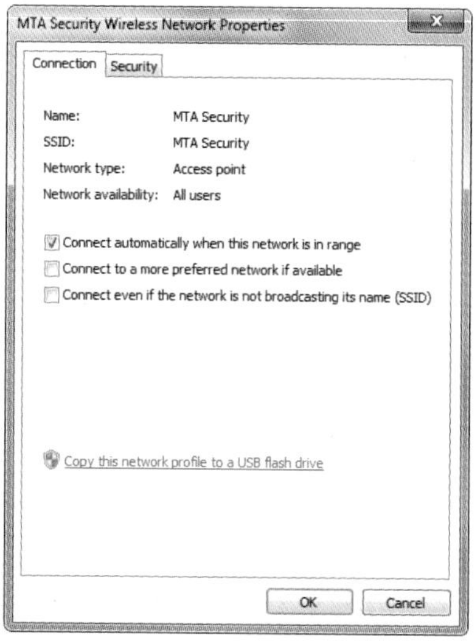

FIGURE 8.8 Viewing the Connection tab of a wireless connection properties page

Configuring Wireless Routers

Most wireless routers have web-based administration pages. You can connect to the page using a web browser such as Internet Explorer with the IP address of the router. For example, many wireless routers use an IP address of 192.168.0.1, 192.168.1.1, or 192.168.2.1. You can type **http://192.168.0.1**, **http://192.168.1.1**, or **http://192 .168.2.1** into the address bar to connect to the web administration page.

You're then prompted to log on using an administrator account. Most wireless routers have a default administrator account named admin. Additionally, wireless routers start with a default password. Table 8.2 shows some of the default IP addresses and passwords used by different vendors.

TABLE 8.2 Default IP Addresses and Passwords

Brand	Default IP Address	Default Password
Netgear	192.168.0.1	*admin*
Cisco (including Linksys)	192.168.1.1	*admin*
3Com	192.168.1.1	*admin*
Belkin	192.168.2.1	Blank (no password)

Vendors can use different defaults for different models. If these defaults don't work on the default router, check the manual.

Most wireless routers also support resetting the passwords of the router. For example, if the password is changed but no longer known, you can reset the wireless router back to the factory defaults.

Changing the Default Administrator Password

One of the first security steps to take is to change this default password. For example, Figure 8.9 shows the Administration Management page for a Linksys wireless router. You can change the password on this page. If you don't change the password, and web access is available, an attacker may attempt to access the router, use the default password, and change any of the settings. In other words, an attacker can lock you out of your own wireless network.

Changing the SSID

The SSID is the name of the wireless network. It's configured on the WAP or wireless router; each wireless device uses the same SSID when connecting to the wireless network.

War Driving

Anyone who has a laptop with Internet access can locate wireless networks. Some attackers drive around looking for wireless networks to exploit. This is called *war driving*. If a network isn't secure, they can try to hack into it.

One of the first things a war driver looks for is unprotected networks, including networks without any security and those using WEP. These networks are easy to find with Windows 7. For example, the following graphic shows wireless networks in range of a Windows 7 computer. You can access this information on a Windows 7 computer with wireless abilities by clicking Start ➤ Connect To.

You can then hover over any of the wireless connections to see details about the connection. For example, in the graphic, I'm hovering over the 54A81 network. The tooltip shows the Name, Signal Strength, Security Type (WEP), Radio Type or wireless standard (802.11g), and service set identifier (SSID; 54A81). Try this at your house. You may be surprised how many wireless networks around you are still using WEP.

If an attacker discovers that WEP is being used, they can then use other tools to crack into the wireless network. If they can't find any systems in this neighborhood that are easy to break into, they can just drive to another neighborhood.

Some dedicated attackers use modified antennas to provide better gain in specific directions. For example, some attackers have been known to connect an empty can with a wire to their wireless antennas. This acts as a directional antenna and can connect to wireless networks that otherwise wouldn't be in range.

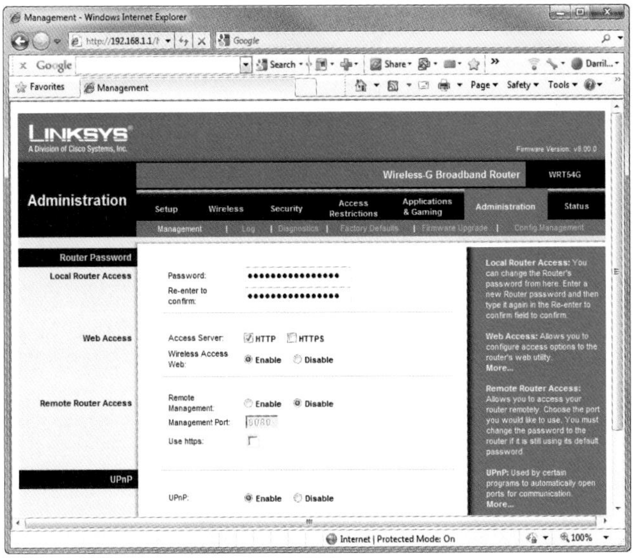

FIGURE 8.9 Changing the default password on a wireless router

Some wireless network devices start with a default SSID that you can rename. For example, some Linksys wireless routers start with an SSID of Linksys-g, and some Netgear wireless routers start with an SSID of NETGEAR. A trend with newer network devices is to give a random name as the SSID, with or without the brand name. Some devices require you to enter the SSID when you first configure the device.

Figure 8.10 shows the wireless settings page for a Linksys wireless router. Notice that the SSID has been renamed MTA Security on this page.

One of the benefits of renaming your SSID is that it no longer identifies the router by brand. If the SSID name is Belkin.475E, the attacker knows it's a Belkin device. If there are known vulnerabilities with a Belkin wireless router, the attacker can try to exploit these. However, if the SSID is MTA Security, the attacker doesn't have a clue about the brand of the device.

> Renaming the SSID from the default is recommended for security.

> The SSID has to be 15 characters or less.

To Broadcast or Not to Broadcast

The SSID can be set to broadcast so that other devices can easily find it; or you can disable broadcast, making it more difficult for other devices to locate it. For example, look back at Figure 8.10, where the SSID was identified for the wireless device. In the figure, you can see that Wireless SSID Broadcast setting is set to Enable, but you can change it to Disable.

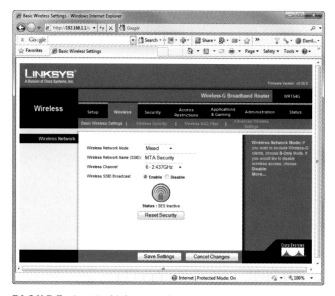

FIGURE 8.10 Linksys wireless settings

When configured to broadcast, the wireless router routinely transmits its name. Other wireless devices use this information to connect to the wireless network. Of course, when you're using security such as WPA and WPA2, connectivity is denied unless the wireless clients are configured with the PSK.

Many security professionals suggest that SSID broadcasts should be enabled. Others suggest that SSID broadcasts should be disabled. Here is some background on these two recommendations:

Disable SSID Broadcast   The idea behind this recommendation is that disabling broadcast makes it harder for an attacker to locate a wireless network. This recommendation is based on the myth that disabling the SSID broadcast enhances security. However, even though the wireless router isn't broadcasting regularly, the SSID is still included in transmitted packets. Wireless sniffers (such as Kismet) can easily capture packets and discover SSIDs, even if SSID broadcast is disabled.

Because the SSID is transmitted in clear text, disabling it doesn't add any security. Worse, you must configure computers so that their privacy might be at risk. Figure 8.11 shows a configuration page in Windows 7. Notice that the last setting is Connect Even If The Network Is Not Broadcasting—Microsoft has added the warning right below it. Because the computer never knows when it's close to the wireless network, it will regularly send out packets looking for this network to connect to. This occurs when the computer's in an airport, a coffee

> Kismet is a wireless network detector, sniffer, and intrusion-detection system. It's available for free via the Internet.

shop, or anywhere else. If an attacker is using a wireless sniffer, it will easily see details on your computer announcing your presence, your IP address, and more.

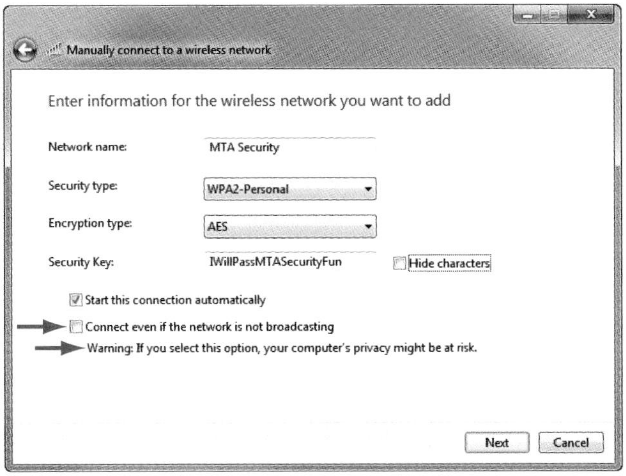

FIGURE 8.11 Configuring a wireless connection in Windows 7

Leave SSID Broadcast Enabled   Security experts stress that disabling SSID broadcast doesn't provide any real security and hampers usability. Additionally, be aware that Microsoft recommends leaving SSID broadcast enabled; so if you're preparing for a Microsoft exam such as Security Fundamentals (Exam 98-367), it's a good idea to know what Microsoft advises. To better understand Microsoft's thoughts on this topic, check out Steve Riley's blog entry "Myth vs. Reality: Wireless SSIDs" here:

> **Microsoft recommends keeping SSID broadcasts enabled.**
> ◀

```
http://blogs.technet.com/b/steriley/archive/2007/10/16/myth-vs-reality
-wireless-ssids.aspx
```

It's important to remember that the frequencies used for wireless transmissions are well known. For example, you saw the base frequencies for 802.11a, b, g, and n at the beginning of this chapter. The transmission frequencies aren't secret. And for any attackers using freely available tools such as Kismet, the SSID isn't a secret, even with SSID broadcasting disabled. The primary security protection against these sniffing tools is the use of a strong security protocol like WPA2.

> **The MAC address is also known as the *physical address*. It includes six pairs of hexadecimal numbers and looks something like this: 00-21-6B-B2-13-D6.**
> ◀

Using MAC Filters

Another feature that is included with most wireless routers is *MAC filtering*. MAC filtering allows you to identify specific media access control (MAC) addresses that you want to allow or block.

For example, Figure 8.12 shows the Wireless MAC Filter page for a Cisco M20 wireless router. The setting is disabled. If it's enabled, the wireless router gives two choices: You can block wireless access for computers with specific MAC addresses and allow access for all others, or block wireless access for all computers except those with specific MAC addresses.

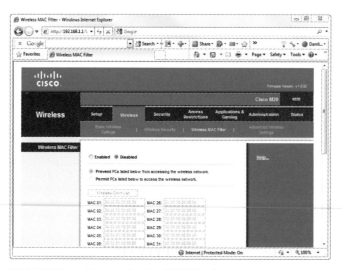

FIGURE 8.12 Configuring MAC filtering

This sounds good. Because MAC addresses are theoretically unique, it's highly unlikely that any two systems will have the same MAC address. If you create a MAC filter that allows only MAC addresses for your computers, you may be lulled into believing that only your computers can access the wireless network. However, this theory has two significant flaws. First, the MAC addresses are broadcast over the air, so it's a simple matter for an attacker to discover what MAC addresses are being used. Second, it's relatively simple for an attacker to spoof a MAC address.

As a reminder, a spoofing attack is any attack where the attacker attempts to impersonate or masquerade as someone or something else. In this case, the attacker spoofs the MAC address of an allowed computer, which in turn allows them to connect. Although the MAC address is burned into the network interface card, it's possible to change the MAC address in many operating systems. The attacker simply changes the MAC address of the attacking computer to a MAC address of an allowed computer. They're then able to access the network.

> **MAC filtering doesn't provide any real security. The best protection is a secure protocol such as WPA2.**

Configuring Windows 7 for Wireless

You can use the following steps to configure a Windows 7 computer to connect to a wireless network:

1. Click Start, type **Network** in the Search Programs And Files text box, and select Network And Sharing Center.

2. Click Manage Wireless Networks in the left pane. Figure 8.13 shows the system connected to a wireless network named MTA Security.

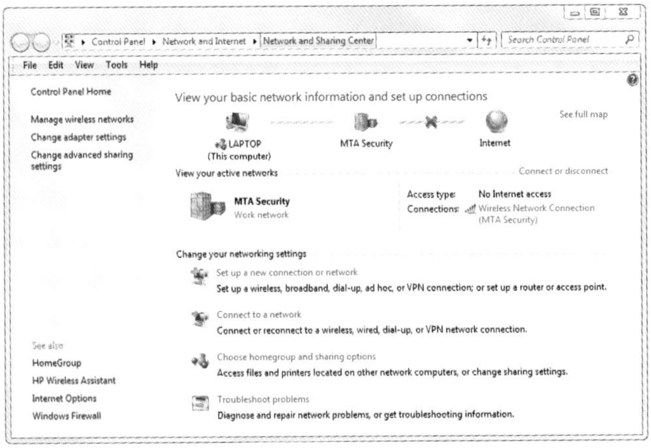

FIGURE 8.13 Windows 7 Network And Sharing Center showing network connectivity

The Manage Wireless Networks link is available only if the system has wireless capabilities. If this link doesn't appear, verify that you have a wireless adapter and that it's enabled.

3. Click Add. Select Manually Create A Network Profile.

4. Type the name (the SSID) of the wireless network in the Network Name text box.

5. Select the security type used by the WAP or the wireless router. As a reminder, WPA2 is stronger than WPA. WPA2-Enterprise is stronger than WPA2-Personal, but it requires an 802.1X authentication server in the network.

6. Select the encryption type. AES is stronger than TKIP.

7. Type in the same passphrase that is used on the WAP or wireless router. Your display will look similar to Figure 8.11, shown earlier.

Notice that you can have your computer connect to this network automatically by selecting the Start This Connection Automatically check box. If SSID broadcast is disabled on the WAP or wireless router, you can select Connect Even If The Network Is Not Broadcasting. As a reminder, Microsoft recommends that SSID broadcast remain on.

8. Click Next. Click Close.

9. Connect to the network by clicking Start ➤ Connect To and selecting the connection.

THE ESSENTIALS AND BEYOND

In this chapter, you learned some basics about wireless devices and wireless security. Devices with wireless adapters can connect to wireless networks. WAPs and wireless routers are used to bridge the wireless devices to the wired network. The primary step you can take to secure a wireless network is to use either the WPA or the WPA2 security protocol. The WEP security algorithm has serious flaws and shouldn't be used. WPA-Personal and WPA2-Personal use a PSK, and WPA-Enterprise and WPA2-Enterprise use an 802.1X authentication server. WPA-Enterprise and WPA2-Enterprise provide more security than WPA-Personal and WPA2-Personal. Disabling SSID broadcast doesn't increase security, and Microsoft recommends leaving SSID broadcast on. MAC filtering can restrict access to computers based on their MAC addresses, but MAC filtering doesn't provide real security. It's relatively easy to discover MAC addresses used in wireless transmissions and spoof them.

ADDITIONAL EXERCISES

▶ List the wireless security algorithms and protocols from the least secure to the most secure.

▶ If you have a wireless network, determine what type of security you're using.

▶ If your wireless network is using WEP, reconfigure it to increase security.

▶ If you have a wireless network, determine if you can enable MAC filtering, and determine if MAC filtering is enabled.

To compare your answers to the author's, please visit **www.sybex.com/go/ securityessentials**.

(Continues)

THE ESSENTIALS AND BEYOND *(Continued)*

REVIEW QUESTIONS

1. True or false: A wireless access point always includes routing capabilities.

2. True or false: Algorithms used by WEP, WPA, and WPA2 are published and accessible to anyone who wants to look at them, and they aren't changed from one transmission to another.

3. Of the following choices, which one provides the best security for a wireless network?

    A. WEP   **C.** WPA2

    B. WPA   **D.** WPA3

4. True or false: WPA2-Enterprise allows clients to authenticate with smart cards.

5. You want to use WPA2-Enterprise. What element is needed for WPA2-Enterprise that isn't needed for WPA2-Personal?

6. You want to provide the strongest security possible for your wireless network. Which one of the following choices provides the strongest wireless security?

    A. WPA-Personal   **C.** WPA-Enterprise

    B. WPA2-Personal   **D.** WPA2-Enterprise

7. A wireless network is identified by its name. The wireless network name is also known as _____.

8. Of the following choices, what can you do with the SSID to increase security for a wireless network?

    A. Rename the default SSID   **C.** Change the SSID password

    B. Disable SSID broadcast   **D.** Remove the SSID

9. True or false: WEP uses AES for encryption.

10. True or false: You can increase security in a network by disabling SSID broadcast.

CHAPTER 9

Understanding Physical Security

One of the basic security steps you can take is to restrict physical access to systems. Most organizations use a variety of different methods to enforce physical security, such as locked doors, cipher locks, guards, and more. Preventing unauthorized personnel from gaining physical access to servers and network devices (such as routers and switches) is an integral step in any comprehensive security plan.

Whereas previous chapters focused on individual Group Policy settings, this chapter expands the explanation of Group Policy. It shows how to organize users in organizational units, create a Group Policy within a domain, and modify the Group Policy to manage users and computers. You'll see how you can use Group Policy to enhance physical security by restricting access to systems. For example, you can use the Deny Log On Locally Group Policy setting to prevent users from logging onto a computer. You can also create a Removable Storage Access policy to restrict what users can do with different types of removable devices, including USB flash drives.

The last section in this chapter addresses security with mobile devices such as cell phones. All of these concepts are covered in the following topics:

▶ **Comparing site security and computer security**

▶ **Using Group Policy to enhance computer security**

▶ **Exploring mobile device security**

Comparing Site Security and Computer Security

The objectives for Exam 98-367, Security Fundamentals, specifically separate site security and computer security in the context of physical security.

Physical security includes all the elements used to protect facilities and Information Technology (IT) resources within a facility. You can think of physical security in two contexts:

Site Security   This includes all the elements used to control movement within an organization. Site security starts at the organization's property line. It can include fences, guards, lighting, cameras, locked doors, motion detectors, and more.

Computer Security   This includes all the elements used to protect IT resources such as servers, desktop computers, and network devices. Organizations typically protect servers and network devices (such as routers and switches) in locked server rooms, and even in locked equipment bays (or racks) within the server room. Additional logical controls are implemented to restrict access, such as who can log onto a computer and what resources they can use when they're logged on.

Group Policy provides several tools an organization can use to enhance computer security. Group Policy is covered in more depth later in this chapter.

Understanding the Importance of Physical Security

A common mantra known by many IT professionals is, "If an attacker has unrestricted physical access to a system, the attacker owns it." There is almost no limit to what an attacker can do given unrestricted access. Some examples include the following:

Chapter 3 mentioned Ophcrack. It's a free tool that attackers can use to crack all the passwords on a system, including the Administrator password.

Reset the Administrator Password   If an attacker can boot the system to a DVD or bootable USB flash disk, they can boot using their own utilities. Many tools are available that can change the password on the built-in Administrator account. The attacker then reboots and logs on as the Administrator account. As the Administrator, the attacker has access to everything on the system.

Install Unauthorized Software   An attacker can install any type of malicious software. This could include malware such as a virus. It could also include a *keylogger* to capture and record keystrokes. The captured data could be stored on the system for later retrieval or sent to the attacker using the Internet or email.

Steal the System   If the attacker steals the system, they now have all the data and the hardware. Although servers can costs thousands of dollars, the data is often much more valuable, and the attacker has unlimited time to access it. If it's a domain controller, the attacker now has access to critical domain secrets that can seriously compromise the security of the domain. Some organizations have been forced to re-create their domains from scratch after a domain controller was stolen.

Physically Damage the System   The attacker could make the system unavailable by damaging it. A system could also be accidentally damaged if it's not protected. For example, if a server were stored under a desk, an accidental coffee spill could damage the machine. However, food and drink restrictions are typically much more stringent in server rooms. It's worth noting that you shouldn't store servers on or under a desk.

Modify Data   An attacker can modify critical data on a system. Audit logs can track all activity on a system, but a knowledgeable attacker could modify the audit logs too, destroying the audit trail. Insiders can also modify data. For example, a disgruntled employee could modify their own performance reviews, payroll data, or critical project data.

Steal Data   Portable USB flash drives can hold 32 GB of data or more on a very small device easily hidden by a thief. The thief could steal proprietary information, research and development data, customer data such as names and credit-card numbers, private employee information, and more.

◀

Chapter 6 presented the use of read-only domain controller (RODCs) that don't store domain secrets. RODCs can be used when a location doesn't have strong physical security.

◀

Chapter 5 covered the different types of auditing. Windows auditing is stored in the Security log.

COMPARING KEYLOGGERS

Keyloggers, also known as *keystroke loggers*, capture keystrokes made by a user. This includes anything typed in, such as usernames and passwords, search phrases, email, and more. The data is stored and can be retrieved by the attacker later, or the data can be transmitted to the attacker.

Some keyloggers have advanced capabilities such as capturing screenshots. For example, a keylogger can capture a picture of every website a user visits and every application a user starts.

Keyloggers can be hardware-based, software-based, or firmware-based. A hardware-based keylogger attaches between the keyboard and computer to capture keystrokes. Software-based keyloggers are applications that start when the computer starts and usually include stealth techniques to stay hidden from the user. Firmware keyloggers are either built into the motherboard or installed into the system by modifying the BIOS. Years ago, many motherboard manufactured in Asian countries had keyloggers built into them; the only way to remove these keyloggers was to install a different motherboard.

Controlling Physical Access

Physical-access controls protect different areas of an organization with various levels of security. Many organizations use a multiple-layer approach to control different physical boundaries. For example, consider Figure 9.1. It shows multiple layers of physical security with multiple physical security elements.

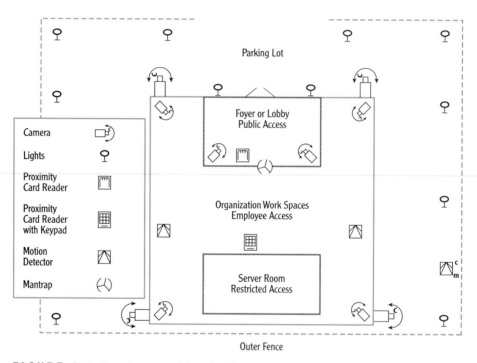

FIGURE 9.1 Boundary control for a building

Protection starts with a fence and includes progressively stronger security to enter the organization's work spaces and the server room. Not every organization will use all of the security methods shown and discussed here, and some organizations will use more. However, the example demonstrates many of the physical security methods that can be used.

The first layer is the fence around the building's parking lot. The parking lot should be well lit and often includes cameras. Cameras can be stationary or movable. Movable cameras can pan, tilt, and zoom (PTZ) to focus in on suspicious activities.

The next layer is the front-door access to the building. Although an organization may allow public access to the building, this is often limited to a foyer or lobby. An organization may also protect this area with cameras.

Employee workspaces are often limited to employees only. In order for people to enter the organization's workspaces, they must pass through some type of physical-access control. For example, the organization could use guards to control access. Security guards may be instructed to only allow employees with employee IDs or identification badges into the employee workspace. Some organizations use cipher locks or proximity cards to control access.

◀

A cipher lock is controlled with a numeric keypad. When the user enters the correct number, the door is unlocked.

CONTROLLING ACCESS WITH PROXIMITY CARDS AND BADGES

A *proximity card* is a small card about the size of a credit card. It has data embedded into it that identifies the carrier. You only need to place a proximity card close to (or in close proximity to) a proximity-card reader.

The proximity card doesn't have a power source. Instead, the proximity-card reader generates an energy field; and when the card is passed over the reader, the electronics on the card are charged, and the card transmits the data. This is the same technology used by some credit cards at some gas stations and some fast food restaurants. You just pass your card over the credit-card reader, and it reads your information.

Some proximity cards double as identification badges and include a picture of the employee similar to the following graphic. Employees wear the badge for identification while walking around in the secure areas. Anyone walking around without a badge quickly raises suspicions. When employees need to access a secure area, they swipe their badge in front of a proximity reader to unlock the door.

◀

Chapter 5 covered auditing in more detail. Card readers that include auditing work on the same principles and record details such as who, what, when, and where.

Chapter 3, "Understanding User Authentication," explained the concept of multifactor authentication, where more than one factor of authentication is used. Some proximity-card readers also have numeric keypads, requiring users to have something (the proximity card) and know something (the number code to enter into the cipher-lock keypad).

Additionally, many readers can be tied into an auditing system that records access. When a user enters, an application records information about the user and the time of entry. More secure areas also require users to use the card to exit, and the system records the time of the exit. This allows security personnel to know exactly when people enter a secure space, how long they stayed, and when they left.

One challenge with physical access control is *tailgating* (or *piggybacking*). Tailgating occurs when more than one user accesses a secure area but only one user provides the credentials. For example, Bob can use his proximity card to open a door, and Mary can follow him in. Bob may even hold the door open for Mary. In this example, Mary is tailgating because she is entering without using her proximity card.

If physical security practices aren't emphasized to employees in routine training, courtesy often takes over. Actually, even when employees are trained about security, courtesy may still take over. Outside of work, Bob may never dream of closing the door on someone following him into a room. It's polite to hold the door open for others and rude to shut the door in their face. Because of this conflict between courtesy and security, tailgating often occurs even when people know the security policy.

One way of preventing tailgating is with a *mantrap*. A mantrap is a physical security device that controls access and only allows a single person to enter or exit a secure area. In its strictest definition, a mantrap has the ability to trap a person. For example, individuals can enter a small room where their credentials are checked, and then they're allowed to exit. Some mantraps resemble cages with revolving doors made of bars. The user swipes their badge in front of a card reader, and they can then enter the cage, and push through the revolving doors. These cages can lock, trapping individuals inside if necessary.

However, using cages that can trap people doesn't always project a very favorable image. Instead, many organizations use a simple turnstile, similar to those used in subways and bus stations. Individuals swipe their badge and can then pass through the turnstile. If a person doesn't have a badge, they can't get through.

After hours, an organization may use motion detectors and cameras to monitor the employee spaces, server rooms, and more. The motion detectors can set off audible or silent alarms, depending on the needs of the organization.

Some other areas within the building require more security. For example, most organizations protect servers and network devices such as routers and switches in locked server rooms and locked equipment bays. Access to a server room is limited to administrative personnel who have a need to access these systems. For example, an organization can protect access to a server room with a proximity-card reader and a keypad. Because a proximity-card reader can identify the individual holding the card, it can be programmed to allow only specific employees into the room. Requiring the employee to have the proximity card and know the code to enter into the cipher lock increases security with multifactor authentication: The user is required to both have something and know something in order to gain access to the room.

Chapter 7 discussed sniffing attacks. If attackers have access to routers and switches, they can connect a sniffer to capture network traffic.

Using Switches Instead of Hubs

Computers connect to each other via switches or hubs in a network. Although hubs are cheaper, most organizations use switches instead for two primary reasons: security and performance.

Consider Figure 9.2. It shows three desktop computers and a server connected together with a hub. While Dawn (a user) is transferring data back and forth with the file server, the hub is sending the same data to every other computer connected to the hub. If an attacker were using a sniffer, the sniffer would capture all the data.

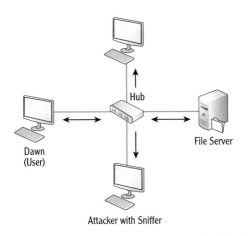

FIGURE 9.2 Computers connected with a hub

However, compare these same computers connected with a switch, as shown in Figure 9.3. A switch has more intelligence and forwards traffic only to specific computers involved in the transmission. If Dawn is transferring data back and forth with the file server, only Dawn's computer and the file server receive the data.

Even if an attacker is running a sniffer on another computer connected to the switch, it won't capture the data. The traffic sent between these two computers never reaches the switch port where the attacker's computer is connected.

Switches also provide performance gains by creating separate collision domains. Because traffic isn't forwarded to each computer connected to the switch, fewer collisions occur. Fewer collisions results in overall better performance.

◄

Switches, hubs, and collision domains are covered in depth in *Microsoft Windows Networking Essentials* (Wiley, 2011), which covers exam 98-366.

Switches provide increased security over hubs. They also provide better performance than hubs due to fewer collisions.

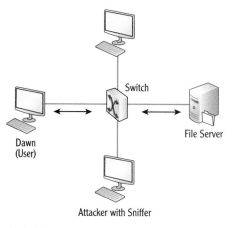

FIGURE 9.3 Computers connected with a switch

Using Group Policy to Enhance Computer Security

Group Policy settings apply to users and computers. Administrators use Group Policy to automate management and administration of user and computer accounts.

Group Policy includes many settings you can use to enhance computer security. For example, you can use some Group Policy settings to restrict what computers a user can log onto. Other settings can control what devices (such as USB flash drives, DVD drives, and more) can be used with computers.

Several chapters in this book have already introduced some Group Policy settings. For example, Chapter 3 covered the use of Group Policy to set a Password Policy and an Account Lockout Policy. Chapter 5, "Using Audit Policies and Network Auditing," covered how to use Group Policy to set an Audit Policy. The goal related to Group Policy in previous chapters was to let you know about some of the settings that are available. With an understanding of some Group Policy settings, it's easier to understand how Group Policy works. This section covers the big picture of Group Policy and how you can use Group Policy to manage users and computers in a domain.

You'll also learn about some specific Group Policy settings you can use to enhance physical security.

Understanding Default GPOs

There are thousands of GPO settings. You're not expected to know them all. However, you should understand the GPO settings covered in this book when preparing for the 98-367 exam.

As a reminder, Active Directory is a database of objects such as users, computers, and groups. Organizational units (OUs) and Group Policy objects (GPOs) are two other types of objects in Active Directory. You can organize objects within OUs, and manage users and computers by utilizing GPOs.

Every domain has two default GPOs:

Default Domain Policy   This GPO is linked to the domain and applies to all users and computers in the domain. It includes several default settings.

Default Domain Controllers Policy   This GPO is linked to the Domain Controllers OU and applies to all domain controllers in the OU. When a server is promoted to a domain controller, it's placed in the Domain Controllers OU.

You shouldn't add any other objects to the Domain Controllers OU or move domain controllers out of this OU.

Designing OUs and GPOs to Manage Users and Computers

You can create OUs in a domain, organize objects in the OUs you create, and create additional GPOs to manage users and computers in these OUs. For example, consider Figure 9.4. It shows a diagram of a domain with three OUs. The two default policies are linked at the domain and at the Domain Controllers OU. Two additional OUs have been added named Servers OU and Sales OU, and two additional GPOs have been added named Server Security and Sales. The Server Security and Sales GPOs have been linked to the Servers OU and the Sales OU, respectively.

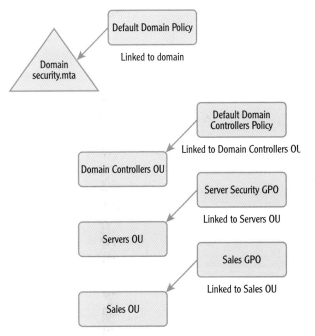

FIGURE 9.4 GPOs linked in a domain

This represents the design, but you need to take several steps to put the design into place. The following high-level steps show what you would need to execute in order to build out this design in your Active Directory environment:

1. Create an OU   For example, if you want to manage a group of servers with security settings, you can create an OU named Servers. If you want to organize users in the Sales department, you can create an OU named Sales. You create OUs with Active Directory Users and Computers.

2. Move the Active Directory Objects into the OU   For example, you can move all the server objects into the Servers OU. Similarly, you can move all the user and computer objects representing users and computers assigned to the Sales department into the Sales OU. You move objects into OUs with Active Directory Users and Computers.

3. Create and Link the GPO   For example, you can create a GPO named Server Security to secure the servers in the Servers OU. Similarly, you can create a GPO named Sales to manage the users and computers in the Sales OU. You create and link GPOs using the Group Policy Management console.

4. Configure the GPO   For example, you can configure the Servers GPO with specific settings to prevent regular users from logging on locally and configure settings for the Sales OU to restrict the use of removable devices. You configure GPOs with the Group Policy Management Editor, which can be launched from the Group Policy Management console.

A domain controller by default has all the tools needed to perform these steps; the following sections assume you're performing the steps on a domain controller. As a reminder, you can download the lab steps to create your own virtual environment from here: **www.sybex.com/WileyCDA/redirect/go/securityessentials**. This lab includes the steps needed to install Virtual PC, download and install Windows Server 2008, and promote it to a domain controller.

Creating OUs in a Domain

You can use the following steps to create two OUs. One is the Servers OU, which will hold server objects. The second is the Sales OU, which will hold user and computer objects for users and computers in the Sales department:

1. Launch Active Directory Users and Computers via the Administrative Tools menu.

2. Select the domain. Right-click the domain, and select New ➤ Organizational Unit.

3. Type in **Servers** as the name, and click OK.

4. Right-click the domain again, and select New ➤ Organizational Unit.

5. Type in **Sales** as the name, and click OK.

6. Leave Active Directory Users and Computers running.

At this point, you have the OUs created, but there aren't any objects in the OUs. The next step is to move appropriate objects into the OUs.

Moving Objects into an OU

You can use the following steps to create a server object and move it into the Servers OU:

1. With Active Directory Users and Computers open, select the Computers container.

2. Right-click over the Computers container, and select New ➤ Computer.

3. Type **Server1** in the Computer name text box, and click OK.

4. Right-click Server1, and select Move. Select the Servers OU, and click OK.

You can follow the same steps for other servers that you want to manage in the Servers OU. Additionally, you can use the same steps to move users and computers into the Sales OU.

The next step is to create and link a GPO to each of the OUs.

Creating GPOs to Manage Users and Computers

You can use the following steps to create and link the Server Security GPO to the Servers OU and the Sales GPO to the Sales OU:

1. Launch the Group Policy Management console via the Administrative Tools menu.

2. If necessary, expand Forest ➤ Domains ➤ *your domain*. Select the Servers OU.

3. Right-click over the Servers OU, and select Create A GPO In This Domain, And Link It Here.

4. Type in **Server Security** as the name, and click OK.

> ◀
>
> **You normally don't have to manually create computer objects. When a computer joins a domain, the computer account is created in the Computers container by default.**

5. Right-click the Sales OU, and select Create A GPO In This Domain, And Link It Here.

6. Type in **Sales** as the name, and click OK.

   At this point, your display will look similar to Figure 9.5. You can see that Security Filtering is set to Authenticated Users for the Sales GPO.

Users are added to the Authenticated Users group automatically when they log on. In other words, the Authenticated Users group includes all members of the domain.

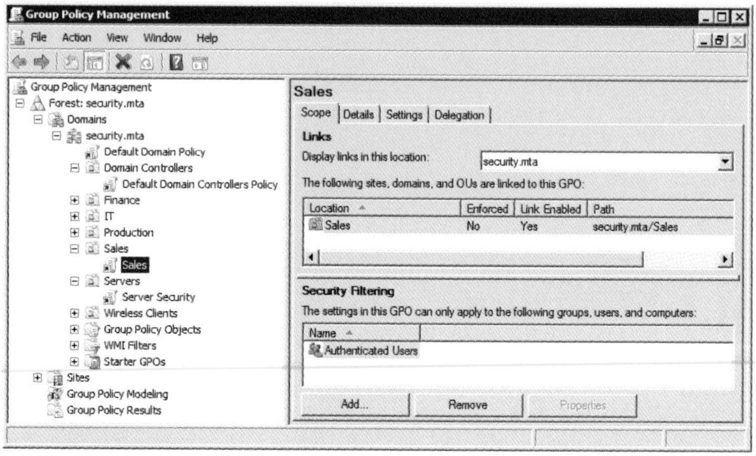

FIGURE 9.5 Group Policy Management with OUs and GPOs

Even though you've created the structure at this point, the Sales and Server Security GPOs are empty. They won't have any impact until you modify the GPO settings. In contrast, the Default Domain Policy has many settings configured by default; they apply to all users and computers in the domain.

Understanding Security Settings in a GPO

You can edit any GPO by right-clicking it in the Group Policy Management tool and selecting Edit. Doing so launches the Group Policy Management Editor. The editor includes settings organized in two nodes: Computer Configuration and User Configuration.

The Computer Configuration node includes settings that apply to a computer, and users logged onto that computer, no matter which user is logged on. The User Configuration includes settings that apply to a user, no matter which computer the user logs onto. Some settings are included in both the Computer Configuration and the User Configuration, whereas other settings are only included in one node or the other.

Figure 9.6 shows the Group Policy Management Editor with the Computer Configuration ➢ Policies ➢ Windows Settings ➢ Security Settings node opened. This node includes many of the settings covered in this book.

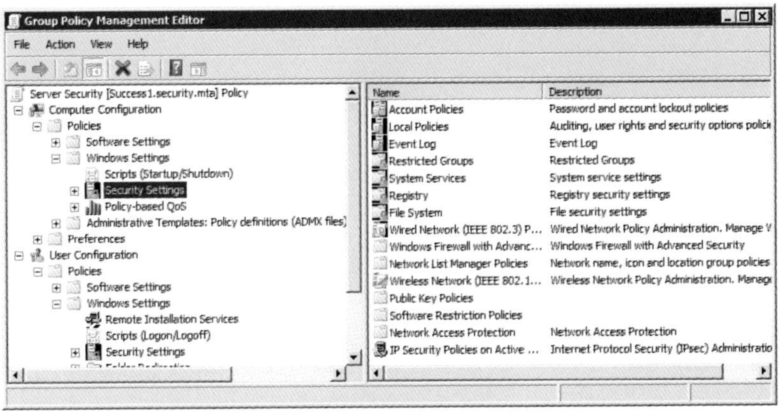

FIGURE 9.6 Group Policy Management Editor

Most GPO settings apply when a GPO is linked to any OU, but there are some exceptions. Specifically, Account Policies (including Password Policy, Account Lockout Policy, and Kerberos Policy) are applied only at the domain level. Figure 9.7 shows the location of these settings.

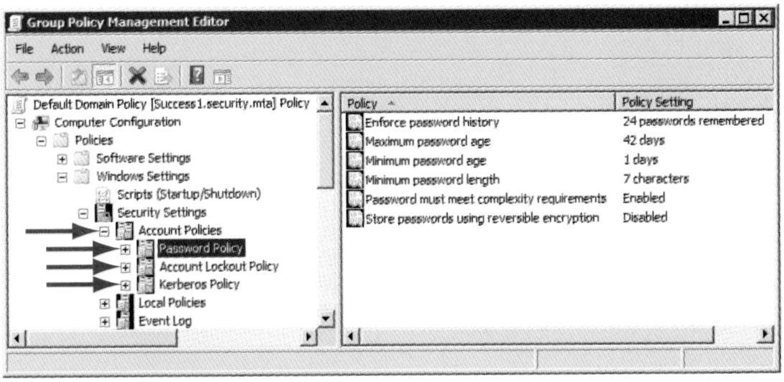

FIGURE 9.7 Account Policies

Account Policies settings apply only at the domain level. Chapter 3 covered the Password Policy node and the Account Lockout Policy node.

You can still modify these Account Policies settings in a GPO and link the GPO to an OU. However, the settings aren't applied to any domain accounts unless the GPO is linked at the domain level.

Windows Server 2008 does include some advanced abilities to apply Password Policy and Account Lockout Policy settings to specific users and groups. For example, if you want to have one password policy for regular users but need a stronger password for administrators, you can create a Password Settings Object (PSO) for the administrators. The implementation of PSOs is beyond the scope of this book and the Security Fundamentals exam.

All other Group Policy settings (except those in the Security Settings ➤ Account Policies node) are applied no matter where the GPO is linked. For example, if you configure an Audit Policy within Security Settings ➤ Local Policies (not the Account Policies node) and link the GPO to an OU named Servers, it will apply to objects (such as server computer objects) in the Servers OU. These servers will have a special Audit Policy that doesn't apply to any other systems.

Disabling Log On Locally with Group Policy

By default, users within a domain can log onto any domain computer except domain controllers. The term *log on locally* refers to a user sitting at the computer and logging onto the console. Other options include logging onto the computer remotely (over the network) or using a Terminal Services or Remote Desktop Services session.

> A *member server* is a server that is a member of a domain, such as file server or database server. However, it isn't a domain controller.

Many organizations restrict the ability of users to log onto some computers. For example, many organizations take steps to prevent non-administrators from logging onto member servers. Additionally, some organizations go a little further and restrict users so that they can log onto only specific computers, such as computers in their department.

You can control a user's ability to log onto a server using the Local Security Policy tool or using the security settings in a GPO. Most of the settings are identical. The difference is that the Local Security Policy tool affects only the local computer. The security settings in a GPO affect all the users and computers within the scope of the GPO, such as the users and computers in the domain, or all the users and computers in a specific OU.

> Rights identify actions users can take, such as changing the system time or logging onto a computer.

Chapter 5 showed how to create an Audit Policy. Right below the Audit Policy settings are the User Rights Assignment settings (shown in Figure 9.8). The User Rights Assignment node includes many settings used to grant and deny specific user rights to users.

Two important settings in the User Rights Assignment node affect who can log onto computers:

Allow Log On Locally   This identifies specific users and groups that are allowed to log on. By default, this setting isn't configured for any computers except domain controllers. When it isn't defined, any user can log onto the computer. When it's defined, only members of groups added to the setting (or individual users added to the setting) are able to log onto the system.

Deny Log On Locally   This identifies specific users and groups that are blocked from logging onto the system. If a user is identified in the Allow Log On Locally setting and also in the Deny Log On Locally setting, deny takes precedence. Because of this, you need to be careful with the Deny Log On Locally settings. For example, if you add the Administrators group to the Allow Log On Locally setting and then add the Authenticated Users group to the Deny Log On Locally setting, no one will be able to log on, including users in the Administrators group.

Figure 9.8 shows the Allow Log On Locally setting that applies to Domain Controllers. This setting is from the Default Domain Controllers Group Policy object.

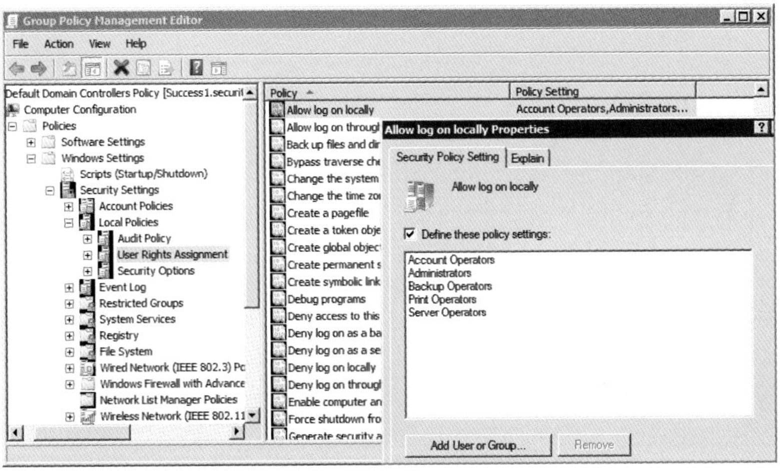

FIGURE 9.8 Allow Log On Locally from Default Domain Controllers Policy

The Allow Log On Locally setting isn't defined by default; and when it isn't defined, any user is allowed to log on. However, when it's defined, only users who are members of the defined groups (or added individually) can log onto the machines impacted by the policy.

In other words, regular users can't log onto domain controllers unless they're added to one of the listed groups. You don't need to explicitly configure Deny Log On Locally to prevent users from logging on. However, if you want to prevent members from any of these groups from logging onto the system, you can add them to the Deny Log On Locally setting.

Deny takes precedence. This is a phrase worth remembering, because it applies to many security scenarios.

Domain Controllers are located in the Domain Controllers OU. The Default Domain Controllers Group Policy is linked to the Domain Controllers OU, so it applies to all domain controllers.

The groups shown in Figure 9.8 are built-in groups. Microsoft domains include these groups by default.

Most organizations create additional groups in Active Directory to organize users, such as the Sales group for all users in the Sales department. Chapter 4, "Securing Access with Permissions," presented the concept of organizing users with groups. You can assign permissions and rights to a group, and all members of the group have those permissions and rights. For example, the IT department can have an IT Admins group, and all IT administrators in the IT department are added to this group. If the IT Admins group is added to this setting, any users in this group can log onto any of the domain controllers in the Domain Controllers OU.

You can use the following steps to restrict who can log onto servers in the Servers OU by modifying the Server Security GPO:

1. Launch the Group Policy Management console via the Administrative Tools menu.

2. If necessary, expand Forest ➤ Domains ➤ *your domain* and the Servers OU created earlier.

3. Right-click the Server Security GPO, and select Edit.

4. Expand Computer Configuration ➤ Policies ➤ Windows Settings ➤ Security Settings ➤ Local Policies, and select User Rights Assignment.

5. Double-click Allow Log On Locally.

6. Select the Define These Policy Settings check box, and click Add User Or Group.

7. Click Browse. Type in **Account Operators**, and click OK twice.

8. Repeat step 7 for the following groups: Administrators, Backup Operators, Print Operators, and Server Operators. When complete, the properties for the Allow Log On Locally will look similar to Figure 9.8, shown earlier.

9. Double-click the Deny Log On Locally setting.

10. Select the Define These Policy Settings check box, and click Add User Or Group.

11. Click Browse. Type in **Guests**, and click OK twice. Your display will look similar to Figure 9.9.

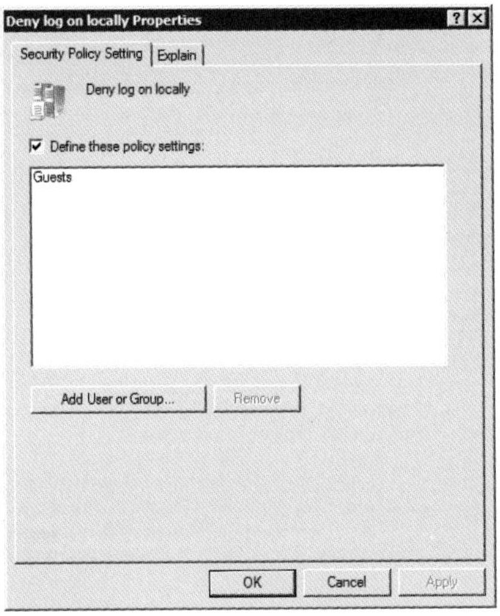

FIGURE 9.9 Deny Log On Locally from Default Domain Controllers Policy

You can add any group to this setting, but you shouldn't add the Everyone, Domain Users, or Authenticated Users group. If you do, no one will be able to log on locally.

Controlling Removable Storage Access with Group Policy

You can control the capabilities of removable devices and drives with a Removable Storage Access policy. Group Policy includes several settings that allow you to deny read access or deny write access to removable devices in the system.

Figure 9.10 shows the Removable Storage Access policy settings. You can view them in Group Policy here: Computer Configuration ➤ Policies ➤ Administrative Templates ➤ System ➤ Removable Storage Access.

The settings are as follows:

Time (In Seconds) To Force Reboot The Removable Storage Access policy settings aren't applied until a system reboots. You can configure this setting to force a reboot if any settings are modified. If you enable it, the default time is 1800 seconds (30 minutes), but this time can be changed.

CD And DVD This controls all CD and DVD drives. It includes both internal and external CD and DVD drives.

Custom Classes You can identify any specific class of removable media using a globally unique identifier. For example, you can identify a specific type of USB flash drive to deny.

These settings can be enforced on Windows Vista, Windows 7, Windows Server 2008, and Windows Server 2008 R2.

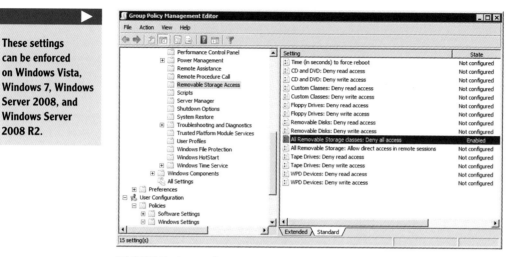

FIGURE 9.10 Removable Storage Access policy settings

Floppy Drives This controls 3.5″ floppy drives. Most systems don't include floppy drives any more, but external floppy drives are still available.

Removable Disks This category includes any external drive connected with a USB or IEEE 1394 (FireWire) connection. It includes hard drives and flash drives.

The Removable Storage Access policy applies only when a system is booted into Windows. The policy doesn't apply if attackers reboot the system using their own operating system.

All Removable Storage Classes This category includes removable media from any of the following classes: CD and DVD drives, floppy disk drives, removable drives, tape drives, and Windows Portable Devices. Users normally don't have access to removable devices when connected in a remote session. However, you can grant this right with the All Removable Storage: Allow Direct Access In Remote Sessions setting.

Tape Drives This category includes both internal and external tape drives.

WPD Devices You can control Windows Portable Devices (WPDs) such as media players, smart phones, and so on with this setting.

You can use the following steps to configure a Removable Storage Access policy. These steps modify the Sales GPO linked to the Sales OU (created earlier in this chapter):

1. Launch the Group Policy Management console via the Administrative Tools menu.

2. If necessary, expand Forest ➢ Domains ➢ *your domain* and the Sales OU created earlier.

3. Right-click over the Sales GPO, and select Edit.

4. Expand Computer Configuration ≻ Policies ≻ Administrative Templates ≻ System ≻ Removable Storage Access.

5. Double-click the All Removable Storage Classes: Deny All Access setting.

6. Select Enabled. Your display will look similar to Figure 9.11.

7. Click OK. Close all open windows.

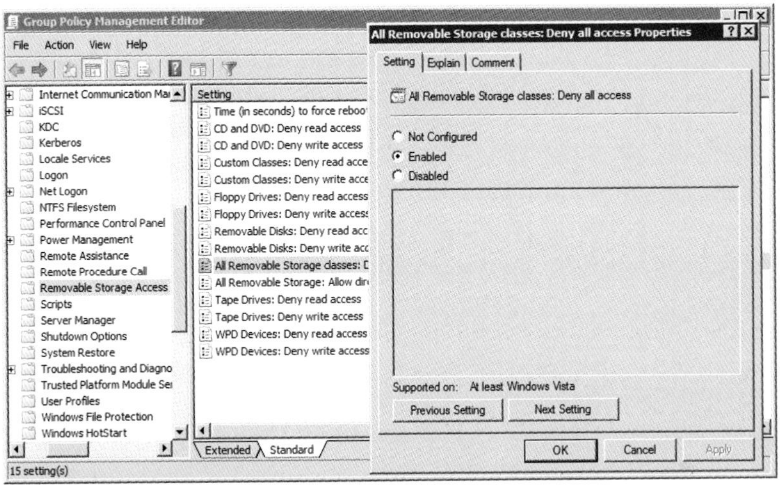

FIGURE 9.11 Denying access for all removable storage classes

Exploring Mobile Device Security

Mobile devices can hold a significant amount of personal information, so including some security practices for these devices is worthwhile. A simple step users can take to protect mobile devices is to password-protect them. This way, if the phone is lost, there's less possibility that someone can easily steal the personal information.

Smartphones today have significant capabilities and features. For example, many smartphones can send and receive email using a Microsoft Outlook interface and tie into Microsoft Exchange servers. Because these smartphones can tie into the network, they also need to be protected. An increasingly important step today is to install antivirus software on these mobile devices. Some mobile devices have unique challenges: For example, Bluetooth-enabled smartphones have specific risks related to discovery mode.

Protecting Mobile Devices Against Malware

Many banks provide access to their online services via mobile devices. Malware installed on mobile devices has the potential to intercept these transactions and capture data.

The good news is that until recently, malware on mobile devices hasn't been much of a threat. The bad news is that malware is beginning to appear on mobile devices. Because many devices now have the ability to surf the Internet and receive email, they're at risk. A computer can become infected by simply visiting a website or opening a malicious attachment. Mobile devices can become infected the same way.

Admittedly, the malware has to be targeted for the operating system running on the mobile device. However, when attackers realize there is money to be made via mobile devices, you can expect more malware for these devices to appear.

Antivirus (AV) software for mobile devices includes a lot of the same capabilities you find in computer AV software. This includes both real-time virus scanning and automatic signature updates. You can find mobile-device software that's currently available by searching on the Internet for **mobile device antivirus** in your favorite search engine.

Minimizing Risks with Bluetooth Devices

It's important to understand Bluetooth vulnerabilities. Bluetooth devices use wireless technologies to connect to each other in small personal area networks (PANs). The process of connecting the devices is known as *pairing*. When you connect two Bluetooth devices, they must be in discovery mode. Discovery mode allows the two devices to easily connect to each other.

However, after connecting the devices, discovery mode should be turned off. If discovery mode is left on, anyone else in range of the Bluetooth device can pair with it. For example, an attacker with a Bluetooth device on a Linux operating system can pair to a Bluetooth device in discovery mode with a simple command.

Discovery mode should be turned off after devices are paired. This reduces the possibility of an attacker taking over the device in a bluesnarfing or blue-jacking attack.

Two of the common Bluetooth attacks are bluesnarfing and bluejacking. *Bluesnarfing* is the unauthorized access of information on a Bluetooth device. Of course, when the attackers access it, they can steal the data; it can include contacts, emails, and any other data the device can store. In a *bluejacking* attack, the attacker hijacks the Bluetooth device and uses it to send messages. Depending on the capability of the Bluetooth device, the attacker may be able to send text messages, or full emails with attachments.

THE ESSENTIALS AND BEYOND

In this chapter, you learned about physical security. Sites are protected with varying levels of physical security depending on the needs of the organization. Physical security can include fences, lighting, cameras, guards, cipher locks, proximity-card readers, motion detectors, mantraps, and more. Computer security can be enhanced with Group Policy. You can organize users and computers in OUs and link GPOs to the OUs. These GPOs can include a wide variety of settings, including some that directly enhance physical security. You can control what computers individual users can log onto with Group Policy. You can also control what removable devices users can use with a Removable Storage Access policy. Other mobile devices such as mobile phones present their own risks. If valuable data is stored on a mobile device, the device should be protected with a password. Additionally, antivirus software can be installed on mobile devices to protect against emerging malware. Bluetooth devices should be switched into non-discovery mode to protect them against attackers.

ADDITIONAL EXERCISES

▶ Explore your environment. List all the physical security mechanisms employed.

▶ Determine whether any hubs are used in your environment.

▶ Create an OU named Testing. Create a GPO named Restrictions. Modify the GPO so that only administrators can log onto any computers in the OU.

▶ If you have a cell phone, determine whether it can be password-protected.

To compare your answers to the author's, please visit **www.sybex.com/go/ securityessentials**.

REVIEW QUESTIONS

1. Of the following choices, what can be used to prevent tailgating?

    A. Cipher lock **C.** Mantrap

    B. Proximity card **D.** Cameras

2. You want to improve basic security with network devices. Which of the following steps can you take?

    A. Replace all hubs with switches. **C.** Replace all routers with switches.

    B. Replace all switches with hubs. **D.** Replace all switches with routers.

3. True or false: You can create GPOs, modify their settings, link a GPO to an OU, and manage all users and computers in the OU with the GPO settings.

(Continues)

THE ESSENTIALS AND BEYOND   *(Continued)*

4. True or false: The Default Domain Controllers policy applies to all users and computers in the domain.

5. You want to restrict what computers a user can log onto. What Group Policy setting should you configure?

6. You have modified the Password Policy settings for a GPO so that passwords must be at least 15 characters long. You have linked the GPO to an OU named IT, which includes administrators working in the IT department. What is the effect on these administrators?

   A. Unable to determine.

   B. The administrators are required to have a password 15 characters long.

   C. This policy is ignored because only a Password Policy linked to the domain will be used.

   D. None. Group Policy settings don't apply to administrators.

7. A user named Joe is in the Administrators group. The Administrators group is added to the Allow Log On Locally Group Policy setting for a server. Joe's account has been added to the Deny Log On Locally setting for this server. What is the effect for Joe?

   A. Unable to determine.

   B. Joe is unable to log on because deny takes precedence.

   C. Joe is able to log on because he's in the Administrators group.

   D. Joe is able to log on locally, but he can't log on remotely.

8. True or false: You can restrict access to removable devices with Group Policy.

9. What can be done to protect mobile devices such as mobile phones? (Choose all that apply.)

   A. Password-protect them.   **C.** Enable discovery mode.

   B. Install antivirus software.   **D.** Add Internet access.

CHAPTER 10

Enforcing Confidentiality with Encryption

A key part of the security triad (confidentiality, integrity, and availability) is confidentiality. Authentication and access controls help protect data from loss of confidentiality, and you can also encrypt data to protect it. The two primary ways of encrypting data are symmetric and asymmetric encryption. You can also provide one-way encryption with hashing functions.

Encryption and cryptographic methods are used to protect many types of data used in day-to-day work by many end users. For example, many users regularly encrypt and digitally sign email to provide different protections. Similarly, many users use the NTFS built-in feature Encrypting File System (EFS) to encrypt important folders and files. BitLocker Drive Encryption is a newer technology that encrypts entire drive volumes. An extension of BitLocker is BitLocker To Go; it allows users to easily encrypt entire USB flash drives. This chapter includes these concepts in the following topics:

▶ **Comparing encryption methods**

▶ **Securing email**

▶ **Understanding EFS**

▶ **Exploring BitLocker Drive Encryption**

Comparing Encryption Methods

Chapter 1, "Understanding Core Security Principles," introduced the security triad of confidentiality, integrity, and availability. Confidentiality ensures that unauthorized individuals aren't able to access data. One of the methods used to prevent the loss of confidentiality is encryption.

Encryption scrambles data so that unauthorized users are unable to read it. There are many different types of encryption protocols and algorithms in use; you've already read about several of them in this book. For example, Chapter 8, "Understanding Wireless Security," provided a short introduction to encryption. As a reminder, most encryption includes an algorithm and a key. The algorithm provides a mathematical formula that identifies how data is to be encrypted. The key is a number that provides randomization for the encryption.

Most encryption algorithms are in one of two categories: symmetric and asymmetric. Hash functions are another type of cryptographic method used to provide one-way encryption of data. Each method is discussed in the following sections.

Although there are hardware devices that will encrypt data, the encryption methods focused on in this chapter are software-based. In other words, software is used to scramble the data.

Understanding Symmetric Encryption

Symmetric encryption uses a single key to encrypt and decrypt data. More specifically, the key that is used to encrypt data is the same key used to decrypt it. For example, if an algorithm uses the key 1A2B3C4D5E6F7A8B9C (a hexadecimal number) to encrypt data, this same key must be used to decrypt it. An important part of symmetric encryption is that both parties must know what the symmetric key is, and this key must be kept secret from other parties. You'll see later in this chapter how asymmetric encryption can help with this.

Figure 10.1 shows the process for both encryption and decryption. The encryption algorithm converts plain-text data into ciphered text. The data can be decrypted using the decryption process of the algorithm with the same key that was used for encryption.

The key used in symmetric encryption is frequently called a *secret key*. This key must be kept secret between the two parties encrypting and decrypting the data. If anyone else discovers the key, they're able to decrypt the data.

Symmetric encryption uses a single key (a secret key) for encryption and decryption. Asymmetric encryption uses two keys (a public key and a private key).

▶

When a strong encryption algorithm is used, an attacker can't decrypt the data without the key within a reasonable amount of time.

▶

▶

The key provides a randomization factor for the ciphered text. When a different key is used, the ciphered text is completely different.

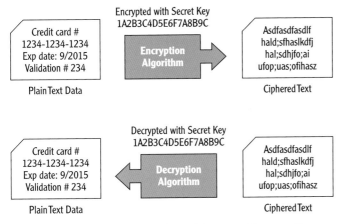

FIGURE 10.1 Encrypting data with symmetric encryption

Symmetric encryption algorithms frequently change the key. For example, one file may be encrypted with a key of 123, and another file may be encrypted with a key of 456. Even if an attacker discovers the key of 123 and can decrypt the first file, the 123 key can't be used to decrypt the second file encrypted with a key of 456.

When weak keys are used or keys aren't kept secret, attackers can potentially steal or obtain the keys and use them to access the data that has been encrypted. Chapter 8 talked about Wired Equivalent Privacy (WEP) and many of its flaws. One significant flaw was that part of an encryption key was transmitted over the air in clear text. Another flaw was that the same keys were reused frequently in the same transmission.

In contrast, a single system using a 256-bit key may never use the same key twice in the lifetime of the system. If you use a key of 16 bits, there are only 65,536 possible keys that can be used. Increase the number of bits to 40, and you increase the number of possible keys to more than a trillion. With 256 bits used for the keys, there are over 1.e+77 possibilities (1 followed by 77 zeroes!).

Some common symmetric encryption algorithms are as follows:

Advanced Encryption Standard (AES) This is the standard used to encrypt a wide variety of data due to its speed and efficiency. It's described in more depth in the following section.

Data Encryption Standard (DES) An older encryption protocol, DES has been cracked and isn't recommended for use. However, some legacy applications still use it.

> The actual keys are much more complex than 123 or 456. Keys are often 128 bits long or longer.

3DES (Triple DES)   Triple DES was introduced to improve DES. However, it's processor-intensive, resulting in slow encryption and decryption times. AES is much quicker and more efficient.

International Data Encryption Algorithm (IDEA)   IDEA was very popular for a period of time. But it's used less today, because newer standards (such as AES) are more efficient.

Blowfish and Twofish   These are two other strong encryption algorithms that are being used less in favor of the more efficient AES.

It's worthwhile noting that end users don't often choose the encryption algorithm. Instead, the encryption algorithm is selected by either the software or an administrator. However, there are some exceptions. For example, in Chapter 8 you saw how AES could be selected for a wireless connection.

Exploring AES

The *Advanced Encryption Standard (AES)* is a very strong, efficient encryption algorithm and uses less computer resources than other algorithms. It was picked from 15 competing algorithms in a 5-year process by the National Institute of Standards and Technology (NIST). It was adopted as a U.S. federal government standard in 2002 and has also been adopted by multiple public sector organizations.

▶

BitLocker and BitLocker To Go are covered later in this chapter.

AES is also used in many nongovernment applications. For example, Kerberos (the primary network-authentication protocol used in Microsoft's Active Directory) uses AES to encrypt data. WPA2 (a wireless encryption protocol mentioned in Chapter 8) uses AES. BitLocker and BitLocker To Go use AES to encrypt hard drives and USB flash drives, respectively.

Most encryption algorithms (including AES) are published and available for anyone to study. For example, if you want to view the AES algorithm, you can use your favorite search engine to search for **AES algorithm**. You'll find a wide assortment of highly technical and complex explanations of the algorithm along with some high-level overviews. In short, the algorithm isn't kept secret. However, the key used to encrypt and decrypt any piece of data *is* kept secret.

If you're a mathematician, you may be interested in the complex algorithm AES uses to shift data in multiple rounds using different substitutions, transpositions, and mixing operations. But at this stage of your learning, the most important thing to realize is that AES is a well-respected standard for symmetric encryption.

AES can use 128-bit, 194-bit, or 256-bit keys. When more bits are used in the encryption keys, the keys becomes harder to guess. In other words, AES-256 is more secure than AES using 128 bit keys.

◄

AES can use multiple different key sizes. However, only AES-256 includes the key size in the name. AES may use 128 or 194 bits, whereas AES-256 uses 256 bits.

ATTACKERS CAN DECRYPT ENCRYPTED DATA

Given enough time and resources, attackers can decrypt data even if they don't know the correct key. One of the goals of encryption is to make this sufficiently difficult that it isn't worthwhile to the attacker. You can ensure that it costs more money than the data is worth and/or ensure that it simply takes too long.

For example, AES can use 128 bits. It's estimated that it would take more than two million, million, million (18 zeros) years to crack this key and then read the data. If an attacker invested millions in multiple supercomputers and networked them together to crack a key, the time might be reduced. But it's still unlikely that the key would be discovered in the attacker's lifetime.

But if the data is important, you can increase the key size. AES can also use 192 bits or 256 bits. If you use AES with 256 bits, it's estimated that it would take more than 10^{51} years to crack the key. (That's 10 with 51 zeros behind it.) In contrast, many early algorithms used 40 bits and could sometimes be cracked within a week.

Similarly, think of data encrypted on the Internet, such as your credit-card number. If an attacker devoted millions of dollars to discover the key and get your credit information, they still wouldn't be able to discover the key in their lifetime. And by the time that single key was discovered, the credit card would most likely no longer be valid.

Understanding Asymmetric Encryption

Asymmetric encryption uses two matched keys, a *public key* and a *private key*. These two keys work together and are useful only when used with the other key in the pair. When the public key is used to encrypt data, only the private key can be used to decrypt the data, and vice versa. When the private key is used to encrypt data, only the public key can be used to decrypt it.

◄

Asymmetric encryption is also known as *public-key encryption*.

The public key is freely shared with others. However, the private key is kept private and never shared. Only one entity (such as a user or a server) has access to the private key. If the private key is shared or compromised, the key pair is no longer safe to use.

Asymmetric encryption is about 1,000 times slower than symmetric encryption. Because of this, asymmetric encryption isn't suitable to encrypt massive amounts of data. But it's ideally suited to encrypt the secret key that is used for symmetric encryption.

As an example, imagine that you wanted to encrypt a 10 MB file and pass it back and forth between two users over a network. If you encrypted it using symmetric encryption, imagine that it would take one second to encrypt and one second to decrypt. (One second is just a reference point; the actual time would be different, but the math is easy to see with one second.) If it took one second with symmetric encryption, it would take 1,000 seconds (almost 16 minutes) to encrypt the data with asymmetric encryption, and 1,000 seconds to decrypt the data with asymmetric encryption.

Clearly, symmetric encryption is quicker. However, the challenge is to let both sides know what the symmetric key is without letting anyone else know. The systems can't just whisper it over the network.

Instead, asymmetric encryption is used to encrypt the symmetric key. Even if the symmetric key is 256 bits long, it's trivial to encrypt and decrypt these 256 bits with asymmetric encryption, especially when comparing the encryption of 256 bits with the encryption of a 10 MB file.

As a reminder, symmetric encryption uses the same key for both encryption and decryption. For secure encryption, the secret key must be kept secret, and it must be changed often. By using asymmetric encryption to encrypt and decrypt the secret key, the key can be privately exchanged between two parties without allowing anyone else to discover it.

Look at Figure 10.2 as you read the following description. Imagine that Maria's computer is trying to establish a secure session with the server. The server has a private key matched with a public key shared with Maria's computer. Remember, the goal is to use asymmetric encryption to privately share the secret key.

The secret key (1A2B in the example) will ultimately be used to symmetrically encrypt data transmitted between the two machines. Maria's system creates the secret key and then encrypts it with the server's public key. The encrypted secret key is then sent to the server that holds the matching private key. If anyone intercepts the encrypted secret key, it isn't useful to them because it can only be decrypted with the matching private key, which is kept private.

> **Asymmetric encryption uses matched key pairs of a public key and a private key. These two keys work only with each other.**

> **The secret key will actually be much longer, but it's shortened to 1A2B here for brevity. Similarly, the public and private keys are really much longer.**

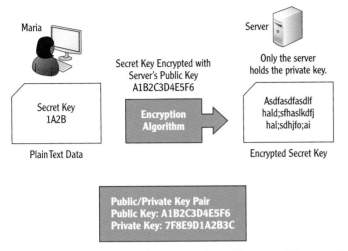

FIGURE 10.2 Encrypting a secret key with asymmetric encryption

Figure 10.3 shows the decryption process. When the server receives the encrypted secret key, it uses the private key in the matched key pair to decrypt the secret key. At this point, both parties know what the secret key is, but no one else knows what it is. The data that is to be transferred between the two machines can then be encrypted and decrypted with the secret key using symmetric encryption.

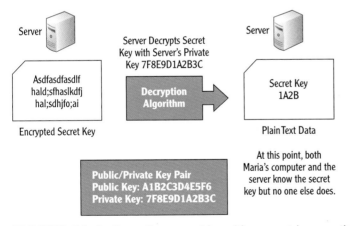

FIGURE 10.3 Decrypting a secret key with asymmetric encryption

Although this process shows how the public key is used to encrypt and the private key is used to decrypt, asymmetric encryption can also work in reverse. In other words, it's possible to use the private key to encrypt and then use the public key to decrypt. The "Securing Email" section later in this chapter shows how both processes can be used to encrypt and digitally sign email.

The following are two common asymmetric encryption algorithms:

▶ RSA (named after Rivest, Shamir, and Adleman, the three individuals who first described it)

▶ Diffie-Hellman (named after Diffie and Hellman)

Using Certificates to Share Public Keys

Chapter 11 covers certificates and certification authorities in more depth.

Certificates are digital files that include several pieces of key data used with cryptography. Certificates are used for a wide variety of purposes including sharing a public key.

Figure 10.4 shows a certificate with the public key selected. You can access it from the Personal certificate store by clicking the Advanced button. Notice that the public key is 1,024 bits long. It's using RSA, an algorithm used for public-key cryptography.

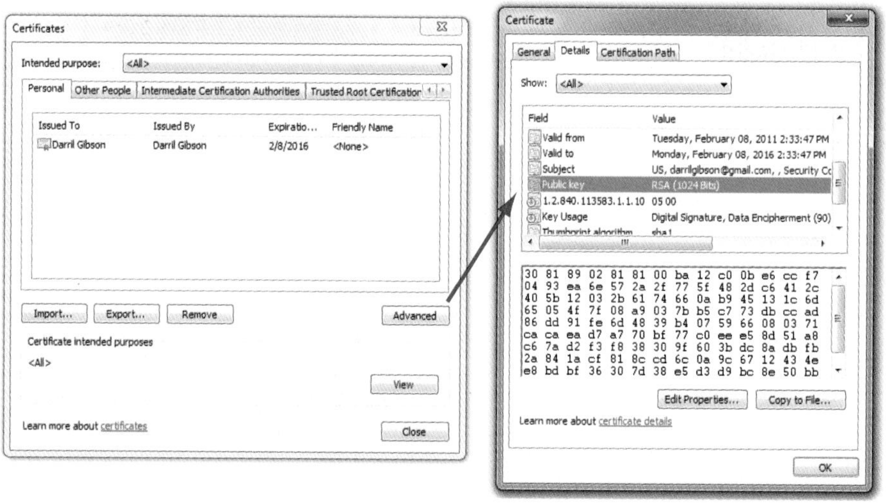

Many public keys used in certificates on the Internet are 2,048 bits long.

FIGURE 10.4 Viewing the public key in a certificate

Any user or computer with a matched key pair can freely share its public key in a certificate. As long as the private key stays private, the public and private keys can be used together for cryptography.

Understanding Hashing

Hashes have been mentioned several times in this book. One point that should be clear is that a *hash* is simply a number. A hashing algorithm is executed against a piece of data to create the hash (the number).

Message Digest 5 (MD5) is a popular hashing algorithm used today. MD5 creates 128-bit hashes, or numbers 128 bits long. It doesn't matter if MD5 is calculating a hash on a small 30 Kb email or a massive 2 GB .iso file—it will still create a 128-bit hash. Secure Hashing Algorithm (SHA) is another popular hashing algorithm. There are several versions of SHA, but SHA-1 is the most popular; it creates 160-bit hashes and is used by the U.S. government.

A key point about hashing is that as long as the content of the data isn't modified, the MD5 hash will always be the same. It doesn't matter how many times the MD5 algorithm is executed against the data. As long as the data remains the same, the resulting hash will always be the same.

There are some distinctive differences with hashing compared with symmetric and asymmetric encryption. Unlike symmetric and asymmetric encryption, a hash function doesn't use a key. Instead, the calculation is always the same and never randomized with a key. Also, a hash function is one-way. In other words, you can use a hash function to create a hash, but you can't re-create the original data from the hash.

Figure 10.5 shows the basic process of hashing for both MD5 and SHA-1. The hash function runs against the file or message, and the output is the hash.

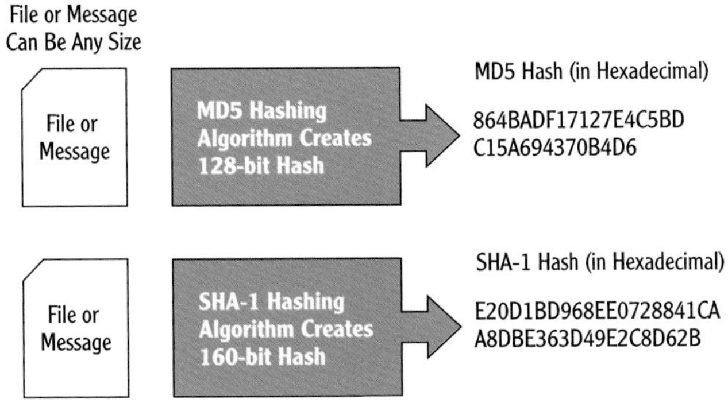

> ◀
>
> **You can use Bing or another search engine to search on calculate hash on files to locate free hash calculators.**

> ◀
>
> **Hashes are often displayed as hexadecimal numbers instead of bits. Each hexadecimal number is created with 4 bits; a 128-bit hash is represented as 32 hex numbers.**

File or Message
Can Be Any Size

File or Message → MD5 Hashing Algorithm Creates 128-bit Hash →

MD5 Hash (in Hexadecimal)

864BADF17127E4C5BD
C15A694370B4D6

File or Message → SHA-1 Hashing Algorithm Creates 160-bit Hash →

SHA-1 Hash (in Hexadecimal)

E20D1BD968EE0728841CA
A8DBE363D49E2C8D62B

FIGURE 10.5 Hashing algorithms create hashes.

Hashing is often used to verify the integrity of data or verify that it hasn't changed. For example, hashing can be used with email to verify that the message hasn't been modified. The following steps explain this process in general terms:

1. An email is created, and a hash is calculated for the email.

2. Both the email and the hash are sent.

3. When the email is received, the hash is calculated again.

If the calculated hash is the same as the received hash, the receiving system knows that the message hasn't been modified—it has retained integrity.

Similarly, you can use hashing to verify the integrity of downloaded files. For example, with a Microsoft TechNet subscription, you can download entire DVD images (as .iso image files). These files are often over 1 GB in size, and if a single bit is lost, the entire file is corrupt. But Microsoft posts the hash for these files.

Figure 10.6 shows a Microsoft TechNet download page with details expanded for a DVD image of a Windows Server 2008 DVD. Notice that the details include a SHA-1 hash. TechNet subscribers can download the files and, after download-ing them, use other tools to calculate the hash. They can then compare the hash displayed on TechNet with the hash calculated by their hashing tool. If the hashes are different, there's a problem.

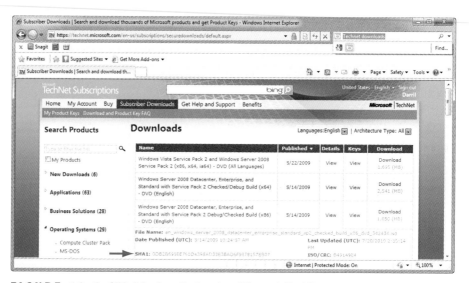

FIGURE 10.6 SHA-1 hashes displayed on Microsoft TechNet

Verifying the hash of a file also verifies that it hasn't been infected by mal-ware. For example, antivirus software can create hashes of uninfected execut-able files on Monday. (An executable file is a file that the computer runs or executes, such as a .exe file.) It can scan these files on Tuesday and calculate the hash again. If the hash on Tuesday is the same as the hash calculated on Monday, the file hasn't changed. If the antivirus software scans the files on

Friday and sees that one of the files has a different hash, it knows that file has been modified. Some files (such as Word documents) change regularly. However, executable files shouldn't change without an authorized update.

Securing Email

One of the common uses of cryptography is to secure email. There are two primary methods of securing email: encrypting messages and digitally signing them.

Email is encrypted to prevent the loss of confidentiality. As long as the data is securely encrypted, it can't be read. Even if an attacker uses a sniffer to capture an encrypted email sent over a network or the Internet, it's highly unlikely that the attacker will be able to read the contents.

◄

Encryption of email prevents loss of confidentiality.

A digital signature provides proof that an email was sent by an individual. For example, an executive of a company may want to send an email and provide assurances to others that the email wasn't spoofed. By digitally signing the email, others know definitively that the executive sent it.

In other words, the digital signature provides authentication of the sender. Digital signatures also provide integrity and nonrepudiation. (Chapter 5, "Using Audit Policies and Network Auditing," introduced nonrepudiation. As a reminder, nonrepudiation provides proof that an individual took a specific action and prevents the individual from believably denying the action.)

In the "Digitally Signing Email" section later in this chapter, you'll see how a digital signature uses hashing and asymmetric encryption together. It hashes the message to provide integrity. When integrity is verified with the hash, the recipient knows that the contents haven't been modified. The digital signature process encrypts and decrypts the hash with asymmetric encryption to provide authentication and nonrepudiation. Nonrepudiation prevents the sender of the email from denying having sent the email. It's worth noting that although a digital signature does encrypt the hash of the message, it doesn't encrypt the actual message. It's possible to encrypt the message, but a digital signature doesn't do so.

◄

Digitally signed email provides authentication, integrity, and nonrepudiation.

Secure/Multipurpose Internet Mail Extensions (S/MIME) is the underlying standard used for most email security. It uses public and private keys to encrypt and digitally sign email. The sender must have a certificate with a public key embedded that matches a private key that only the sender can access. Within an Active Directory domain, administrators often create a certification authority (CA) to issue and manage certificates. Additionally, public CAs issue and manage certificates that are commonly used on the Internet and elsewhere.

Encrypting Email

Most email programs such as Microsoft Outlook include the ability to encrypt email. Users are issued certificates that include a public key matched to a private key. The public key is publically available in a certificate. The private key is kept private and is available to only a single user.

When used in this way, the public key encrypts the email, and the private key decrypts it. For example, if you wanted to encrypt an email and send it to someone else, you would need a copy of their public key. Or more specifically, you'd need a copy of the certificate that holds their public key. Take a look at Figures 10.7 and 10.8. Figure 10.7 shows the process of the sender encrypting the email, and Figure 10.8 shows the process of the recipient decrypting the email. The steps are as follows:

▶

The secret key will be more complex, but A1B2 is used for brevity.

1. The sender creates a secret key for symmetric encryption.

   For example, the sender can create a secret key of A1B2. At this point, only the sender knows the secret key.

2. The sender encrypts the email using the secret key and symmetric encryption.

   The email can be decrypted only with this secret key, so the sender must also securely transmit the secret key to the recipient.

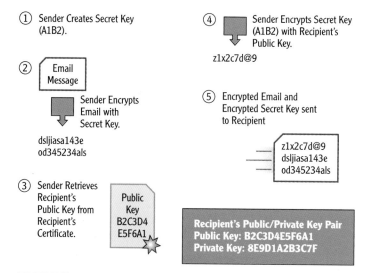

FIGURE 10.7 Sender process when encrypting email

3. The sender retrieves the recipient's certificate, which contains the recipient's public key.

4. The sender encrypts the secret key with the recipient's public key.

   At this point, the secret key A1B2 is encrypted to something like z1x2c7d@9. The encrypted key can't be used by anyone until it's decrypted, and it can be decrypted only with the recipient's private key.

5. The sender sends both the encrypted email and the encrypted secret key.

   Because the email and the secret key are both encrypted, nothing is readable even if an attacker captures the email with a sniffer.

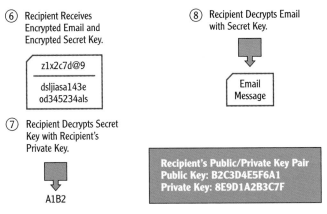

FIGURE 10.8 Recipient process when decrypting email

6. The recipient receives the encrypted email and the encrypted secret key.

7. The recipient decrypts the secret key using the recipient's private key.

8. The recipient uses the decrypted secret key to decrypt the contents of the email.

A common question many people have about this process is, "Why not use asymmetric encryption for the entire process?" In other words, instead of creating a secret key (step 1), encrypting the data with the secret key (step 2), and then encrypting the secret key with the public key (step 4), why not just encrypt the entire email with the public key?

It's a good question, but remember that asymmetric encryption is 1,000 times (or more) slower than symmetric encryption. It's much more efficient to use symmetric encryption to encrypt the data and only use asymmetric encryption to encrypt the secret key. Additionally, the symmetric key can be changed each time another email is sent. The symmetric keys are randomly generated for each email, which adds to the security of the transmission.

The wonderful part about this process is that it's automated. Within a Microsoft domain, applications can query Active Directory to locate certificates for other people. For example, if a user is using Microsoft Outlook, they select the Encrypt Message Contents And Attachments check box as shown in Figure 10.9 to encrypt the email. Microsoft Outlook then handles all the underlying details. When the email is received, the other user opens it, and the decryption is automatic.

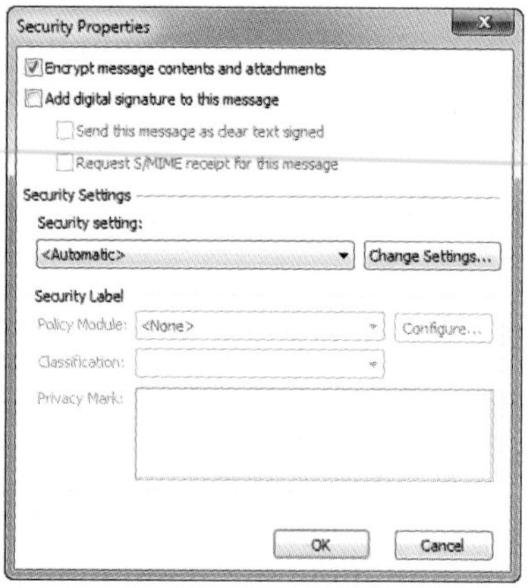

> **The process is automatic for users in the same domain. However, when users are outside a Microsoft Active Directory domain, the certificates must be exchanged manually.**

FIGURE 10.9 Encrypting an email with Microsoft Outlook

> **Chapter 5 describes how audit logs provide nonrepudiation by logging user activities. Digital signatures provide nonrepudiation for email.**

If two individuals wanted to send email, they could exchange certificates privately. The process is different for different applications; but in general, they would each create a certificate, exchange these certificates, and then install the certificates on their computers. Although it takes a lot more manual intervention to get this to work, a benefit is that it can work with different email programs. For example, both users wouldn't need to be running Microsoft Outlook.

Digitally Signing Email

A digitally signed email includes a digital signature. This provides proof that a specific person sent the email. It also provides nonrepudiation and integrity.

Digital signatures use hashing to provide integrity. The hash is calculated at the source and at the destination; as long as they're the same, the recipient has verification that the message hasn't been modified.

Public and private keys are used with digital signatures, but the process works a little differently than it does when you encrypt email. As a reminder, when you encrypt email, you retrieve the recipient's public key and use it to encrypt the email. In contrast, a digital signature is signed by the sender with the sender's private key.

Look at Figures 10.10 and 10.11 when reading through the following steps. Figure 10.10 shows the process of the sender digitally signing the email. Figure 10.11 shows the process of the recipient validating the digital signature.

1. The sender creates the email.

   For this example, the email doesn't need to be kept confidential. If it did need confidentiality, it could be encrypted. However, this example is focused only on the digital signature.

2. The email content is hashed.

   In this example, the hash is 1A3B5C7E9. If this were MD5, it would be 32 hexadecimal numbers; and if it were SHA-1, it would be 40 hexadecimal numbers. It's shortened here for brevity.

3. The hash of the email is encrypted with the sender's private key.

   In the example, this gives a result of 43c0lm120p. This encrypted hash is used as the digital signature.

> It's possible to only digitally sign an email, only encrypt an email, or both digitally sign it and encrypt it.

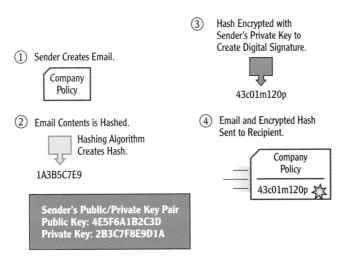

FIGURE 10.10 Sender's process when digitally signing email

4. The unencrypted email and the encrypted hash (the digital signature) are sent to the recipient.

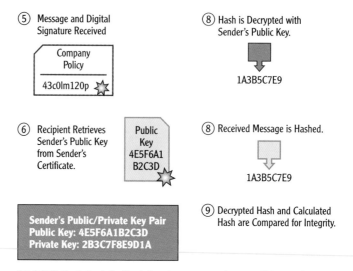

⑤ Message and Digital Signature Received

Company Policy
_____
43c0lm120p ☆

⑥ Recipient Retrieves Sender's Public Key from Sender's Certificate.

Public Key
4E5F6A1
B2C3D ☆

Sender's Public/Private Key Pair
Public Key: 4E5F6A1B2C3D
Private Key: 2B3C7F8E9D1A

⑧ Hash is Decrypted with Sender's Public Key.

1A3B5C7E9

⑧ Received Message is Hashed.

1A3B5C7E9

⑨ Decrypted Hash and Calculated Hash are Compared for Integrity.

FIGURE 10.11 Recipient's process when verifying a digital signature

5. The recipient receives both the message and the digital signature.

6. The recipient retrieves the sender's public key from the sender's certificate.

In some situations, the recipient may already have the sender's certificate. In other situations, the recipient may have to retrieve the certificate as well.

▶
If the public key can decrypt the hash, the hash must have been encrypted with the matching private key. This authenticates the sender and provides nonrepudiation.

7. The recipient decrypts the received hash with the sender's public key.

If the public key can't decrypt the encrypted hash, this indicates it wasn't encrypted with the sender's private key. However, if the public key can decrypt the encrypted hash, it proves that the hash was encrypted with the sender's private key. This authenticates the sender identified in the certificate. Also, the sender can't later deny sending the message (providing nonrepudiation), because the sender's private key was used to encrypt the hash.

In this example, the decrypted hash is 1A3B5C7E9 (the hash that was calculated and encrypted by the sender).

8. The received message is hashed.

   In this example, the resulting hash is 1A3B5C7E9.

9. The decrypted hash (1A3B5C7E9) from step 7 is compared against the recalculated hash (1A3B5C7E9) from step 8. If they're both the same, it verifies that the message hasn't lost integrity. In other words, it verifies that the message hasn't been modified.

Just as with the email and the encryption and decryption process, the digital signature process occurs with very little user interaction. For example, if a user is using Microsoft Outlook, they simply select a check box to add a digital signature to a message (shown in Figure 10.9 earlier). Microsoft Outlook then handles all the underlying details. When the email is received, the other user opens it, and the digital signature is verified. If there are any problems, the user that received the message is notified.

Understanding EFS

Chapter 4, "Securing Access with Permissions," introduced NTFS. NTFS provides security such as assigning permissions to files and folders to restrict access. Another feature of NTFS is Encrypting File System (EFS). On an NTFS volume, you can use EFS to encrypt NTFS files and folders. When a file is encrypted with EFS, only specific users can access it.

You can encrypt folders and files with EFS using the following steps:

1. Launch Windows Explorer, and browse to the folder.

2. Right-click the folder, and select Properties.

3. With the General tab selected, click the Advanced button.

4. On the Advanced Attributes page, select the Encrypt Contents To Secure Data check box, as shown in Figure 10.12.

5. Click OK. When prompted, select Apply Changes To This Folder, Subfolders, And Files.

When an authorized user opens an encrypted file, it's automatically decrypted without any user interaction. The following section shows the steps you can follow to encrypt and decrypt files. In addition to these steps, a lot of other activity is going on behind the scenes to encrypt and decrypt files with EFS.

> Microsoft recommends that you encrypt folders instead of individual files. All files within the folder are automatically encrypted.

◄

> It's possible to configure a Group Policy setting to remove the ability to encrypt files with EFS. If EFS isn't showing, this could be why.

◄

◄

> Encrypted folders and files appear with green text in Windows Explorer.

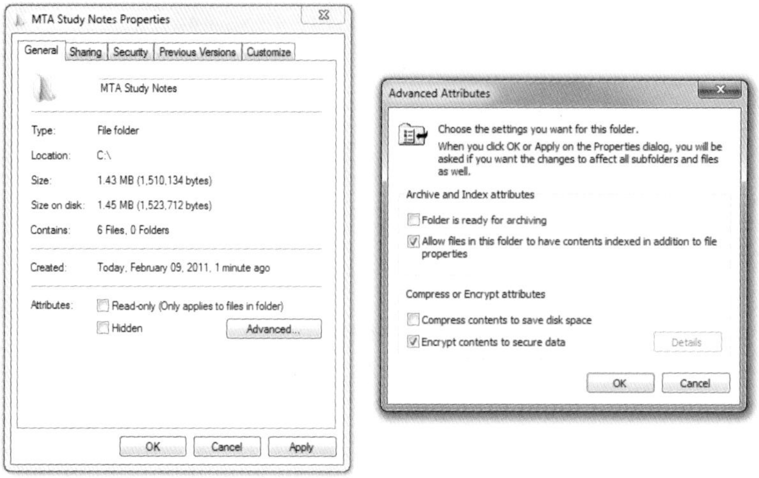

FIGURE 10.12 Encrypting a folder with EFS

Encrypting and Decrypting Files with EFS

EFS uses a combination of both symmetric and asymmetric encryption to encrypt files. It creates a different symmetric secret key for each file it encrypts. It then encrypts this secret key with asymmetric encryption. The following steps show the overall process when a file is encrypted with EFS:

1. EFS creates a symmetric secret key to encrypt the file.

   A different symmetric secret key is used for each file. Even if an attacker somehow discovers the secret key for one file, they can't use this same key to decrypt other files.

2. EFS retrieves the user's public key.

   The first time a user encrypts a file, EFS works with the operating system to create an EFS encryption certificate for the user. The certificate includes a public key for the user. The user is granted exclusive access to a matching private key.

3. EFS encrypts the symmetric secret key with the user's public key.

4. The encrypted symmetric secret key is included in the header of the encrypted file.

When a user double-clicks a file to open it, EFS takes the following steps:

1. The encrypted symmetric secret key is retrieved from the file.

> **EFS is only as secure as the user's password. If the user's password is discovered, an attacker can log on as the user and open encrypted files.**

2. The user's private key decrypts the symmetric secret key.

3. EFS decrypts the file with the decrypted symmetric secret key.

Again, this process is automatic. As long as users don't lose access to their private keys, the files are decrypted automatically without any other user interaction.

End users will rarely manipulate their secret key. However, if the password for a local user (not a domain user) is reset, the private key associated with the account is lost. The user won't be able to decrypt any files encrypted with the previous password. This doesn't occur if a user changes their password, only if the password is reset, such as by an administrator. Additionally, just as with a file, the end user's private key can become corrupt and no longer usable.

Understanding the Recovery Agent

If the user's private key is lost or becomes corrupt, the user can no longer decrypt the files. But EFS includes a recovery procedure to mitigate the risk of lost data.

By default, the built-in Administrator account on a system is the designated recovery agent (DRA) for EFS. As the DRA, an administrator can decrypt files. In some organizations, another individual (instead of the administrator account) is assigned the role of DRA.

The DRA capability can be disabled. For some organizations, the risk of the DRA account being used to access encrypted data is greater than the risk of losing data due to lost keys. In this case, the DRA isn't enabled; and if a user's private EFS key is lost or corrupted, the data is lost forever.

Understanding Behavior When Files Are Moved or Copied

Chapter 4 stressed the behavior of permissions when files are copied or moved. As a reminder, you can use two simple rules to identify the permissions on moved or copied files:

▶ If you move a file on the same partition, the originally assigned permissions are retained.

▶ Any other time, the originally assigned permissions are lost, and only the inherited permissions apply.

Chapter 3 covered how to create a password reset disk. If this exists, the user can reset the password without administrator help and without losing access to the encrypted files.

▶

When you're moving or copying files, encryption always wins. If there is any way the file can be encrypted in the process, it's encrypted.

EFS works a little differently. The one rule to remember with EFS is *encryption always wins*.

The idea here is that you've determined a file is important enough to encrypt it to protect it. The operating system won't decrypt it automatically if you move it or copy it to any other NTFS drive. If the file started out encrypted, or the target folder has encryption enabled, the file will be encrypted.

For example, if the `C:\Encrypted` folder has the `encrypted` attribute enabled, then all files moved or copied into this folder will be encrypted. If an encrypted file is moved or copied from this folder to any other location on an NTFS file system, it will stay encrypted.

Table 10.1 shows the result for different encryption states. With encryption, it doesn't matter if the file is moved or copied. The result is always the same: encryption wins.

TABLE 10.1   Effect on encryption when files are moved or copied

Original State of Encryption	Target Location Encryption Setting	Result
Encryption enabled	Encryption enabled	Encrypted
No encryption	Encryption enabled	Encrypted
Encryption enabled	No encryption	Encrypted
No encryption	No encryption	No encryption

If you're using FAT (or FAT32) drives, things work a little differently. As a reminder, FAT doesn't support any of the security features of NTFS, including encryption. FAT doesn't have the header of an NTFS file, so it can't store the keys needed to decrypt the file.

If you're an authorized user of the file and you move it or copy it to a FAT drive, EFS decrypts it and stores it in unencrypted format. However, if an unauthorized user moves or copies an encrypted file to a FAT drive, the file is copied in the encrypted format. Also, because FAT doesn't store the encryption keys, the encryption keys for the file are lost, and the file will stay encrypted forever.

Exploring BitLocker Drive Encryption

BitLocker Drive Encryption uses encryption to protect data on entire volumes. In contrast, EFS encrypts individual files. There are two flavors of BitLocker: BitLocker and BitLocker To Go.

You can use BitLocker to encrypt entire volumes within Windows 7, Windows Vista, Windows Server 2008, and Windows Server 2008 R2. You can also use BitLocker To Go to encrypt removable USB flash drives on Windows 7 and Windows Server 2008 R2 systems.

Figure 10.13 shows the BitLocker Drive Encryption page in the Control Panel on a Windows 7 system. In the figure, you can see that BitLocker isn't enabled on the system volume. However, BitLocker To Go is enabled on one of the USB flash drives inserted into the computer.

◄ **BitLocker encrypts volumes or partitions. If a single hard drive is configured as two partitions (such as C: and D:), BitLocker can encrypt D: without encrypting C:.**

◄ **BitLocker is available only on the Ultimate and Enterprise versions of Windows 7 and Windows Vista.**

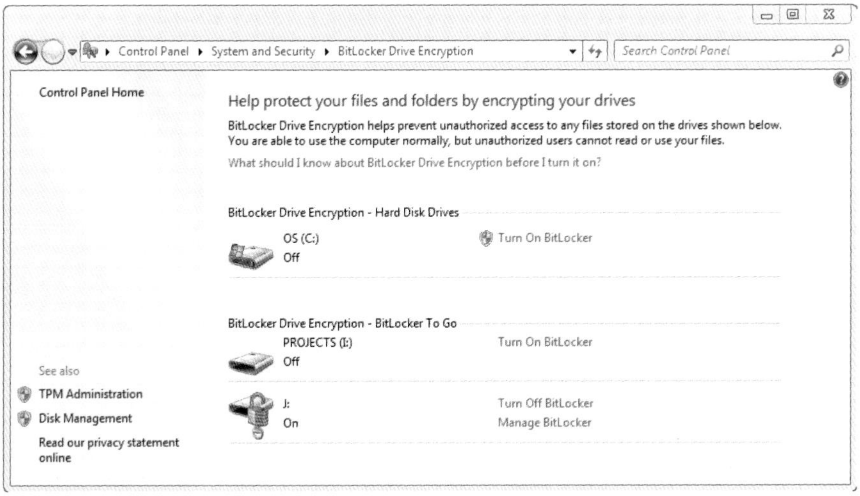

FIGURE 10.13 BitLocker Drive Encryption in the Control Panel

◄ **BitLocker uses AES to encrypt disk drives.**

Understanding BitLocker Requirements

Both BitLocker and BitLocker To Go are available by default in Windows 7 Enterprise and Ultimate editions, but they aren't available by default in Windows Server 2008 or Windows Server 2008 R2. You can add BitLocker as a feature using the Server Manager. This enables BitLocker on Windows Server 2008 and both BitLocker and BitLocker To Go on Windows Server 2008 R2.

If a computer is stolen and the hard drive is moved to another system, it will remain locked and protected.

BitLocker can use a Trusted Platform Module (TPM) version 1.2 or a removable USB storage device to lock and unlock the drive. The TPM is a chip on the computer's motherboard. It includes a program used to check the hardware on a system for suspicious modifications, and it stores and protects the key used to unlock the volume. The TPM examines different aspects of the environment such as ensuring that boot files haven't been modified. If these checks pass, the TPM module releases the key to unlock the volume. If the checks don't pass, the volume remains locked. Even though the TPM is hardware, the drive is still encrypted using software methods. The TPM uses the hardware (the TPM chip) to protect the key if the checks fail.

Not all systems have a TPM. Additionally, the TPM isn't enabled by default in many BIOS systems. If your system doesn't have a TPM, it's possible to use a USB flash drive that includes a startup key. When the system is booted, you insert the USB flash drive, and BitLocker reads the startup key. BitLocker then unlocks the drive. It's highly recommended that the USB flash drive not be stored with the computer. Otherwise, a thief can steal the computer and the USB flash drive.

You can also implement additional authentication methods with BitLocker to increase security. The following combinations are supported:

TPM and a Personal Identification Number (PIN)   A user has to be present to enter the PIN on bootup.

TPM and a USB Flash Drive   The USB should be removed after the system is booted. A user can then insert the USB when the system needs to be rebooted.

TPM, a PIN, and a USB Flash Drive   The user inserts the USB flash drive on boot and also enters the PIN when prompted.

Understanding Recovery Keys

You can use a recovery key to recover data on a BitLocker drive if the drive becomes locked. For example, if the computer suffers a hardware failure, you can move the hard drive to a different computer and unlock it with the recovery key.

When you enable BitLocker on a drive, you're prompted to save the recovery key. You can store the key as a file or print it. If you store it as a file, it needs to be stored on a different drive than the encrypted drive.

If you want to make an additional copy of the recovery key at any time, you can do so via the Manage BitLocker window in the Control Panel. But you need to be able to unlock the drive to make a copy of the recovery key.

Using BitLocker To Go

BitLocker To Go is a very convenient capability built into Windows 7 and Windows Server 2008 R2. It allows you to easily encrypt USB flash drives. You can use the following steps to encrypt an individual USB drive using BitLocker To Go on a Windows 7 system:

1. Insert the USB flash drive that you want to encrypt into your computer USB slot.

2. Launch the Control Panel from the Start menu.

3. Type **BitLocker** in the Search Control Panel text box. Select BitLocker Drive Encryption.

4. Locate your USB Flash drive in the list, and select Turn On BitLocker.

5. Select the Use A Password To Unlock The Drive check box.

6. Enter a password in the Type Your Password and Retype Your Password text boxes. Click Next.

7. On the How Do You Want To Store Your Recovery Key page, select Save The Recovery Key To A File.

8. Browse to a location where you want to save the recovery key, and click Save.

9. Click Next. Click the Start Encrypting button. The encryption process begins. Depending on the size of the USB drive and the speed of your system, this could take a while.

10. When the encryption process is complete, click Close.

Files on this drive are encrypted at this point. If you remove the USB flash drive and put it back into a Windows 7 or Windows Server 2008 R2 system with BitLocker enabled, you'll be prompted to enter the password. Enter the password and click Unlock, and you can use the drive normally.

You can also access the files from systems that don't have BitLocker enabled. For example, you can insert the USB flash drive into a Windows XP system and browse to it with Windows Explorer. After double-clicking the BitLocker To Go application, you'll be prompted to enter a password, as shown in Figure 10.14, to launch the BitLocker To Go Reader. Enter the correct password and click Unlock, and you can access the files.

◄

You can also configure BitLocker to automatically unlock the removable drive when you insert it into a compatible computer with BitLocker installed.

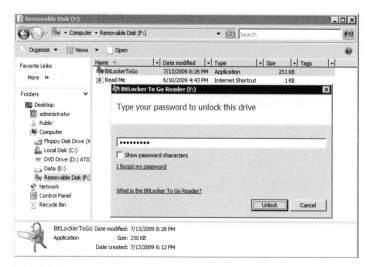

FIGURE 10.14 Using the BitLocker To Go Reader

> You can only read and copy files from a BitLocker To Go encrypted drive with the BitLocker To Go Reader. You can't modify them or copy files back to the USB drive.

You won't be able to modify the files from the USB drive when using the BitLocker To Go Reader. Additionally, you can't copy files to the USB drive with the BitLocker To Go Reader. However, the BitLocker To Go Reader lets you copy files from the drive to a drive on another computer.

THE ESSENTIALS AND BEYOND

In this chapter, you learned about different methods of encrypting data. Symmetric encryption uses a single key to encrypt and decrypt data. Asymmetric encryption uses two keys (a public key and a private key) to encrypt and decrypt data. Asymmetric encryption is about 1,000 times slower than symmetric encryption, and it's typically used only to encrypt and decrypt symmetric keys. AES is a strong, efficient symmetric encryption used in many situations including in Kerberos and BitLocker. Hashing provides one-way encryption and is used for integrity. MD5 and SHA-1 are two common hashing algorithms. You can secure email by encrypting it and digitally signing it. Both require the use of certificates to publically share the public key. EFS is built into NTFS and allows users to encrypt folders and files. EFS uses a combination of asymmetric and symmetric encryption. BitLocker Drive Encryption can encrypt entire volumes. It can be used with or without a TPM v1.2 module built into the motherboard. BitLocker To Go can be used to encrypt data on USB flash drives.

(Continues)

THE ESSENTIALS AND BEYOND *(Continued)*

ADDITIONAL EXERCISES

▶ List the key difference between symmetric and asymmetric encryption algorithms.

▶ Determine whether your email supports digital signatures.

▶ Encrypt a folder in NTFS. Copy an unencrypted file to the folder, and determine whether it's encrypted.

▶ Encrypt a USB flash drive with BitLocker To Go.

To compare your answers to the author's, please visit **www.sybex.com/go/ securityessentials**.

REVIEW QUESTIONS

1. Name the type of encryption that uses a single key for encryption and decryption.

2. Name the key (or keys) used by asymmetric encryption.

3. Of the following choices, which one provides the strongest symmetric encryption?

    A. RSA   **C.** DES

    B. AES   **D.** MD5

4. Of the following choices, which is a one-way hashing function?

    A. RSA   **C.** SHA-1

    B. AES   **D.** WPA2

5. You want to provide confidentiality for email. What should you do?

    A. Encrypt it using S/MIME.   **C.** Encrypt it with BitLocker.

    B. Digitally sign it.   **D.** Encrypt it with EFS.

6. A user encrypted a file with EFS. The user's certificate became corrupt, and the user can no longer open the file. Who, if anyone, can access the file?

    A. The user, with the user's password-recovery disk   **C.** The user, with a recovery key

    B. An administrator, as a designated recovery agent   **D.** An administrator, with a recovery key

7. You've moved an encrypted file from one NTFS partition to another. What is the state of the encryption attribute?

(Continues)

THE ESSENTIALS AND BEYOND *(Continued)*

8. Of the following choices, what does a TPM do?

   A. Secures the key for BitLocker   **C.** Secures the key for RSA

   B. Secures the key for AES   **D.** Ensures that the private key is publically available

9. True or false: You can use BitLocker to encrypt a hard drive even if the system doesn't have a TPM.

10. True or false: BitLocker To Go can encrypt USB flash drives.

CHAPTER 11

Understanding Certificates and a PKI

A Public Key Infrastructure (PKI) includes all the pieces required to issue, use, and manage certificates. Certificates (also called public key certificates) are used for a wide variety of purposes to provide different types of security. For example, certificates are used to digitally sign and encrypt email, as mentioned in Chapter 10, "Enforcing Confidentiality with Encryption."

The certificate includes details about who issued it, who it was issued to, and when it expires, as well as unique data such as a public key and a serial number. Because the certificate can be used to provide security assurances, it's checked each time it's used to ensure that the certificate hasn't expired, wasn't tampered with, or has been revoked. If the certificate doesn't pass these checks, the user sees an error detailing the problem.

The certification authority (CA) is an important element of the PKI. The CA issues certificates to users and computers, and it regularly responds to queries about the certificates to validate them. The CA can also revoke certificates if they become compromised to let users know that the certificate has a problem. This chapter includes these concepts in the following topics:

▶ **Understanding a certificate**

▶ **Exploring the components of a PKI**

Understanding a Certificate

A *certificate* is a file that is used for a variety of security purposes. The certificate can be issued to a person and associated with a user account. For example, users may have smart cards for authentication. The certificate file is embedded into the smart card, allowing the user to carry the certificate with them from system to system. It can also be issued to a device such

Most certificates are files with an extension of `.cer`. The files are formatted in a special X.509 format.

as a server, workstation, or mobile phone, and will stay with that device for the lifetime of the certificate. Within a domain, certificates are normally issued to users automatically with little, if any, user interaction. However, administrators often request and install certificates on servers manually.

A certificate includes several key pieces of data, including the following:

▶ Who it was issued to

▶ Who issued it

▶ Its purpose(s)

▶ Validity dates (including an expiration date)

▶ Its unique serial number

▶ Public key

The public key embedded in the certificate is matched with a private key. The private key is kept private while the public key is shared in the certificate.

As an example, Figure 11.1 shows several certificates installed on a Windows 7 computer along with the general details of one of the certificates. Notice that you can import or export the certificate files from here. You can also select any of the certificates and click View to see the details on the certificate.

Steps in the "Viewing Certificate Properties" section later in this chapter show you how to view the properties of a certificate.

FIGURE 11.1 Viewing a certificate

Certificates are used for several purposes. The following list shows some common usages:

Authentication   Certificates help users and computers prove their identity. When a certificate is issued to a person or a server from a trusted entity, any system utilizing the certificate as a source of authentication has assurances that the other party is who they claim to be. For example, a certificate can be issued to an Internet web server such as the one hosting the Dell website. If you connect to `dell.com` to purchase a product, the web server presents the certificate to your web browser as proof that it actually is a Dell web server.

Encryption The certificate may be used to encrypt and decrypt data at rest and during transmission in order to prevent unauthorized disclosure of data. Encrypted data can't be read by others unless they have the correct keys to decrypt the data.

Digital Signatures A digital signature can be added to an email to provide proof to the recipient of who sent the email. It provides authentication, integrity, and nonrepudiation.

Code Signing Active content used on Internet web pages can be digitally signed to identify the author and verify that the code hasn't been modified. Attackers don't want to be identified, so they won't sign their malicious code. However, legitimate companies use code-signing certificates to sign active content and add legitimacy to the code. It's possible to block all unsigned code from running within a web browser such as Internet Explorer.

Certificates are issued and managed by certification authorities (CAs). A CA can be a public organization or a private entity within an organization. For example, VeriSign is a company that provides public CA services and that issues certificates that are widely used on the Internet. However, you can also create a private CA with Microsoft's Active Directory Certificate Services (AD CS) by adding the AD CS role to a Windows Server 2008 server. Administrators can then manage the server running AD CS in their environment to issue and manage certificates.

Comparing Public and Private Keys

Public and private keys were introduced in Chapter 10. As a reminder, these two keys are created in matched pairs and used for asymmetric encryption. Anything encrypted with a public key can be decrypted with the matching private key. Similarly, anything encrypted with a private key can be decrypted with the matching public key.

The private key is always kept private and never shared. If the private key is compromised and unauthorized personnel have access to it, the key pair shouldn't be used anymore. When a private key is compromised, the CA can revoke the certificate holding the matching public key.

In contrast, the public key is freely shared. The public key is embedded in a certificate, and the certificate is accessible to anyone who needs it. In a Microsoft

Chapter 10 presented several different encryption methods, including ones using certificates.

Chapter 10 explained how digital signatures are used to sign email.

CAs are explained in more depth in the "Exploring the Components of a PKI" section later in this chapter.

The keys in the pair can work only with each other. Keys from one pair can't decrypt data encrypted with a key in a different matched pair.

domain, the certificate with the public key can be automatically retrieved when needed. As an example, if a user wants to encrypt email using Microsoft Outlook, the user simply clicks a button. Outlook then queries Active Directory to locate the recipient's certificate and encrypts the email with the user's public key embedded in the retrieved certificate. On the Internet, the certificate holding the public key is sent to the recipient when it's needed.

As an example, Figure 11.2 shows the process of how a public key and a private key are used on the Internet to privately share a secret key for an HTTPS session. Imagine a user has subscribed to Microsoft's TechNet. Before the user signs onto the website, an HTTPS session is initiated to ensure that the user's name and password are encrypted before they're sent over the Internet.

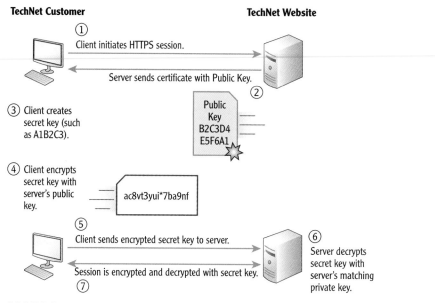

FIGURE 11.2 Creating an HTTPS session

The following steps show the overall process:

1. The client clicks a link or types in a URL to initiate the HTTPS session. Although this example shows how this works for a secure TechNet session, it works the same for any session secured with HTTPS.

2. After receiving the request, the server sends the client its certificate with the public key embedded. As a reminder, the public key is matched with a private key kept private on the server.

3. The client creates a secret key (such as A1B2C3), which will ultimately be used to encrypt the session data. The secret key will actually be much longer, but it's shortened here for brevity.

4. After creating the secret key, the client encrypts it with the server's public key. The secret key is now encrypted to cipher text (such as ac8vt3yui*7ba9nf), and only the server's private key can decrypt it.

5. The client sends the encrypted secret key (ac8vt3yui*7ba9nf) to the TechNet server. If anyone on the Internet captures the encrypted key, they won't be able to read it because it can be decrypted only with the server's private key.

6. When the server receives the encrypted secret key, it decrypts the key with the server's matching private key. At this point, both the client and the server know what the secret key is, but no one else knows it.

7. The HTTPS session is encrypted and decrypted with the secret key.

In this context, the secret key is sometimes called the *session key*. It will only be used for this session. The process repeats with a new session key for any other sessions.

WHY BOTHER WITH THE SECRET KEY?

A common question is, "The public and private keys are already being used, so why not use them to encrypt and decrypt the entire session?" On the surface, this sounds like it may be more efficient.

However, as mentioned in Chapter 10, asymmetric encryption with the public and private keys is about 1,000 times slower (and sometimes even slower than that) than symmetric encryption with a single symmetric key. It's much more efficient to only use the asymmetric process to privately share the secret key. When both parties know what the secret key is, they then switch to only using the secret key to encrypt and decrypt the session.

Understanding Certificate Errors

Several checks can occur to verify that a certificate is valid before it's accepted for its intended usage by a machine. These checks are typically automatic, but the user often sees an error if one of the checks fails.

For example, each time a certificate is passed to a client, the client may check with the CA to ensure that the certificate hasn't been revoked. The CA publishes a certificate revocation list (CRL, pronounced "crill") in the form of a certificate, as shown in Figure 11.3. The CRL includes the serial number of all revoked certificates and the date of revocation. A CRL is always published in a special certificate format known as a *version 2 certificate*. In contrast, other certificates are published in a different format known as a *version 3 certificate* or an older version 1 certificate.

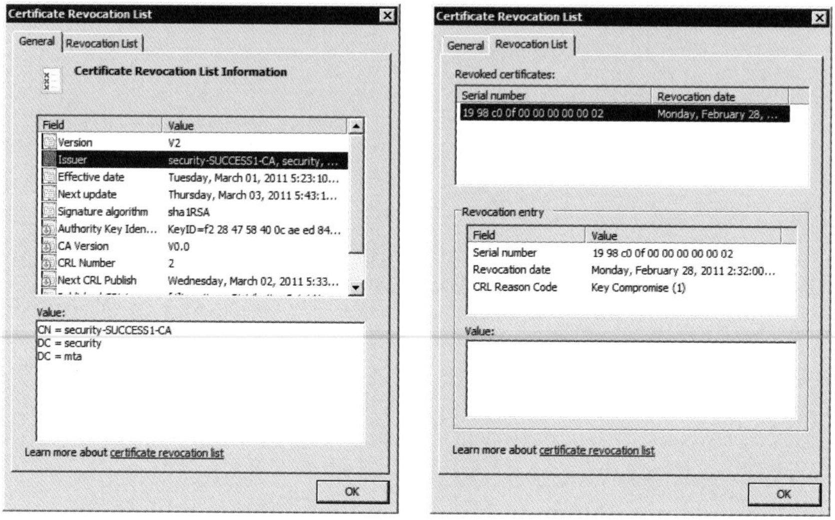

FIGURE 11.3 Viewing the CRL

There are other ways a client can check to see if a certificate has been revoked. However, the most important point to realize is that the certificate is checked.

One way a client can check to see if a certificate has been revoked is to retrieve a copy of the CRL. If the certificate in question is listed on the CRL, then it has been revoked by the issuing CA and shouldn't be trusted. In the figure, only a single certificate has been revoked; but it's not uncommon for the CRL to include multiple certificates.

Figure 11.4 shows the overall process of how a client validates a certificate:

1. The server sends the certificate to the client.
2. The client verifies that the certificate hasn't expired and checks to ensure that the name in the certificate matches the name of the server.
3. The client queries the CA that issued the certificate to determine if the certificate has been revoked.

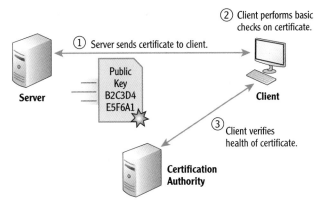

FIGURE 11.4 Checking the validity of the certificate

The following list shows some errors you may see that indicate a certificate has a problem:

"This website's security certificate has been revoked."   This indicates that the private key has been compromised or the certificate is being used fraudulently. If it's revoked, the original certificate owner wouldn't use it, but a malicious attacker may be fraudulently using it.

"This website's security certificate is out of date."   This indicates that the certificate has expired. Expired certificates aren't validated by CAs, so they shouldn't be trusted. As a reminder, Figure 11.4 shows how a certificate is validated each time it's used. This certificate could have been revoked because it was stolen and is being used fraudulently; but because it's not validated by the CA, you'll never know.

"This website's security certificate isn't from a trusted source."   This indicates that the certificate hasn't been issued from a trusted CA. It's common to see this error from malicious phishing attempts.

"Internet Explorer has found a problem with this website's security certificate." Miscellaneous problems will trigger this error. For example, if the certificate was modified, tampered with, or is unreadable, this error occurs.

"There is a problem with this website's security certificate."   This indicates that the certificate was issued to one website, but another website is using it. Figure 11.5 shows the error you'll see in Internet Explorer when this validation step fails.

All of these errors indicate problems with the certificate, and the certificate shouldn't be used.

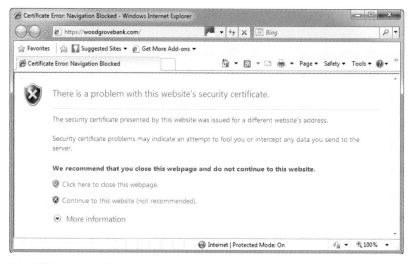

FIGURE 11.5 Error from a certificate

You may also see the Address bar in your web browser turn red with the message "Certificate Error" in the Security Status bar (next to the Address bar). It's not recommended that you continue when you see any type of problem with the certificate. However, you can click Continue To This Website (Not Recommended). If you do continue, you shouldn't enter any private information. If attackers are fraudulently using the certificate, they will be able to view any private information you submit, even if an HTTPS session is established.

Viewing Certificate Properties

You can view a certificate and its properties with the following steps:

These steps are written for Internet Explorer 8, but they will also work with Internet Explorer 7.

1. Start Internet Explorer.

2. Select Tools ➤ Internet Options.

3. Select the Content tab.

4. Click the Certificates button.

5. Select the Trusted Root Certification Authorities tab. Your display will look similar to Figure 11.6.

6. Select one of the certificates in the Trusted Root Certification Authorities store.

7. Click Advanced. Scroll through the Certificate Purpose list, as shown in Figure 11.7. Notice that the certificate can be used for several different purposes, such as server authentication and code signing.

8. Click Cancel.

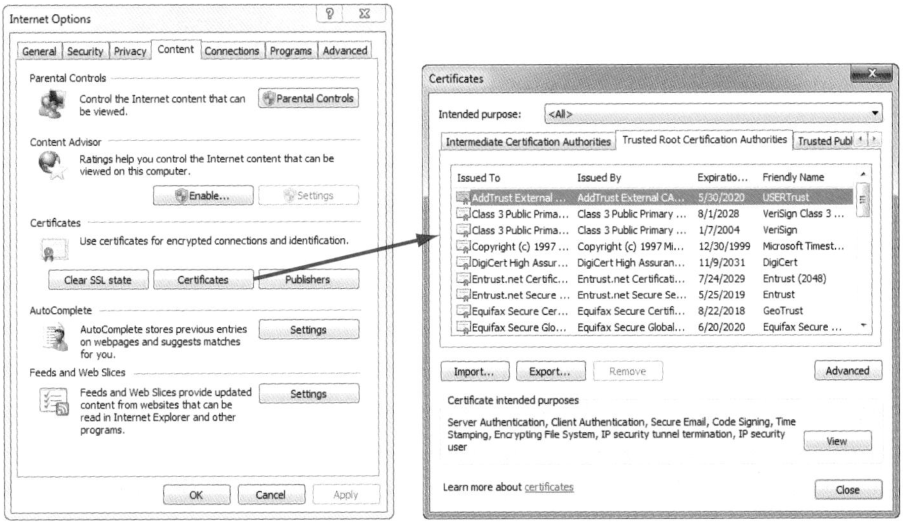

FIGURE 11.6 Viewing the Trusted Root Certification Authorities store

Certificates issued by CAs with certificates existing in the Trusted Root Certification Authorities store are automatically trusted.

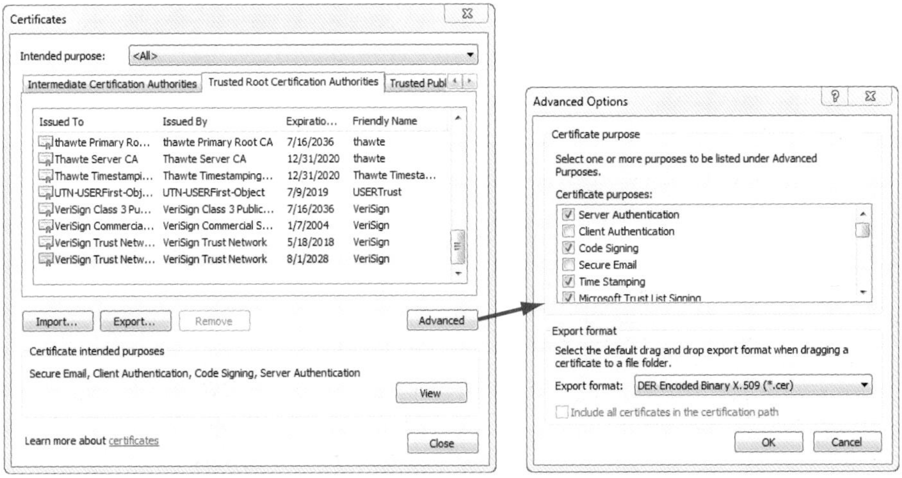

FIGURE 11.7 Viewing the purposes of a certificate

9. Click the View button. Your display will look similar to Figure 11.1 (shown earlier in the chapter). Notice that the General tab shows the purposes of the certificate in simple bullet form. It also shows who the certificate was issued to, who it was issued by, and the validity dates for the certificate.

10. Click the Details tab, and select Issuer. Your display will look similar to Figure 11.8. You can also see other details here such as the serial number, the public key, and more.

11. Scroll through the different fields and values on the Details tab. When you select any item, the value displays in the bottom pane of the window.

12. Click the Certification Path tab. Your display will look similar to Figure 11.9. This shows the path to the root CA, which is also known as the *certificate chain*. When the certificate was issued by the root CA, there is only one certificate listed in the chain—the CA that issued the certificate. When multiple certificates are listed, it shows the path to the root CA.

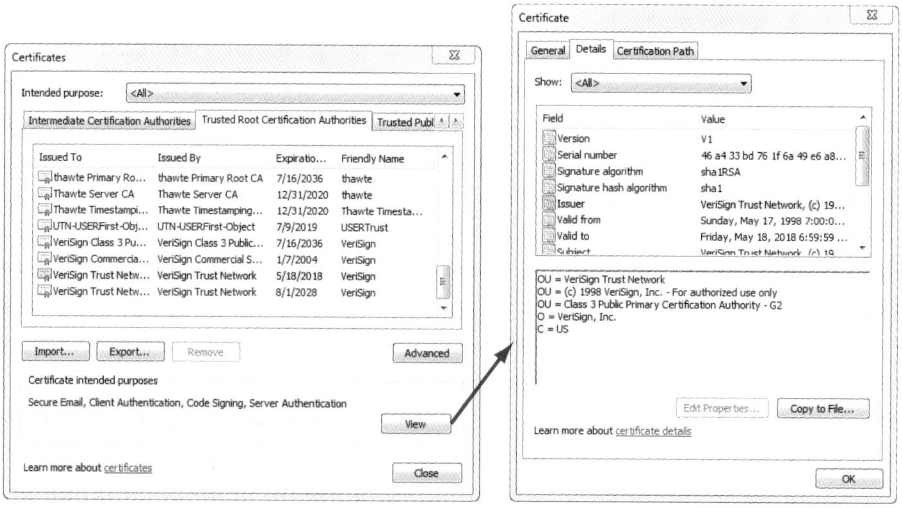

FIGURE 11.8 Viewing the details of a certificate

FIGURE 11.9 Viewing the certificate path

The certificate path is also known as the certificate chain. The certificate chain is explained in the "Understanding the Certificate Chain" section later in this chapter.

Exploring the Components of a PKI

A Public Key Infrastructure (PKI) includes all the components necessary to issue, manage, verify, and use certificates for different purposes. A PKI includes the following components:

Public/Private Key Pairs   The public/private key pair is a matched set of keys used for encryption and decryption of data. These matched key pairs will work with each other but not with keys from other key pairs. Applications are commonly used to generate these matching key pairs.

Certificates   A certificate is an electronic file. It includes details such as who issued it, who it was issued to, validity dates, and the public key.

Certification Authority (CA)   The CA issues and manages certificates. If a certificate or a private key becomes compromised, the CA revokes the certificate holding the matching public key. The CA answers queries to verify the status of certificates.

Registration Authority (RA)   An RA is optional, but in large organizations it can take some of the load off the CA. The RA accepts certificate requests and validates the credentials of the requestors. After the request has been verified, the RA forwards the request to the CA. The RA never issues certificates.

Root CA   The first CA in a certificate chain is called the root CA. The root CA can issue certificates to subordinate CAs, and these CAs are considered to be in the same certificate chain. If a computer trusts the root CA, it trusts all certificates issued by any CAs in the certificate chain. Microsoft systems store certificates from many public root CAs in the *Trusted Root Certification Authority store*.

Understanding the Certificate Chain

Figure 11.1 earlier in this chapter showed the contents of the Trusted Root Certification Authorities store. Each certificate in this store represents a trusted root CA.

Figure 11.10 shows an example of a certificate trust chain. The root CA is the first CA in the chain. It issues itself a self-signed certificate. It can then issue certificates to intermediate CAs. The intermediate CAs can issue certificates to subordinate CAs. Certificates are issued to clients from the subordinate or issuing CAs.

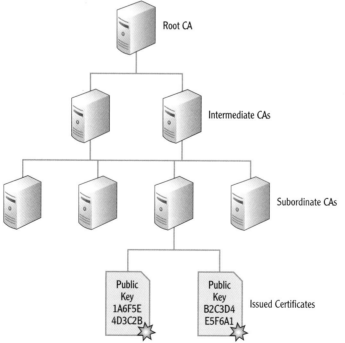

FIGURE 11.10 A certificate chain

The benefit of the certificate chain is that if the root CA is trusted, all the certificates issued by any of the CAs in the chain are also trusted. The root CA is trusted by placing the root certificate into the Trusted Root Certification Authorities store.

Microsoft has agreements with many public CAs (such as VeriSign) and places certificates for the public CAs in the Trusted Root Certification Authorities store of the company's operating systems. Companies doing ecommerce on the Internet purchase their certificates from these public CAs. Then, when the ecommerce company sends you a certificate, your system checks to see if the certificate was issued by a trusted CA in your Trusted Root Certification Authorities store. If the certificate was issued by a trusted CA, it's trusted. If the certificate wasn't issued by a trusted CA, it isn't trusted. As an example, if you purchase a product from Amazon.com, Amazon will send you a certificate that it purchased from VeriSign. Because you trust VeriSign (it's in the Trusted Root Certification Authorities store), you trust the certificate sent from Amazon.

The concept is similar to the trust given to a driver's license. If you present your driver's license at a bank as your proof of ID, it's trusted. People at the bank trust that the Department of Motor Vehicles (DMV) took adequate steps to verify your identity; and because they trust the DMV, they trust that your ID is valid. On the other hand, if you purchase an ID from FlyByNight IDs, the ID likely won't be accepted by the bank because there may not be a trusted relationship between the bank and FlyByNight IDs.

Similarly, if an ecommerce site purchases a certificate from FlyByNight certificates, the certificate may not be trusted by default. Because the certificate of the FlyByNight root CA isn't in the Trusted Root Certification Authority store by default, any certificates issued by this CA also won't be trusted.

Although Figure 11.10 shows a lengthy certificate chain, this isn't required. For example, Figure 11.11 shows a simple CA configuration. A single CA is created as the root CA, and it issues certificates to clients.

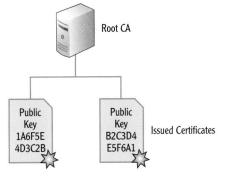

FIGURE 11.11 A single CA in a certificate chain

Figure 11.11 shows the common way that a CA is created in an internal organization such as in a Microsoft domain. A single server is configured as a CA and used to issue certificates within the organization.

The root certificate from this CA is placed in the user's Trusted Root Certification Authority store with Group Policy or through other automated methods.

Comparing Certificate Services

You can add Microsoft's *Active Directory Certificate Services (AD CS)* to create a CA. AD CS is added to Windows Server 2008 as a role; it can be added as either an *enterprise CA* or a *standalone CA*. In general, an enterprise CA is used to issue certificates only within the organization, whereas a standalone CA can be used to issue certificates in or out of the organization:

Standalone CA   The CA can be used to issue certificates within an organization or publicly. The CA isn't required to be a member of a Microsoft Active Directory domain, but it can be. Certificate requests are submitted manually and are manually approved.

Enterprise CA   This is used within a Microsoft domain and requires Active Directory Domain Services (AD DS). An enterprise CA is used to issue certificates only within the company or enterprise. One of the benefits of an enterprise CA is that administrators can configure autoenrollment for the certificates so that certificates are automatically issued based on the configuration of the CA. Credentials are checked using authentication in Active Directory.

Figure 11.12 shows an enterprise CA created on a Windows Server 2008 server. You can create a CA on a Windows Server 2008 server by adding the Active Directory Certificate Services role. In the figure, this CA has issued one certificate to a domain controller for authentication purposes.

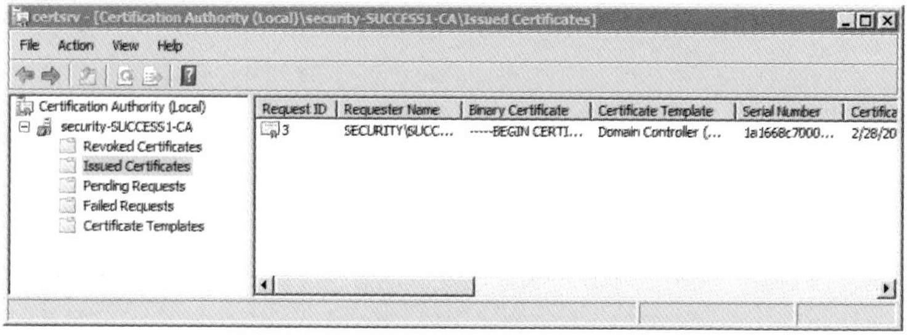

> When an organization creates its own CA, it doesn't have to buy certificates from a public CA that are used internally.

> An enterprise CA is used within a domain to issue certificates to internal users and computers.

FIGURE 11.12 Enterprise CA in Windows Server 2008

The choice you use depends on the purpose of the certificates. For example, if an organization needs to generate certificates for smart cards that will be used for authentication within the domain, it makes sense to create an enterprise CA.

On the other hand, if the CA will be used to issue certificates to users or computers outside the organization, a standalone CA should be used.

Either way, though, the certificate from the root CA should be in the Trusted Root Certification Authority store of the client computers. This ensures that any certificates issued from the CA are trusted by clients.

THE ESSENTIALS AND BEYOND

In this chapter, you learned about certificates and the components of a Public Key Infrastructure (PKI). Certificates are used for a wide variety of purposes including authentication, encryption, digital signatures, and code signing. Public keys are included within certificates, and the public and private key pairs are used for asymmetric encryption. For example, HTTPS sessions start with asymmetric encryption to privately share a secret key and then use the secret key for symmetric encryption of the session. Before a certificate is used, several validation checks may be completed to ensure that the certificate isn't expired, revoked, or being misused. If these checks fail, the user may see an error. You can view the properties of any certificate and see that they include the name of who issued it, who it was issued to, the validity dates, the serial number, the public key, and more. A PKI includes all the components necessary to issue, manage, and use certificates. A certification authority (CA) issues certificates. The first CA in the certificate chain is the root CA. When the certificate from the root CA is placed in the Trusted Root Certification Authority store, all certificates issued by this CA (or any CAs in the certificate chain) are automatically trusted. You can install Active Directory Certificate Services on Windows Server 2008 to create your own CA. An enterprise CA requires Active Directory Domain Services, but you can create a standalone CA with or without Active Directory Domain Services.

ADDITIONAL EXERCISES

▶ Determine whether your system has any root certificates from Microsoft.

▶ Determine whether your system has any root certificates from VeriSign.

▶ Visit **https://woodgrovebank.com**. Determine whether there is an error with the certificate.

To compare your answers to the author's, please visit **www.sybex.com/go/securityessentials**.

(Continues)

THE ESSENTIALS AND BEYOND *(Continued)*

REVIEW QUESTIONS

1. True or false: A server will give out its certificate containing its private key.

2. Which of the following are valid uses of a certificate? (Choose all that apply.)

   A. Authentication   C. Digital signatures

   B. Encryption   D. Antivirus scanning

3. True or false: A certificate issued to a web server with one name can be used on another web server with another name without any problems.

4. How are certificates uniquely identified?

   A. Public key   C. Version number

   B. Issuer   D. Serial number

5. You want all certificates issued by a CA to be trusted. Where should you place its root certificate?

6. A CA issues itself the first certificate in the trust chain. What is the CA called?

   A. Root CA   C. Enterprise subordinate CA

   B. Self-signed CA   D. Standalone subordinate CA

7. An organization wants to create a CA that will be used internally with a Microsoft domain, with the ability to automatically enroll certificates for users. What should be created?

   A. Standalone CA   C. Enterprise CA

   B. Public CA   D. RA-enabled CA

8. What role is added to a Windows Server 2008 server to create a CA?

   A. Certification Authority role   C. Active Directory Certificate Services

   B. Active Directory Domain Services   D. File services

CHAPTER 12

Understanding Internet Explorer Security

Internet Explorer (IE) is the primary web browser used on Windows Server 2008 and Windows 7. Because it's so common to use the Internet to research and to do regular work, it's important to understand some of the security risks and some of the security mechanisms that help protect users. InPrivate Filtering and InPrivate Browsing help you control what data is stored on a system. You can also delete browsing history to erase the data that is stored on your system. When a user visits a website, IE automatically detects the zone and applies different security settings based on this detected zone. Most browsing sessions will automatically run in the Internet zone, but there are some exceptions. There are also some additional tools such as the SmartScreen Filter and Protected Mode that help a user avoid many of the problems associated with malicious websites. This chapter includes these concepts in the following topics:

► **Exploring browser settings**

► **Comparing security zones**

► **Using IE tools to identify malicious websites**

Exploring Browser Settings

Internet Explorer (IE) version 8 is installed by default on Windows 7 and Windows Server 2008 R2; this chapter focuses on IE version 8.

On the surface, IE is a web browser that lets you surf the Internet. However, if you dig just a little bit, you'll see that there is a lot you can manipulate and

►

Windows Server 2008 (not R2) includes IE version 7 by default. However, it can be upgraded to version 8 or version 9.

configure. Figure 12.1 shows IE opened to Bing with some items highlighted. These highlighted items are explained next:

Address Bar   This shows the address of the site being visited. When a secure session is established, the address starts with https (instead of http). The *s* indicates that the site is secure. More specifically, it indicates that the site is using Hypertext Transfer Protocol over Secure Sockets Layer (HTTP over SSL).

When HTTPS is used, an icon of a lock appears at the end of the address bar.

Page Drop-Down Menu   This menu allows you to manipulate and view some elements of the web page and also save it. As an example, you can select Page ➢ Properties and then click the Certificates button to view any certificates associated with the displayed page.

Safety Drop-Down Menu   This menu includes several security-related settings you can use to improve the security of a browsing session. For example, it includes settings for InPrivate Browsing, InPrivate Filtering, and the SmartScreen Filter.

InPrivate settings and the SmartScreen Filter are explored in the "Using IE Tools to Identify Malicious Websites" section later in this chapter.

Tools Drop-Down Menu   This menu includes many selections used to manipulate the default behavior of IE. Here you can access the Internet Options selection, which provides most of the settings you can configure for IE.

FIGURE 12.1 Internet Explorer

Zone Indicator   This indicates which zone you're currently connected to: Internet, local intranet, trusted sites, or restricted sites. Security settings are automatically adjusted based on the zone.

Protected Mode Indicator   Protected Mode helps prevent malware from being installed on your system. It's turned on by default for the Internet and restricted sites zones. It's turned off by default for the local intranet and trusted sites zones.

The "Comparing Security Zones" section later in this chapter explores these zones in more depth.

Understanding IE Enhanced Security Configuration

If you're running IE from within Windows Server 2008 or Windows Server 2008 R2, you may notice that many websites don't display as expected. The reason may be that IE Enhanced Security Configuration (ESC) is preventing the sites from being displayed properly. This setting is enabled by default and is intended to provide an added layer of protection for the server by preventing many attacks from web-based content by blocking different types of web content and scripts.

You can tell if IE ESC is enabled when you first launch IE. A display similar to Figure 12.2 appears by default when you launch IE. If ESC has been disabled, a different display will let you know that it's disabled.

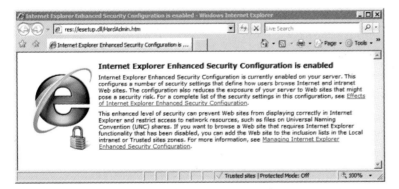

FIGURE 12.2 IE ESC display

You can use the following steps to disable IE ESC on a Windows Server 2008 or Windows Server 2008 R2 server:

1. Launch Server Manager. Ensure that Server Manager is displayed.

2. Scroll down to the Security Information section, and click Configure IE ESC. Your display will look similar to Figure 12.3.

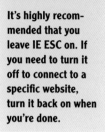

It's highly recom-
mended that you
leave IE ESC on. If
you need to turn it
off to connect to a
specific website,
turn it back on when
you're done.

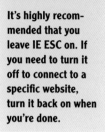

FIGURE 12.3 Enabling or disabling IE ESC

3. Change the setting to Off for Administrators, Users, or both depending on your needs. Click OK.

4. Close all open windows.

Selecting Cookies Settings

Figure 12.4 shows the Internet Options Privacy tab. The Settings section identifies how cookies are handled and has a default setting of Medium. *Cookies* are
small text files that a website places on your computer and that can be used to
track your preferences and activity.

You can adjust these settings with selections from Accept All Cookies to Block
All Cookies, with several settings in between High, Medium High, Medium, and
Low. In general, though, the Medium setting meets most users' needs when they
are surfing the Internet.

Although it's possi-
ble to block all cook-
ies from websites
from being placed on
your computer, you'll
find that then many
sites won't function
or will constantly
harass you to enable
cookies.

You need to understand some terms for these settings to make sense:

First-Party Cookie   A first-party cookie is placed on your system by a site you
visit. For example, if you visit `www.msn.com`, and `www.msn.com` places a cookie on
your system, it's a first-party cookie.

Third-Party Cookie   A third-party cookie is placed on your system by a different site than the one you're visiting. For example, when you visit `www.msn.com`,
several advertisements are displayed from companies other than Microsoft. These
advertisers may also place cookies on your system. In this scenario, `www.msn.com`

and you are the first party and the second party, respectively. The advertiser is a third party.

Compact Privacy Policy   A compact privacy policy is a summary of a company's privacy policy that is embedded in the web page in XML format. You can also view the privacy policy summary of a website (if it has published one) by clicking Safety ➢ Web Page Privacy Policy, selecting the site, and clicking Summary, as shown in Figure 12.5. The summary includes a link to the full privacy policy.

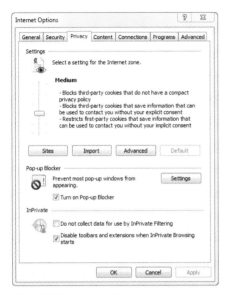

FIGURE 12.4 Viewing settings for cookies

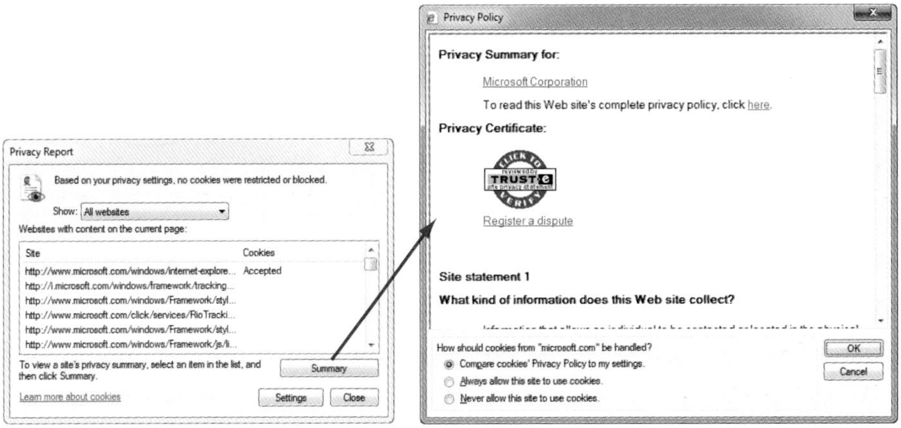

FIGURE 12.5 Viewing a privacy policy summary

If you're not satisfied with the privacy policy for any site, you can adjust the settings so that cookies are never allowed for the site. If you need to access a site and allow cookies but your Privacy Policy settings are more secure and blocking most cookies, you can adjust the settings so that cookies are always allowed for a specific site.

You can view the folder used to store cookies (and other temporary files) with the following steps:

1. Start Internet Explorer.

2. Select Tools ➢ Internet Options.

3. With the General tab selected, select Settings in the Browsing History section.

4. Click the View Files button. Windows Explorer opens in a protected mode so you won't be able to accidentally launch malicious content in this window. If you double-click any file in this window, a Windows Security Warning window appears, indicating that the action may be unsafe.

Most web developers are responsible and don't put private data into a cookie. However, some developers either don't know any better or don't care and still put private data into cookies.

▶

Cookies are generally meaningless to users. However, they have embedded codes that are used by various websites. For example, the following text is from a cookie named `Darril@msn` on my system:

```
MC1V=3&GUID=9e9e7be2baf84727b1731a0792a4fa49
msn.com/1054132824196309148983728271209127155*
```

About the only text that is clear is `msn.com`. The rest of the information is generally a group of different codes that are only meaningful to **www.msn.com** developers. On the other hand, when a website developer puts clear text data into the cookie, such as username and password, the cookie presents other risks. If someone is able to read the text in the cookie, they can discover your credentials for specific sites.

Manipulating the Pop-up Blocker

▶

Pop-up windows can appear on top of a web page or behind a web page. A pop-up that appears behind a web page is called a *pop-under*.

Most pop-ups are automatically blocked by IE's built-in pop-up blocker. A *pop-up* is a small web browser window that some websites use to bring attention to an advertisement. Pop-ups can be harmless (although irritating) ads, but they can also be malicious.

For example, Figure 2.1 in Chapter 2, "Understanding Malware and Social Engineering," showed an example of a malicious rogueware pop-up. It tries to scare a user into thinking their system is infected with malware and encourages them to click to scan their system. However, clicking instead results in malware being installed on the user's system.

Although you probably want to block pop-ups such as the malicious rogueware pop-up, there may be times when you want to allow pop-ups from specific sites. For example, if your bank uses pop-ups, you may want to allow pop-ups from the bank. You can change the settings for the pop-up blocker with the following steps:

1. Start Internet Explorer.

2. Select Tools ➢ Pop-up Blocker ➢ Pop-up Blocker Settings.

3. Type in the address of the website that you want to allow, and click Add.

4. The default Blocking Level is Medium. If desired, you can select a different blocking level from the Blocking Level drop-down menu, as shown in Figure 12.6. (Microsoft doesn't offer a more detailed explanation of the levels than the options shown here.)

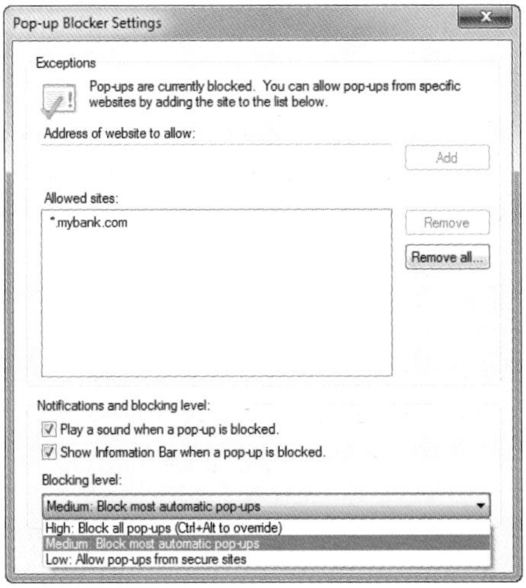

FIGURE 12.6 Modifying the Pop-up Blocker settings

Using InPrivate Filtering and InPrivate Browsing

Two features in IE that you can use to help enhance browsing security are *InPrivate Filtering* and *InPrivate Browsing*. Although they both start with *InPrivate*, they do different tasks.

InPrivate Filtering works by analyzing content on a web page to determine whether the same content is being used on a number of different websites. If the same content is being used by many websites, it's likely provided by a third party, and information about you could be shared with the third party and others. InPrivate Filtering helps prevent these third-party websites from collecting information about you. InPrivate Filtering is off by default.

You can use the following steps to turn on InPrivate Filtering:

1. Start Internet Explorer.

2. Select Safety ➤ InPrivate Filtering. The first time you select this, you'll see a display similar to Figure 12.7. You can automate InPrivate Filtering by clicking Block For Me, or you can select Let Me Choose Which Providers Receive My Information.

   After you make a choice, you can modify the settings by selecting Safety ➤ InPrivate Filtering Settings.

3. You can toggle InPrivate Filtering on and off by selecting Safety ➤ InPrivate Filtering or pressing Ctrl+Shift+F.

If you close all browser sessions and start another one, the InPrivate Filtering setting will default to the Off setting. You must set InPrivate Filtering anew for each browser session.

FIGURE 12.7 Enabling InPrivate Filtering

InPrivate Browsing lets you browse websites without leaving any trail of the websites you visit. This can be especially useful when you're using a public computer or using a computer shared with others. InPrivate Browsing prevents your browsing history, temporary Internet files, form data, cookies, usernames, and passwords from being stored on the computer.

You can use the following steps to begin an InPrivate Browsing session:

1. Start Internet Explorer.

2. Select Safety ➤ InPrivate Browsing (or press Ctrl+Shift+P). This launches a new web browser window. The title bar and the beginning of the address bar both indicate that the session is using InPrivate Browsing settings, as shown in Figure 12.8. All data collected during the session will be discarded as soon as the session is closed.

FIGURE 12.8 Starting an InPrivate Browsing session

Deleting Browser History

IE automatically stores information each time you visit a website. This includes a list of the websites you've visited, data you've entered into website forms, copies of web pages, images, and other media.

It's often useful to leave this data (including the web pages, images, and other media) on your personal computer. Doing so can improve page loads if the information exists locally and doesn't have to be retrieved from the original website from the Internet. Additionally, you won't have to enter the same information each time you visit a website. However, if you're using a public computer or one shared by others, you may want to delete the browser history when you step away from the computer.

You can delete the browser history with the following steps:

1. Start Internet Explorer.

2. Select Tools ➤ Internet Options.

3. If necessary, select the General tab. Click the Delete button. Your display will look similar to Figure 12.9.

4. Pick the items that you want to delete, and click Delete.

◄

You can also delete browsing history by selecting Tools ➤ Safety ➤ Delete Browsing History, or simultaneously pressing the Ctrl+ Shift+Del keys.

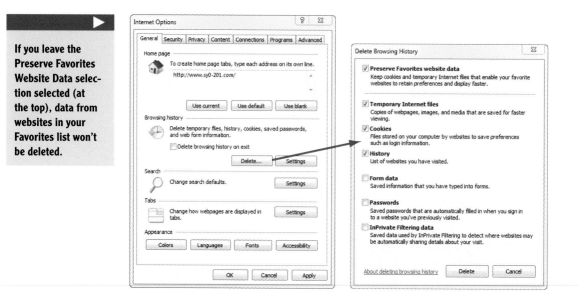

If you leave the Preserve Favorites Website Data selection selected (at the top), data from websites in your Favorites list won't be deleted.

FIGURE 12.9 Deleting browser history

Managing Add-ons

One of the key features of IE is its extensibility. You can install a wealth of *Internet Explorer add-ons* to provide additional features and abilities to IE. For example, Microsoft Silverlight can be added to IE (and to other browsers as a plug-in) to provide enhanced graphics and animations. Silverlight allows web developers to create engaging interactive web applications that go way beyond basic HTML pages.

Figure 12.10 shows the Manage Add-ons page. Although the graphic shows add-ons from Microsoft Corporation, many other companies write and publish add-ons. For example, Adobe publishes several different add-ons such as Shockwave and Flash, which are popular with many users. Notice that you can enable and disable add-ons by selecting them and clicking Enable or Disable.

Add-ons can improve the user's experience, but they can sometimes cause IE to become unstable or even unusable. This most commonly occurs when two or more add-ons conflict with each other or if an add-on hasn't been properly tested by its developer.

If an add-on causes problems, you should disable it. However, if you have multiple add-ons and can't figure out which ones are causing the problems, you can reset IE to its original state to eliminate all the add-ons. The following steps show how to reset IE settings:

    1. Start Internet Explorer. Select Tools ➢ Internet Options.

If you're unable to start IE, you can access the Internet Options page with the following steps:

a. Click Start, and type **inetcpl.cpl** in the Search Programs And Files text box.

b. Select `inetcpl.cpl`.

2. Select the Advanced tab.

3. Click the Reset button. Your display will look similar to Figure 12.11.

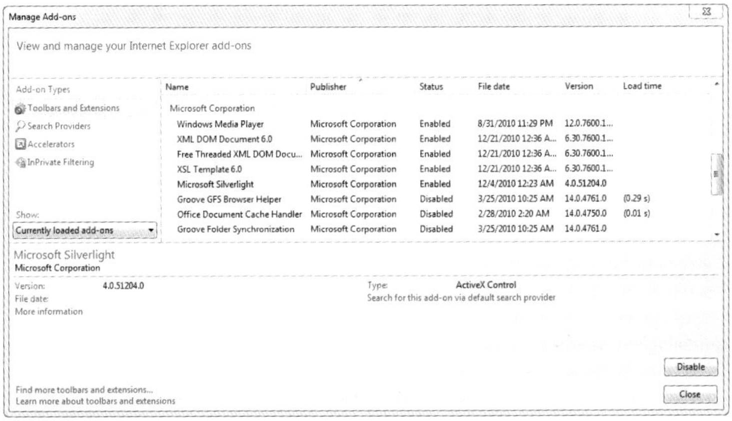

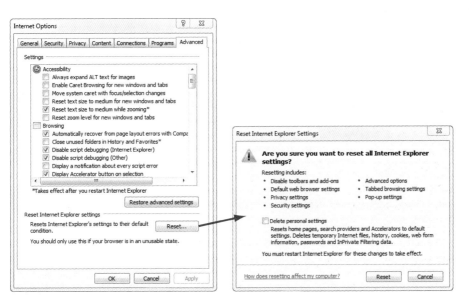

FIGURE 12.10 Managing add-ons in IE

FIGURE 12.11 Resetting IE to the default state

Notice that you can choose to delete all of your personal settings too, but that check box isn't selected by default.

4. Click Reset. All the settings are reset. This may take a moment.

5. When it completes, click Close. Click OK. Close all open windows.

Exploring Advanced Security Settings

Group Policy was covered in more detail in Chapter 9.

IE includes several different security settings that you can adjust based on your needs. These settings are automatically configured, so it's not common to change them. However, some administrators do take the time to control them with Group Policy to ensure that end users don't modify them.

Figure 12.12 shows these settings. Notice that they're on the Internet Options properties page with the Advanced tab selected. You can access this page with IE open by selecting Tools ≻ Internet Options, and selecting the Advanced tab.

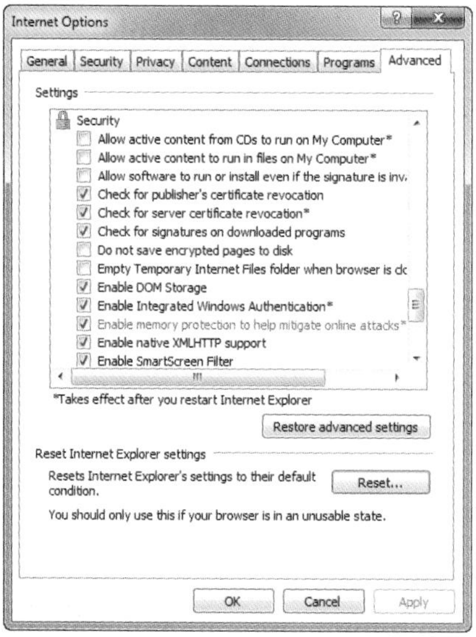

FIGURE 12.12 IE advanced security settings

Several settings are enabled by default. For example, Chapter 11, "Understanding Certificates and a PKI," presented information about how certificates are automatically checked. You can see in Figure 12.12 that the first two enabled settings are directly related to checking certificates. Additionally, further down the list (not shown in the figure), another setting is enabled by default to warn the user if the certificate address doesn't match the website.

The settings on the Advanced tab apply to all security zones. However, additional settings are configured differently for different security zones. The various security zones are described in the following section.

Comparing Security Zones

The different *Internet Explorer security zones* provide default security settings for different security purposes. For example, if your organization hosts a website on your internal network (your intranet), then you can consider it relatively safe from malware. By configuring the site to run in the local intranet, it will run with relaxed security, providing greater usability. In contrast, websites on the Internet are generally suspect because it's so easy for an attacker to create a malicious website. Sites from the Internet run in the Internet security zone, which provides a higher level of security than the local intranet zone.

Figure 12.13 shows the Security tab of the Internet Options properties page, and the following list describes these zones:

Internet   The Internet zone is used for any websites that aren't on your local computer or your local intranet or are not assigned to another zone. The Internet hosts countless malicious websites. If not blocked in some manner, malicious websites can run malware on your system. This includes malicious scripts embedded in a web page, ActiveX controls, or other software that is automatically downloaded onto your system when you visit. The default security level for the Internet zone is Medium High, which helps block much of the malicious content on the Internet.

Websites are controlled by the Internet zone if they're not in another zone and don't meet the narrow requirements to be identified as an intranet site.

Local Intranet   Websites hosted on an organization's internal network (the intranet) are run with this zone setting. Some internal sites are automatically placed in this zone. For example, if the site name doesn't include periods (such as http://success) or was accessed via a Universal Naming Convention (UNC) path of \\servername\sharename\pagename, it will be recognized as an intranet zone. However, if a site is placed in either the trusted sites zone or the restricted sites zone, those settings will take precedence. Additionally, IE will default to the Internet zone if you use an IP address or a fully qualified domain name (FQDN) such as http://security.mta. The default security level for the local intranet zone is Medium Low, which is the lowest security level of the four zones.

FIGURE 12.13 Viewing the security zones

Trusted Sites   Many times, an organization will host a website on the Internet for the use of the organization's employees. For example, several large companies host websites that employees can access from home or while traveling. These websites may have scripts or applications that enhance the user's experience but these extras won't run from within the Internet zone. When the user places the website into the trusted sites zone, the lower security level allows the extra features to run. The default security level for the Internet zone is Medium.

Restricted Sites   Some sites are well known for hosting malware, but there are times when they need to be visited. For example, law enforcement and security professionals often visit known malicious websites. By placing these websites in the restricted sites zone, these users have a higher level of protection. The default security level for the restricted sites zone is High.

Although each of these zones has default settings, you can dig into the settings a little deeper and modify the settings for any specific zone. For example, Figure 12.14 shows some of the advanced settings for the Internet zone related to ActiveX controls. You can access this page by selecting Tools ➢ Internet Options, selecting the Security tab, and clicking the Custom Level button.

In the figure, you can see that many ActiveX controls and plug-ins are disabled by default. If you open this page and scroll down a little, you'll see that unsigned ActiveX controls are disabled but that signed ActiveX controls can be downloaded after prompting the user.

A signed ActiveX control is signed with a certificate. The certificate identifies the author or distributor of the certificate and verifies the ActiveX control hasn't been modified.

It's not typical to modify these settings. However, they do give you granular control over the behavior of IE if you need it for special purposes.

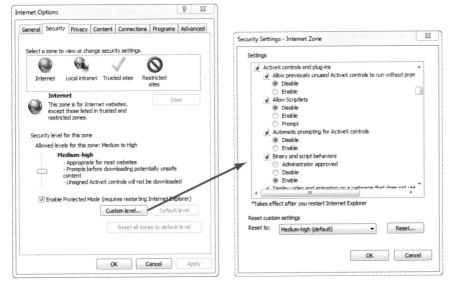

FIGURE 12.14 Viewing security settings for the Internet zone

UNDERSTANDING ACTIVEX CONTROLS AND CODE SIGNING

An ActiveX control is a small program that can run in a web browser. Many are helpful add-ons that enhance the user's experience, such as by providing animation or displaying a Microsoft Excel spreadsheet in a web page. However, attackers can also write malicious ActiveX controls. A malicious ActiveX control could include any type of malware.

One method of providing a measure of safety when working with ActiveX controls is to only allow signed ActiveX controls. Chapter 11 introduced the concept of using a certificate for code signing. A legitimate developer can purchase a certificate to sign an ActiveX control. When the control is executed, the certificate verifies that the ActiveX control is valid and that the ActiveX control has not been modified.

A criminal won't purchase a certificate to sign an ActiveX control because the certificate will also identify the author. In other words, only legitimate ActiveX controls are signed. Some security settings prevent unsigned ActiveX controls from running.

Using IE Tools to Identify Malicious Websites

IE includes several security features that help protect you from malicious websites. The best protection against malicious websites is to simply not visit them. The SmartScreen Filter helps you identify malicious websites before the page is displayed. Protected Mode helps protect your system from malicious activity if you do visit a malicious website. Both are described in more detail in this section.

Understanding the SmartScreen Filter

Phishing is a technique used by attackers to trick users into giving up personal information. Sometimes they want you to reply to an email, but more often, they try to trick you into clicking a link. The built-in *SmartScreen Filter* helps protect you from phishing attacks such as spoofed websites and websites that distribute malicious software.

Chapter 2 introduced phishing.

The SmartScreen Filter is turned on by default. It includes a set of technologies to detect malicious websites and provides a warning when it detects you going to a known malicious website. The background of the screen turns red, and a warning appears indicating that the website has been reported as unsafe.

It's highly recommended that you don't click links from phishing emails. Said another way, consider every hyperlink embedded in an email suspect. Sometimes just visiting the site can result in a drive-by download infecting your system.

UNDERSTANDING DRIVE-BY DOWNLOADS

A *drive-by download* is any download initiated by a website when a user visits. The user doesn't do anything to initiate the download other than visit the site, such as by clicking a link in a phishing email or a pop-up advertisement.

This software can then be installed on the system without the user's knowledge. The software is rarely innocent. Instead, it's usually some type of malware such as a virus, spyware, or even a keylogger.

Although features such as User Account Control (UAC, described in Chapter 6, "Protecting Clients and Servers"), Protected Mode, and zone security settings help protect systems, attackers are constantly modifying their methods. As one protection is implemented, attackers discover or invent other methods to circumvent it. Of course, an added layer of protection is antivirus software, as described in Chapter 2.

Another feature of the SmartScreen Filter is that it blocks downloads that have been reported as unsafe. For example, if a user chooses to visit a phishing website even after being warned by the SmartScreen Filter, the SmartScreen Filter will continue to monitor for risky downloads. This includes downloads that a phishing website may try to perform automatically (as a drive-by download) and also downloads that a user may try to initiate.

Modifying Protected Mode

Protected Mode runs IE with restricted privileges to provide a layer of protection from malicious websites. It reduces the ability of a malicious website to write, alter, or destroy data on a user's system, or to install any type of malware.

By default, Protected Mode is enabled for the Internet and restricted sites zones. It's disabled by default for the local intranet and trusted sites zone. Although it's possible to disable Protected Mode for the Internet and restricted sites zone, doing so isn't recommended. Additionally, many administrators use Group Policy to ensure that Protected Mode remains enabled and can't be changed by users.

You can enable or disable Protected Mode with the following steps:

◄

Protected Mode came out with IE 7 but it doesn't work on Windows XP. It works only on Windows 7, Windows Vista, Windows Server 2008, and 2008 R2.

1. Start Internet Explorer.

2. Select Tools ➤ Internet Options.

3. Select the Security tab.

4. Select the zone where you want to change Protected Mode.

5. Select or deselect the Enable Protected Mode check box. Click OK. If you're disabling Protected Mode, you'll see a warning indicating that you're putting your computer at risk. Click OK.

6. Close Internet Explorer. When you restart it, the settings will take effect.

THE ESSENTIALS AND BEYOND

In this chapter, you learned about many of the built-in security features of Internet Explorer. IE includes a wealth of built-in security features, and you can also manipulate many of these settings based on specific user needs. Cookies are stored on the local machine and can be used to track a user's behavior online, and you can use InPrivate Filtering and InPrivate Browsing to control what cookies are stored on a user's system. You can also delete the browser's history to remove cookies and other data collected

(Continues)

THE ESSENTIALS AND BEYOND   *(Continued)*

from browser sessions. IE automatically detects one of four security zones (Internet, local intranet, trusted sites, and restricted sites) and sets default security based on the risks of the zone. IE also includes the SmartScreen Filter and Protected Mode to help prevent users from visiting phishing sites and to block malicious downloads.

ADDITIONAL EXERCISES

▶ View the cookies currently stored on your system.

▶ Delete the browsing history on your computer, and then view the cookies that are stored on your system.

▶ Launch an InPrivate Browsing session, and browse some websites.

▶ Identify whether ActiveX controls can run in the restricted sites zone.

To compare your answers to the author's, please visit **www.sybex.com/go/securityessentials**.

REVIEW QUESTIONS

1. You have launched Internet Explorer on Windows Server 2008, and you've noticed that some websites aren't displaying correctly. What is causing this?

   A. InPrivate Filtering

   B. InPrivate Browsing

   C. IE Enhanced Security Configuration is enabled.

   D. IE Enhanced Security Configuration is disabled.

2. True or false: A cookie is an executable file that tracks a user's behavior.

3. What can be used to block all cookies from being stored on a user's computer during a browsing session?

   A. InPrivate Browsing   **C.** Pop-up blocker

   B. InPrivate Filtering   **D.** Protected Mode

4. True or false: It isn't possible to remove the history of browsing sessions.

5. An add-on is causing IE to become unstable, but you're unsure which add-on is causing the problem. What should you do?

(Continues)

THE ESSENTIALS AND BEYOND *(Continued)*

6. Which zone is used by default for a website with a fully qualified domain name?

   A. Internet   C. Restricted sites

   B. Local intranet   D. Trusted sites

7. Which IE security zone has the most relaxed security settings?

8. Which one of the following helps detect phishing sites?

   A. InPrivate Browsing   C. SmartScreen Filter

   B. InPrivate Filtering   D. Protected Mode

Answers to Review Questions

Chapter 1

1. **Risk occurs when threats have the potential to exploit vulnerabilities.** A more detailed definition comes from NIST SP 800-30: "Risk is a function of the likelihood of a given threat-source's exercising a particular potential vulnerability, and the resulting impact of that adverse event on the organization."

2. **True** Vulnerabilities are weaknesses, and by reducing vulnerabilities, you reduce risk.

3. **D** Confidentiality ensures that only authorized people have access to data. Confidentiality is ensured with access controls and encryption.

4. **C** Preventing the loss of integrity ensures that unauthorized changes are detected. Audit logs and hashing techniques are the primary methods.

5. **The principle of least privilege** The principle of least privilege states that users, resources, and applications should be given the rights and permissions to perform necessary tasks, and nothing else.

6. **B** You can reduce the attack surface of a system by removing unneeded protocols and disabling unneeded services (not needed services). Disabling the firewall doesn't reduce the attack surface.

7. **C** SCW creates an XML file that can be applied to a system. It includes recommended secure settings for services, firewall rules, the registry, audit policies, and more.

8. **A** Malicious software (malware) includes viruses, worms, and Trojan horses. Antivirus software attempts to detect and block malware.

Chapter 2

1. **C** Viruses require a user to execute an infected program. Worms can spread to other computers using the network without any user intervention. Both are malware.

2. **True** A buffer overflow occurs when a program receives unexpected code that causes an error, overflowing the application's memory buffer and exposing system memory.

3. **B** A Trojan horse appears to be one thing such as a utility or a game, but it has a hidden malicious component.

4. **False** Botnets continue to grow. One botnet (the Rustock botnet) includes more than 1 million clones and sends out more than 40 billion spam emails a day.

5. **Botnets** It's estimated that 88 percent of spam is sent by botnets and about 89 percent of all email is spam.

6. **Microsoft Security Essentials** Microsoft Security Essentials (not Security Essentials 2010) is a free product for home users and for small businesses with up to 10 devices.

7. **True** Security Essentials 2010 is a type of Trojan horse known as rogueware. It was purposely given a name similar to Microsoft's Security Essentials free AV tool, which is a valid AV product.

8. **C** The Microsoft Windows Malicious Software Removal Tool is the only free tool from Microsoft that will remove malware threats on Server 2008. Security Essentials 2010 is malware. Microsoft Security Essentials is free for desktop systems such as Windows 7, but it doesn't work on Server products. Microsoft Forefront is a family of products used for server security, but they aren't free.

9. **Cache poisoning** Pharming redirects victims to undesired websites by modifying one of the name-resolution methods. DNS cache poisoning places incorrect entries into the DNS cache and is one method of pharming.

10. **A, B, D** Antivirus software protects against malware. Disabling automatic display of graphics protects against web beacons verifying email addresses. Educated users are less likely to follow phishing attempts. Pharming is malicious and can't be enabled or disabled in email.

Chapter 3

1. **C** Identification is when a user professes an identity, such as with a user name; and authentication proves the identity, such as with a password. They aren't the same, and identification by itself doesn't authenticate an individual.

2. **Passwords** Passwords can be discovered through social engineering, dictionary attacks, and brute-force attacks.

3. **False** A smart card is an example of the *something you have* authentication factor.

4. **D** *Pa$$w0rd* includes all four character types: uppercase, lowercase, symbols ($$), and a number (0). The others include only one, two, or three of the four character types.

5. **True** Group Policy includes Password Policy settings in the Security Settings node.

6. **Password-reset disk** If a user has created a password-reset disk, the user can reset their password with this disk.

7. **Something you are** Biometrics methods such as fingerprint checks authenticate users using the *something you are* factor of authentication.

8. **Time-skew** A time-skew error prevents clients from accessing resources on the network and will occur if Kerberos detects a client's time is not within five minutes of other computers.

9. **D** Remote Authentication Dial-in User Services (RADIUS) servers can provide central authentication for dial and VPN systems, wireless clients as an 802.1x server, and port-based authentication for 802.1x network devices. It doesn't provide authentication for database servers, and 802x isn't a valid standard.

10. **B** LAN Manager (LM) is the oldest and weakest of the identified protocols. NTLMv1 is an improvement, and NTLMv2 is better. Kerberos is the default network authentication protocol used in Microsoft domains.

Chapter 4

1. **True** The basic Read permission includes Read Data, Read Permissions, Read Attributes, and Read Extended Attributes.

2. **C** Permissions are cumulative, and because Modify includes Read, the effective permission is Modify. It's possible to determine the permissions because Maria is a member of groups that are assigned permissions. Full Control permissions aren't granted unless they're assigned.

3. **False** Modify includes delete, but Write doesn't include delete.

4. **A** Deny takes precedence. If a user is assigned both Allow and Deny, Deny is the effective permission. Read permissions don't override this, and membership in the Administrators group doesn't override this.

5. **Inheritance** Permissions are inherited from parent folder to all files and folders within the folder.

6.   **C** The Finance group has Full Control permission over the C:\Budget folder. When moving files, the permissions stay the same when moved on the same partition. Every other time, they're inherited from the new location. Because the file was copied, the permissions are inherited from the new location (C:\Budget).

7.   **C** The Finance Group has Full Control, inherited from the target folder (D:\Budget) on the different partition. When moving files, the original permissions are retained when moved on the same partition. Every other time, the original permissions are lost and permissions are inherited from the new location. Because the file was moved to a different partition, the original permissions are lost and only the inherited permissions from the new location apply.

8.   **B** Users will have Read permissions. When combining NTFS and share permissions, the more restrictive permissions apply, and Read is more restrictive than Full Control.

9.   **True** The Delegation of Control Wizard in Active Directory Users and Computers can be used to assign permissions for specific tasks, such as resetting passwords in specific OUs.

10.   **False** Permission inheritance is disabled by default for most keys in the Registry.

Chapter 5

1.   **A** The three As (AAA) of security are authentication, authorization, and accounting. They work together to provide accountability. Accountability, access control, and auditing aren't part of the AAA of security.

2.   **False** Object Access auditing is a two-step process. You need to enable Object Access auditing in the Audit Policy and then configure the SACL on the individual folder.

3.   **A** The Logon Events audit setting records any time a user logs on to a local system. Account Logon Events records when a user logs on to a domain. System Events and Process Tracking don't record logon events.

4.   **C** Directory Service Access auditing records changes to Active Directory. Account Management events can record modifications to user, computer, and group accounts, but not other modifications to Active Directory. The other choices don't monitor Active Directory.

5.   **System Events** System Events auditing records when a system is shut down or restarted.

6.   **Event Viewer** You can view audited events in the Security log with the Event Viewer. The tool is the Event Viewer, and the log is the Security log.

7. **D** Event subscriptions can forward events from multiple servers to a central server. None of the other choices can change where events are collected.

8. **True** Write Once Read Many (WORM) media is one method used to ensure that audit logs aren't modified.

9. **MBSA is available free from Microsoft's download site** (**www.microsoft.com/downloads**).

10. **True** MBSA can detect several different vulnerabilities, including weak passwords.

Chapter 6

1. **User Account Control (UAC)** UAC dims the Desktop until the user responds. This prevents an application from taking actions that aren't approved by the user.

2. **False** Files aren't automatically encrypted in offline folders. However, you can encrypt the Offline Folders location.

3. **D** DNS can't be used to update a system, but each of the other choices can be used to update a system.

4. **True** You can configure a Group Policy setting once and have it apply to all the computers in the domain.

5. **False** If updates aren't deployed to the clients, the client remains vulnerable.

6. **B** PTR (pointer) records resolve IP addresses to host names. A (host) records resolve host names to IP addresses. SPF records identify authorized mail servers for a domain. MX records identify mail servers.

7. **C** RODCs have limited information stored on them and are recommended for use in branch offices with limited physical security. Secure dynamic updates won't prevent secrets from being stored on a domain controller, and it's not possible to remove Administrator accounts from a domain controller.

8. **False** It's common (and recommended) to install DNS on a domain controller. When you do, you can enable secure dynamic updates to enhance security.

9. **True** Terminal Services (Remote Desktop Services in Windows Server 2008 R2) should be separated from Active Directory for enhanced security.

10. **True** The two requirements for secure dynamic updates are that DNS must be installed on a domain controller, and the zone must be configured as an Active Directory–integrated zone.

Chapter 7

1.   **False** A distributed denial of service (DDoS) attack comes from multiple computers.

2.   **A sniffing attack** Attackers can use protocol analyzers (also called sniffers or packet sniffers) to capture and analyze network traffic in a sniffing attack.

3.   **LAND** A LAND attack spoofs the source address in a TCP SYN packet. If not detected and stopped, it causes the system to repeatedly reply to itself.

4.   **C** LDAP uses port 389, and secure LDAP uses port 636. SNMP uses ports 161 and 162. Terminal Services and Remote Desktop Services use port 3389. HTTP uses port 80, and HTTPS uses port 443.

5.   **True** Hardware-based firewalls are more efficient than software-based firewalls.

6.   **D** A perimeter network (also called a DMZ) provides a layer of protection for Internet-facing servers. If the web server is placed in the intranet, other resources in the intranet are at risk. If it's directly on the Internet, it's more vulnerable to direct attacks from the Internet. Placing a web server on a firewall isn't recommended because the services have conflicting security requirements.

7.   **B** A Unified Threat Management (UTM) firewall provides protection for multiple elements. A Secure Content Management (SCM) firewall is primarily focused on filtering email. A stateful or packet-filtering firewall provides only a single feature versus protection for multiple threats.

8.   **B, C, D** NAP can't inspect and isolate Linux clients. Windows XP requires Service Pack 3, and Windows Vista and Windows 7 work with NAP by default.

9.   **C** IPsec can encrypt traffic on internal networks. The other three protocols are tunneling protocols used for VPNs and aren't used within a network.

10.   **DNSSEC** DNSSEC is a group of security extensions for DNS. One of the benefits of DNSSEC is the ability to digitally sign DNS records.

Chapter 8

1.   **False** A wireless router includes a wireless access point, but not all wireless access points include routing capabilities.

2.   **True** Algorithms stay the same, but keys should be kept secret and changed frequently.

3.   **C** WPA2 provides the best security. WEP has known vulnerabilities, and WPA was created as an interim replacement. WPA2 is more secure than WPA. WPA3 isn't a valid wireless security protocol.

4.   **True** WPA2-Enterprise requires an 802.1X server, and an 802.1X server can require authentication with smart cards.

5.   **An 802.1X server** WPA2-Enterprise uses an 802.1X authentication server to provide an extra layer of security.

6.   **D** WPA2-Enterprise provides the strongest wireless security. It combines the strength of WPA2 with an 802.1X authentication server.

7.   **The service set identifier (SSID)** The service set identifier (SSID) is the name of the wireless network.

8.   **A** It's recommended that you rename the default SSID for security. Disabling the SSID broadcast doesn't provide security and isn't recommended by Microsoft. The SSID doesn't have a password, and it can't be removed.

9.   **False** WEP uses RC4 for encryption, which is relatively easy to crack. WPA2 and some implementations of WPA use AES.

10.   **False** Disabling SSID broadcast doesn't increase security and isn't recommended by Microsoft.

Chapter 9

1.   **C** A mantrap is often used to prevent tailgating. It ensures that only one person can pass through an entry point at a time, and it requires other personnel to use their own credentials to gain access.

2.   **A** By replacing hubs with switches, you can reduce the possibility of sniffing attacks and also improve performance. Although it's possible to replace routers with special Layer 3 switches, doing so doesn't improve security. You can't replace switches with routers.

3.   **True** These are the basic steps to manage users and computers with a GPO.

4.   **False** The Default Domain Controllers policy is linked to the Domain Controllers OU and applies only to objects in this OU. Only domain controllers should be in this OU.

5.   **Allow Log On Locally (or Deny Log On Locally)** The Allow Log On Locally and Deny Log On Locally settings can control which computers users can log onto.

6. **C** Any settings in the Account Policies node (including the Password Policy and Account Lockout Policy nodes) apply only when linked at the domain level. When linked at an OU level, they're ignored for domain user accounts. Group Policy settings do apply to administrators.

7. **B** If both the Allow Log On Locally and Deny Log On Locally settings apply to a single user, deny takes precedence. Joe won't be able to log on locally.

8. **True** The Removable Storage Access policy settings can control what removable devices users can use.

9. **A, B** Two steps that you can take to protect mobile devices are to password-protect them and install antivirus software. Discovery mode should be disabled on Bluetooth devices. Adding Internet access doesn't provide any protection.

Chapter 10

1. **Symmetric** Symmetric encryption uses a single key for encryption and decryption. Asymmetric encryption uses two keys (a public key and a private key) for encryption and decryption.

2. **Public and private keys** Asymmetric encryption uses public and private keys for encryption and decryption.

3. **B** AES provides strong, efficient symmetric encryption. RSA is used with asymmetric encryption. DES is a weak symmetric encryption. MD5 is a one-way hashing function.

4. **C** SHA-1 is a one-way hashing function. RSA is used with asymmetric encryption. AES provides strong, efficient symmetric encryption. WPA2 is an encryption protocol used with wireless.

5. **A** Email can be encrypted using S/MIME to provide confidentiality. A digital signature provides authentication, integrity, and nonrepudiation. BitLocker encrypts hard drives. EFS encrypts files on NTFS drives.

6. **B** The designated recovery agent (the administrator by default) can access EFS-encrypted files. The password-recovery disk is used to change a password when the user forgets their original password. BitLocker uses recovery keys, but EFS doesn't use recovery keys.

7. **Encrypted** An encrypted file will stay encrypted when it's moved or copied to any NTFS partition.

8.   **A** A TPM is a chip on a motherboard, and it secures the key used with BitLocker. When the system boots, the TPM ensures that key boot files haven't been modified; if so, it releases the key to unlock the hard drive.

9.   **True** BitLocker supports encrypting a hard drive using a startup key stored on a USB flash drive.

10. **True** BitLocker To Go encrypts USB flash drives. BitLocker encrypts hard drives.

Chapter 11

1.   **False** A server will give out its certificate containing its public key but not its private key. The private key is always kept private.

2.   **A, B, C** Valid uses of a certificate include authentication, encryption, and digital signatures. Certificates aren't used for antivirus scanning.

3.   **False** This will result in an error that encourages the client to not use the certificate.

4.   **D** Certificates are uniquely identified by their serial number. The public key is very likely unique, but it isn't used to identify the certificate. The issuer will issue multiple certificates; the common versions are 1 and 3 (which aren't unique).

5.   **In the Trusted Root Certification Authority store** When the root certificate of a CA is placed into the Trusted Root Certification Authority store, all certificates issued by it will be trusted.

6.   **A** A CA that issues itself the first certificate in the trust chain is a root CA. This certificate is also called a self-signed certificate (not a self-signed CA). A root CA issues certificates to subordinate CAs. In other words, a subordinate CA doesn't issue itself a certificate.

7.   **C** An enterprise CA uses Active Directory and supports autoenrollment for certificates. A standalone CA doesn't support autoenrollment. A public CA is for public use, not internal use. There is no such thing as an RA-enabled CA.

8.   **C** You can create a CA on Windows Server 2008 by adding the Active Directory Certificate Services role. There is no such thing as a Certification Authority role. Active Directory Domain Services is hosted on a domain controller, but it doesn't create a CA. The file services role doesn't create a CA.

Chapter 12

1.   **C** IE Enhanced Security Configuration (IE ESC) is enabled by default, and it will prevent many websites from displaying correctly. InPrivate Filtering and InPrivate Browsing must be enabled on a per-session basis.

2.   **False** A cookie is a text file that tracks a user's behavior. A text file can't be executed.

3.   **A** InPrivate Browsing lets you browse the Internet without leaving a trail, such as from cookies or your browsing history. InPrivate Filtering only blocks third-parties from tracking your behavior. The pop-up blocker blocks pop-ups, and Protected Mode helps prevent malicious downloads from automatically installing from a browsing session.

4.   **False** You can delete the browser history to remove files that are normally stored after a browsing session.

5.   **Reset the Internet Explorer settings.** You can reset IE to the default condition from the Advanced tab of the Internet Options property page.

6.   **A** IE will use the Internet zone for any website not in another zone and with a fully qualified domain name.

7.   **Local intranet zone** The local intranet zone has the most relaxed security settings. By default there aren't any sites in the local intranet zone.

8.   **C** The SmartScreen Filter helps detect phishing sites. When you attempt to go to a known phishing site, it will give you a warning to let you know about the malicious nature of the site. InPrivate Browsing lets you browse the Internet without leaving a trail, such as from cookies or your browsing history. InPrivate Filtering only blocks third parties from tracking your behavior. Protected Mode helps prevent malicious downloads from automatically installing from a browsing session.

Microsoft's Certification Program

Since the inception of its certification program, Microsoft has certified more than 2 million people. As the computer network industry continues to increase in both size and complexity, this number is sure to grow—and the need for *proven* ability will also increase. Certifications can help companies verify the skills of prospective employees and contractors.

Microsoft started with the Microsoft Certified Professional (MCP) program, which validated individuals' knowledge and expertise on a wide variety of products. Microsoft then expanded these certifications into multiple categories:

Microsoft Technology Associate (MTA)   The MTA certifications are entry-level certifications that are available only at academic institutions. They validate an individual's knowledge and basic understanding of key technology concepts. The three IT professional series certifications are Networking Fundamentals, Security Fundamentals, and Windows Server Administration Fundamentals. There are also several developer certifications. You must take and pass one exam to earn each MTA certification.

Microsoft Certified Technology Specialist (MCTS)   The MCTS is the next level of certification. For people who are not in an academic institution, these can be the first certifications they earn. The MCTS certification program targets specific technologies instead of specific job roles. You must take and pass one to three exams to earn an MCTS certification in different technologies.

Microsoft Certified IT Professional (MCITP)   The MCITP certification is a Professional Series certification that tests network and system administrators on job roles rather than only on a specific technology. The MCITP certification program generally consists of one to three exams in addition to obtaining an MCTS-level certification.

Microsoft Certified Professional Developer (MCPD)   The MCPD certification is a Professional Series certification for application developers. Similar to the MCITP, the MCPD is focused on a job role rather than on a single technology.

The MCPD certification program generally consists of one to three exams in addition to obtaining an MCTS-level certification.

Microsoft Certified Master (MCM)   The MCM program is for experienced IT professionals who want to deepen and broaden their technical expertise on specific Microsoft server products. It includes three weeks of highly intensive classroom training, three computer-based tests, and one lab-based exam for each of the MCM certifications. There are five separate MCM certifications.

Microsoft Certified Architect (MCA)   The MCA is Microsoft's premier certification series. Obtaining the MCA requires a minimum of 10 years of experience and passing a review board consisting of peer architects.

Certification Objectives Map

Table B.1 provides objective mappings for the Microsoft Technology Associate (MTA) Security Fundamentals exam (98-367). It identifies the chapters and sections where the 98-367 exam objectives are covered.

TABLE B.1   Exam 98-367 objectives map

Objectives	Chapter and Section
Understanding Security Layers	**Chapters 1, 2, 8, 9, 12**
• Understand core security principles. This objective may include but is not limited to: confidentiality; integrity; availability; how threat and risk impact principles; principle of least privilege; social engineering; attack surface	Chapter 1: Understanding Risk, Exploring the Security Triad, Enforcing the Principle of Least Privilege, Implementing a Defense-in-Depth Security Strategy Chapter 2: Thwarting Social-Engineering Attacks
• Understand physical security. This objective may include but is not limited to: site security; computer security; removable devices and drives; access control; mobile device security; disable Log On Locally; keyloggers	Chapter 9: Comparing Site Security and Computer Security, Using Group Policy to Enhance Computer Security, Exploring Mobile Device Security

(Continues)

TABLE B.1 (Continued)

Objectives	Chapter and Section
• Understand Internet security. This objective may include but is not limited to: browser settings; zones; secure Web sites	Chapter 12: Exploring Browser Settings, Comparing Security Zones, IE Tools to Identify Malicious Websites
• Understand wireless security. This objective may include but is not limited to: advantages and disadvantages of specific security types; keys; SSID; MAC filters	Chapter 8: Comparing Wireless Devices, Comparing Wireless Security Methods, Configuring Wireless Routers, Configuring Windows 7 for Wireless
Understanding Operating System Security	**Chapters 2, 3, 4, 5, 10, 11**
• Understand user authentication. This objective may include but is not limited to: multifactor; smart cards; RADIUS; Public Key Infrastructure (PKI); understand the certificate chain; biometrics; Kerberos and time skew; using Run As to perform administrative tasks; password reset procedures	Chapter 3: Comparing the Three Factors of Authentication, Using Passwords for Authentication, Using Smart Cards and Token Devices for Authentication, Using Biometrics for Authentication, Starting Applications with Run As Administrator, Preventing Time Skew with Kerberos, Identifying RADIUS Capabilities Chapter 11: Understanding a Certificate, Exploring the Components of a PKI
• Understand permissions. This objective may include but is not limited to: file; share; registry; Active Directory; NTFS vs. FAT; enabling or disabling inheritance; behavior when moving or copying files within the same disk or on another disk; multiple groups with different permissions; basic permissions and advanced permissions; take ownership; delegation	Chapter 4: Comparing NTFS Permissions, Exploring Share Permissions, Identifying Active Directory Permissions, Assigning Registry Permissions
• Understand password policies. This objective may include but is not limited to: password complexity; account lockout; password length; password history; time between password changes; enforce by using group policies; common attack methods	Chapter 3: Using Passwords for Authentication

(Continues)

TABLE B.1   *(Continued)*

Objectives	Chapter and Section
• Understand audit policies. This objective may include but is not limited to: types of auditing; what can be audited; enabling auditing; what to audit for specific purposes; where to save audit information; how to secure audit information	Chapter 5: Exploring Audit Policies, Enabling Auditing, Managing Security Logs
• Understand encryption. This objective may include but is not limited to: EFS; how EFS encrypted folders impact moving/copying files; BitLocker (To Go); TPM; software-based encryption; MAIL encryption and signing and other uses; VPN; public-key/private key; encryption algorithms; certificate properties; certificate services; PKI/certificate services infrastructure; token devices	Chapter 10: Comparing Encryption Methods, Securing Email, Understanding EFS, Exploring BitLocker Drive Encryption Chapter 11: Understanding a Certificate, Exploring the Components of a PKI
• Understand malware. This objective may include but is not limited to: buffer overflow; worms; Trojans; spyware	Chapter 2: Comparing Malware
Understanding Network Security	**Chapters 6, 7**
• Understand dedicated firewalls. This objective may include but is not limited to: types of hardware firewalls and their characteristics; why to use a hardware firewall instead of a software firewall; SCMs and UTMs; stateful vs. stateless inspection	Chapter 7: Exploring Firewalls
• Understand Network Access Protection (NAP). This objective may include but is not limited to: purpose of NAP; requirements for NAP	Chapter 7: Exploring Network Access Protection

(Continues)

TABLE B.1   *(Continued)*

Objectives	Chapter and Section
• Understand network isolation. This objective may include but is not limited to: VLANs; routing; honeypot; perimeter networks; NAT; VPN; IPsec; Server and Domain Isolation	Chapter 6: Protecting Servers Chapter 7: Exploring Firewalls, Exploring Network Access Protection, Identifying Protocol Security Methods
• Understand protocol security. This objective may include but is not limited to: protocol spoofing; IPSec; tunneling; DNSsec; network sniffing; common attack methods	Chapter 7: Identifying Protocol Security Methods, Identifying Common Attack Methods
Understanding Security Software	**Chapters 1, 2, 3, 5, 6**
• Understand client protection. This objective may include but is not limited to: antivirus; User Account Control (UAC); keeping client operating system and software updated; encrypting offline folders; software restriction policies	Chapter 2: Protecting Against Malware Chapter 6: Understanding User Account Control, Keeping Systems Updated, Protecting Clients
• Understand e-mail protection. This objective may include but is not limited to: antispam; antivirus; spoofing, phishing, and pharming; client vs. server protection; SPF records; PTR records	Chapter 1: Installing Antivirus Software Chapter 2: Protecting Email, Protecting Against Malware Chapter 6: Exploring DNS Security Issues
• Understand server protection. This objective may include but is not limited to: separation of services; hardening; keeping servers updated; secure dynamic DNS updates; disabling unsecure authentication protocols; Read-Only Domain Controllers; separate management VLAN; Microsoft Baseline Security Analyzer (MBSA)	Chapter 1: Hardening a Server Chapter 3: Identifying Unsecure Authentication Protocols Chapter 5: Auditing a Network with MBSA Chapter 6: Protecting Servers, Exploring DNS Security Issues

INDEX

Note to the Reader: Throughout this index **boldfaced** page numbers indicate primary discussions of a topic. *Italicized* page numbers indicate illustrations.